BLOOD OF TWO STREAMS

BLOOD OF TWO STREAMS

GENDER BALANCE IN PARENTAL LEGACY

Francis Mading Deng

Refuge Press, New York, 2021

ISBN#13: 978-0-8232-9762-7 (Paperback)
ISBN#13: 978-0-8232-9763-4 (ePub)
ISBN#13: 978-0-8232-9764-1 (WebPDF)

Cover photo and book design: Mauro Sarri
Photographs of the Abyei Community Referendum and the Funeral of John Garang: Phillip Dhil.

Printed in the United States of America.

To my dear wife, Dorothy L. Deng, the devoted mother of our four sons, and my closest life partner without whom I could not have done what I have done since our wedding. The wedding took place in the United Nations Chapel in New York on February 19, 1972. The way the marriage was covered by the international and national media seemed to reflect a moment of global acceptance of racial intermarriage. Chief Arol Kachuol of Gok Dinka captured this emergent spirit when he said to us in Juba in 1972 shortly after our marriage: "The way we see it, God has brought peace and reconciliation into your hearts. If a man secures a wife, as you have done, it is for him to bear his own blood and to bear the blood of his wife's kin. When that happens, whatever hostility might have existed between people, should no longer be allowed to continue. Relationship kills those troubles and begins the new way of kinship...Man is one single word with God." Over the years, Dorothy has received lavish praise from relatives, friends and colleagues at home and abroad, that nearly always ends with—"You are blessed." And indeed, Dorothy has been a blessing for, without her, I repeat that I could not have done all that I have done since we were joined in matrimony.

Acknowledgements

This book has had a long gestation period, more immediately traceable to the interviews I conducted with family members and elders since the early 1970s, but the origins of which go much farther, predating my conception and birth. Although it would be grossly hazardous to venture to identify individuals who have directly contributed to its conceptualization and realization, a few must be mentioned. Without the understanding and support of Dr. Kevin Cahill and Brendan Cahill of the Institute of International Humanitarian Affairs, the book could not have gained recognition and acceptance for publication across the many cultural boundaries it has ventured to bridge. I am deeply grateful to them.

Members of my immediate family have always been my first sounding board for my writings. I was specifically pleased that the manuscript passed the scrutiny of my Dinka daughter-in-law, Atong Demach Deng, who saw in the book the authenticity of Dinka values in the cross-cultural context which our family now enjoys. Jeffrey Campbell, a close friend of the family, has been an invaluable source of technical and intellectual assistance.

As I was finalizing the manuscript of the book, Atong and our son Daniel Jok, her husband, informed me that their expected first born was a boy and asked me to suggest a name. I immediately thought of proposing the name of my maternal grandfather, Mijok, whose prayers, love, vision, and prophesy, on behalf of his lineage, together with the leadership and legacy of my paternal lineage, account for my very being and have been a source of inspiration for all that I have done and tried to do throughout my life. Members of my paternal kin objected to the naming as a violation of the ancestral code of nomenclature. But I never had a second thought. I hoped that the book and the naming of my grandson would be an expression of my deep appreciation and gratitude for my paternal and maternal legacy of *Blood of Two Streams*.

I sincerely hope that our extended families and the wider readership will find in this book values and principles that are more universally shared as guidelines for our increasingly universalizing and yet diversifying world. As I have often argued, there can be no globalization without localization. The nuclear family only makes sense as an element of the extended and ultimately global family.

Table of Contents

Foreword   13

Introduction   15

One   Setting The Stage   21

Two   Heritage In Crisis   39

Three   A Family Of Multitudes   63

Four   Legends of the Forefathers   75

Five   Feuding Over Power   115

Six   Contest for the Sacred Spears   151

Seven   The Maternal Link   169

Eight   In the Eyes of a Sister   231

Nine   A Legacy at the Crossroads   269

Conclusion   277

Special Thanks   282

Sources   289

Foreword

Kevin M. Cahill, M.D.

This is the third book by Dr. Francis Mading Deng to be published by the Institute of International Humanitarian Affairs (IIHA) and for which I am glad to write a foreword. The first of Dr. Deng's three books with the IIHA, *Sudan at the Brink*, tried to balance promoting unity while realistically predicting separation, and stipulating conditions for ongoing cooperation between the two countries. The second book, *Bound by Conflict*, elaborated on the measures needed for cooperation in resolving internal conflicts within the two countries in order to foster peaceful coexistence and promote regional peace and security.

Dr. Deng's third book, *Blood of Two Streams*, offers a different perspective that merges cultural, historical, political, and literary themes in the experience of the Dinka generally, and the Ngok Dinka on the border between Sudan and South Sudan specifically. As the subtitle, *Gender Balance in Parental Legacy*, suggests, the book aims to correct the paradoxical bias that favors the paternal line in patriarchal societies. As Dr. Deng explains, Dinka culture dictates that the child be closer to the father as a function of the mind, while remaining intimately attached to the mother as a function of the heart. The mind is supposed to override the heart. As Dr. Deng explains, among the Dinka, to call a boy a son of a woman is a grave insult not even a mother would want for her son.

I met Dr. Deng over half a century ago when, as a young medical doctor, I witnessed both the challenges of tropical diseases and the richness of the culture that fortified the resilience of the people against a harsh environment. I developed a special admiration for the Dinka people, and Dr. Deng's books have renewed that deeply rooted connection to the people and their culture. Although the book is centered on the Dinka and merges the paternal and maternal legacies in the person of the author, it is likewise cross-culturally applicable and indeed compelling.

Dr. Deng's three books effectively contribute to the Institute's global outreach aimed at a flexible form of research and documentation to promote understanding of diverse human experiences that are both contextually specific and widely universal. That indeed is the core of the Institute's approach to global partnership for addressing humanitarian challenges of our diversified and yet normatively unifying world. *Blood of Two Streams* is a powerful message that cuts across cultural divides and embodies the universal values of parental dualistic bonds of love and affection.

Introduction

By Douglas H. Johnson
"This man is at the UN"— the note from my supervisor read. "You should go see him." It was attached to a publisher's flier for a new book, *Tradition and Modernization: A Challenge for Law among the Dinka of the Sudan*, whose author, Francis Mading Deng, was then working with the United Nations Human Rights Commission. I was finishing my B.A. dissertation on the history of the southern Sudan at Haverford College, near Philadelphia, only a short train journey from New York. That was nearly fifty years ago and served as my introduction to both the man and his work.

Since that time, Francis has continued to write about the Dinka and Sudan. His first book was soon followed by a second general work, *The Dinka of the Sudan*. This was joined by books on Dinka culture (*The Dinka and Their Songs, Dinka Folktales*), and books of interviews with chiefs and elders (*Dinka Cosmology, The Recollections of Babo Nimr*), developing the method employed here. Increasingly, his books described and analyzed Sudan's attempts to find a way to be at peace with itself (*Dynamics of Identification: A Basis for National Integration in the Sudan*, and *Africans of Two Worlds: The Dinka in Afro-Arab Sudan*), and the fractures that led to a long and devastating civil war (*War of Visions: Conflict of Identities in the Sudan*).

But the book closest to his heart, in many ways his most important book and the background to this current work, is his biography of his father (*The Man Called Deng Majok: A Biography of Power, Polygyny, and Change*). Deng Majok was a towering figure in the system of Native Administration the British applied throughout Sudan. He displayed great diplomatic skill in dealing with his neighbors within Sudan's long, and sometimes fractious, borderland. While widely respected, his decisions also could be controversial, and many South Sudanese have blamed him for the current political crisis over Abyei. In following his father's reliance on diplomacy to resolve disputes, Francis Deng, too, has often been criticized and his motives misrepresented. In the biography of his father, Francis presented both an explanation and a defense of his father's diplomacy in local political affairs. In this book, he explains how his own pursuit of diplomacy is rooted in his family background.

The importance of the Ngok Dinka and the Abyei area in Sudan and South Sudan's recent history rests, in part, on geography. The Ngok inhabit a network of waterways that flow eastwards into the Bahr el-Ghazal and White Nile. It is a meeting place of peoples, especially of cattle-keeping pastoralists who rely on its dry season pastures and water, and the Ngok Dinka have long been the gatekeepers to their own section of the waterways and to the land to the south. This, inevitably, has brought them into contact not only with other Dinka peoples in what is now South Sudan, but with Arabic-speaking pastoralists from Kordofan and Darfur.

The Ngok are one of a related group of Padang Dinka that includes their eastern and southern neighbors, the Ruweng and Twich, as well as some of the more distant Dinka peoples living along the White Nile. The Ngok are further subdivided into nine *wot* (sing. *wut*): territorial sections or chiefdoms that are sometimes even referred to as tribes. These are the Abyor, Achaak, Achueng, Alei, Anyiel, Bongo, Diil, Mareng, and Mannyuar. Within each *wut* are several exogamous clans or kin groups. Members of the same clan can be found spread throughout the different sections, but specific clans provide the chiefs for each section, such as the Pajok clan of the Abyor, and the Dhienagou of the Bongo. Each *wut* is administered by a hierarchy of chiefs (pl. *bany*, sing. *beny*), using the Arabic terms *omda* for the head chief of the section and *sheikh* for the sub-chiefs of the sub-sections.

The Ngok Dinka are said to have entered their current homeland nearly three centuries ago, prior to their contact with the Arab pastoralist Misseriya or Rizeigat. The Arab pastoralists often used the southern waterways and swamps as a temporary refuge from the tax demands of the Darfur sultanate, which is how the river known to the Dinka as the Kiir became known to the outside world as the Bahr el-Arab, the river of the Arabs. Power along the borderlands began to shift away from the Dinka in the nineteenth century following Egypt's invasion of Sudan and their opening of the southern Sudan to a new internal and international slave trade. It was during this time that Francis Deng's ancestors, the chiefs of the Abyor section, took the lead in defending the Ngok from incursions by new enemies. His great-grandfather, Arob Biong, in particular, sought to build alliances with his neighbors, including some Arabs, in order to safeguard his people.

When British administrators arrived in the region after the defeat of the Mahdist state in 1898, it was Arob Biong they dealt with as one of the most important chiefs in the borderlands. After he and the neighboring chief Rehan of the Twich complained of Humr Misseriya attempts at slave-taking and extortion, the government decided to include them all in Kordofan province so that a single administration could resolve their disputes. Arob Biong and his descendants, Kwol Arob and Deng Majok, became the main administrative mediators between their people and the government. As the administrative system increasingly differentiated between Arab/Muslim and non-Arab peoples, and the Twich and Ruweng Dinka were absorbed into the neighboring southern provinces of Bahr el-Ghazal and Upper Nile, the Ngok remained as an anomaly—a "southern" (non-Muslim) people in a northern ("Arab") province.

As documented in this book and Francis' earlier biography of his father, Deng Majok built up alliances with the ruling family of the Misseriya to the north and with neighboring Dinka communities. As Sudanese independence approached in the early 1950s, he had to make a choice between becoming part of a large coalition of Dinka tribes in the southern province of Bahr el-Ghazal or remaining as part of a non-Muslim minority in Kordofan. Deng Majok chose the latter, a decision that was much criticized by some members of the Ngok at the time, and more widely within South Sudan since. The presence of the Ngok of Abyei in Kordofan might have become the foundation of a bridge between two different parts of the country, northern and southern Sudan, but nationalist politics undermined this. In the pre-independence elections, the local Umma party fielded as their candidate a relative of Sayyid Abd al-Rahman al-Mahdi, the son of the nineteenth century Mahdi and leader of the Ansar sect, and secured their political alliance with the Misseriya by marrying a daughter of the al-Mahdi family to Babo Nimr, the head of the Misseriya tribe. This effectively froze Deng Majok and the Ngok out of any real representation in Khartoum.

National politics took a turn for the worse in the 1960s as the civil war in southern Sudan expanded across the border and the Ngok were sucked into it. After Deng Majok's death, his son and successor as paramount chief of the Ngok was assassinated. The Addis Ababa Agreement of 1972 that ended Sudan's first civil war brought some respite for the Ngok, but not for long. The terms of the agreement offered the Ngok the possibility of voting to change their administrative jurisdiction and become part of the semi-autonomous Southern Region, but this was resisted not only by the Misseriya, who depended on Ngok pastures during the dry season, but by the national government in Khartoum. Ngok advocates of a referendum were arrested and detained, and Ngok were among the first to join the Sudan People's Liberation Movement/Army (SPLM/A) when it was formed at the outbreak of Sudan's second civil war in 1983. Successive regimes in Khartoum armed groups of Misseriya as local militia to drive the Ngok out of their homes and to raid into those areas of southern Sudan where the SPLA drew their support.

In the lengthy negotiations that ultimately ended Sudan's second civil war in 2005, the Ngok of Abyei were not included in the main provision of the Comprehensive Peace Agreement (CPA) recognizing South Sudan's right to self-determination. Instead, the CPA included a separate protocol for Abyei that provided for the Ngok Dinka (defined by their nine chiefdoms) to hold their own referendum to finally determine whether they would join the rest of South Sudan or remain as part of what was now Southern Kordofan. The problem with this protocol was that it left the territory of Abyei undefined. Not only were local Misseriya opposed to an Abyei referendum and the prospect of losing access to dry season grazing, but since oil had been discovered in the region, the government in Khartoum was determined that these oil reserves not be ceded to South Sudan. The report of a boundary commission was rejected by Khartoum and sent to The Hague for arbitration. A new boundary was drawn but never demarcated on the ground, and the promised referendum did not take place. In the disturbances in the Abyei area since South Sudan's independence in 2011 Kwol Deng, yet another son and successor to Deng Majok, was killed by Misseriya militia. The future of the Ngok people and the Abyei area remain unresolved and in doubt. If Abyei was ever to be a bridge between North and South Sudan, that bridge has been well and truly burned.

Francis Deng is one of a small number of Deng Majok's numerous progeny who were sent to school and went on to higher education in Sudan and elsewhere. His life as a legal scholar and diplomat has taken him out of his native Abyei, but in many ways he has never left it. It was partly due to his suggestion, on the sidelines of the 1972 Addis Ababa negotiations, that the right to a referendum for peoples culturally related to South Sudan (including the Ngok Dinka) was inserted in the Addis Ababa Agreement. Without that precedent, it is unlikely that a right to a referendum would have been included in the CPA's Abyei Protocol. He has continued to support projects for conflict resolution and reconciliation during frequent return visits to his home area, some of which he describes in this book. More broadly, he has contributed to efforts to bring peace to South Sudan and peace between South Sudan and Sudan. While others have often despaired, he has kept the faith, with an optimism tempered by experience, firmly believing that these conflicts can be resolved, and justice restored.

Francis' career as a diplomat in both his native land and internationally is sometimes traced back to the influence of his father, but here Francis takes us beyond the Dinka patriline and the patriarchal gaze to remind us of the importance of women in Dinka society, and to record the part his mother Achok played in his own development. Anthropologists have analyzed the role of maternal kin in Nilotic societies such as the Dinka and have stressed the special bond that exists between a mother's brother and a sister's son, so vividly illustrated here in Francis' conversations with his maternal uncle, Ngor Mijok. A child's character and personality are derived as much from the mother as the father. A woman with a good heart will pass that on to her children, both through heredity and education. "Heredity from a woman is by far more important than heredity through a man," Francis' sister Ayan reminded him. "If a mother has given all her children her single heart, then you, the children of such a woman, will live united and guided by that single heart." As Matet Ayom later explained—"You are the product of two persons... If anyone would associate you with your mother, he will not have associated you with a bad side." This book helps to reset the balance between the paternal and maternal sides Dinka society generally and of Francis Deng's own well-documented family.

One

Setting The Stage

The saying that "no man is an island unto himself" has become a cliché whose wisdom we take for granted and therefore need not be defended. But precisely because we take it for granted, we may risk losing it. This is why I have sought to demonstrate that, in degrees varying with the context, the society, the culture, and the individuals involved, what we are is the contribution of many generations in many differing ways and over a long span of time. Our heritage is not merely our own accomplishment, but the result of a collective effort from an endless chain of people: some of whom have disappeared into the past and may no longer be traceable; some of whom are members of ancestral lines that are traceable by individual names; many of whom are our contemporaries, although not all are directly and visibly connected with our efforts and destiny; and even more of whom belong to the untapped future and a part of the unknown. This, in a sense, is my idea of culture and heritage. And it is the driving force behind this volume.

The book aims at two principal objectives. The first, as is evident from the title, is a tribute to the duality of human identity, and the legacy of both parents through their respective genealogies. In both patriarchal and matriarchal societies, the tendency is to place emphasis on one of the two, to the subordination, if not the total exclusion, of the other. The reality is that there can be no life without both parents. The heritage of dual lineage is merely an extension of the identities of the parents.

The second objective of the book is to record oral history and literature, which have been severely undermined by our modern system of education, especially in Africa. This is, in essence, a continuation of an objective I have pursued for decades and which has resulted in numerous publications. The materials in those publications accrued from many tape-recorded interviews about various aspects of oral history and culture and from a wide variety of sources: Ngok Dinka

21

tribal leaders and elders, and representatives of neighboring communities with shared history and culture. Recording indigenous cultures, however, remains an ongoing challenge worthy of continued attention. In my translation of these recordings, I have tried to retain the authenticity of language, not only as a means of communication, but also as a manner of speech with its distinctive literary value and integrity.

To give an example, I once got into a stimulating discussion with an anthropologist who was assisting me with the translation of Dinka Songs into English for my book, *The Dinka and Their Songs,* published in the series of the Oxford Library of African Literature, of which he was one of the General Editors. The precise issue was how to translate the Dinka morning greeting, *Ci yi bak,* which is literally—"Are you dawned?" I wanted to use the phraseology in the main text with "Good morning" in the footnote, while he wanted the reverse. To me, there was more to the wording than the shared greeting. The Dinka implies having survived the risks of the night, while the English reflected qualitatively on the state of the morning, probably related to the weather. So, there is a contextual relativity to the wording.

Beyond these two principal objectives, I hope the book will also have implications for the promotion of indigenous knowledge as a source of social and moral values. Recently, during discussions with UN officials in Juba, South Sudan, in support of a leadership dialogue and inter-generational dynamics, I was asked by one of the facilitators, Catherine Shin, to share my reflections "given the positive impact the wisdom of the elders in the country could have in advancing peace and building bridges" in our young nation. I decided to structure my contribution along the theme of "Paradoxes." I identified four interconnected paradoxes contrasting the situation in traditional society with the changes resulting from the process of modernization.

The first paradox relates to the changing patterns of education among age groups and their implications to the normative concept of wisdom. Traditionally, wisdom accrued with age and experience with the resulting accumulation of knowledge, and the process of acculturation through which the cultural and moral values were informally transmitted. "Knowing the words"—the Dinka conceptualization of knowledge, was inherently normative and value-oriented, with a well-established moral code of conduct. In the modern context, knowledge is acquired through formal education which, at least at the initial phases, has reversed the age order in favor of youth, who have begun to be viewed as the custodians of appropriate knowledge and related wisdom.

The second paradox is that modern knowledge, which is primarily Eurocentric, is externalized and separates the young recipients from their social and cultural background and value system. Knowledge is also becoming viewed as a value-free accumulation of information, contrary to the morally oriented transmission of knowledge as a source of wisdom.

The third paradox relates to the division of age-related functional roles in the management of society. Traditionally, the Chiefs and elders were the peacemakers, and the youth were organized into warrior age-sets to defend society against external threats, but in the modern context, elders are now the military leaders—commanders and generals who recruit and lead the youth into war.

The fourth paradox is that the close bond between communalism and individualism is being increasingly transformed in favor of individualism. I have always made a contrasting comparison between the Western and African approaches to the balance between the interests of the individual and those of the community. In the Western context, the individual is free, and enjoys maximum privacy, but with relative insignificance to the community. In Africa, the individual is more connected to the community, less free, with hardly any privacy, but has strong social bonds and significance. Which one is a more appealing model is a matter of personal preference. For me personally, and I believe for most of our people in South Sudan and Africa, the value of the individual is largely determined by family and kinship bonds and service to the community and the society.

The implication of conceptualizing the situation in terms of paradoxes is that there is a need to bridge the gulfs involved. The age issue is resolving itself in that the modern educated youth are aging and becoming elders. But the supposed source of knowledge and assumed wisdom remains modern education, which is externally oriented and culturally disconnected from tradition. This can only be remedied by reorienting the curriculum to be more relevant to the traditional cultural value system.

The traditional division of functional roles between the elders as peacemakers and the youth as warriors also requires adjustment in the modern context. The previously separated roles of elders and youth need to be integrated. The unifying objective should be the quest for peace, unity, harmony, and complementarity of roles. The use of force should then be a last resort pursued through a professional army, with the youth as soldiers under commanders who are their seniors in rank and age. This modernizing arrangement should then be regulated by appropriate laws and norms of war.

In the end, the ability to bridge the gulf reflected in these paradoxes is ultimately individual within the community. But even within one family and among siblings, there can be significant differences determined by a variety of factors, including variations in personal upbringing and influences.

While these paradoxes and the needed remedies pose a pervasive challenge in most traditional societies, especially in Africa, they need to be contextualized into particular cultural situations to give the material a human face, both collectively and individually.

I have personally devoted much of my academic and professional life to this challenge. While documenting this personal experience may run the risk of chauvinism and parochialism, given the prevalence of diverse ethnic identities and correlative cultural pluralism, to assume that there is homogeneity that warrants an inclusive and undifferentiated approach would not only obscure useful specificities, but would also be presumptuous. This would indeed be detrimental to the wealth and integrity of diversity.

That is why I have been unabashedly committed to focusing on the culture of my people, the Dinka, in the Southern part of what was the Republic of Sudan, now divided into Sudan and South Sudan.

This book is even more microcosmic in that it focuses on my paternal and maternal lineages, and, by extension, on the history and biographies of the Ngok Dinka, for whom these lineages have provided generations of leaders. Abyei was, and remains, poised between what was then the North and the South of the then Sudan, now the two countries of Sudan and South Sudan. Addressing and resolving the crises of the area in this strategic and sensitive border location remains one of the major challenges of decision making.

Needless to say, it is both flattering and humbling to see myself as part and parcel of a long chain of generations in the dual lineages of father and mother in the wider ethnic circle of the Dinka and in the even wider national and global community, given, in particular, the way my own family has expanded internationally through intermarriages.

It is in this spirit that I have made a selection of materials from my various interviews and reproduced it in this volume. Of course, I intend the selection to support the concept of continuity in change, but I also value the material as a dynamic and flexible form of literature which must now be reduced into writing or else be lost. The price to be paid for writing it down is that the element of fluidity and flexible adjustment to specific circumstances of communication will be compromised.

While the book should be of particular interest to the Ngok Dinka and South Sudanese generally, though predictably controversial in those circles, this story is about an area that is not only of strategic importance to Sudan and South Sudan, but also to Africa, the Middle East, and indeed the international community. As Douglas Johnson notes in his introduction to this book,

"The importance of the Ngok Dinka and Abyei area in Sudan and South Sudan's recent history rest, in part, on geography. The Ngok inhabit a network of waterways that flow eastwards into Bahr el-Ghazal and White Nile. It is a meeting place of people, especially of cattle-owning pastoralists who rely on its dry season pastures and water; the Ngok Dinka have for long been the gatekeepers of their own section of the waterways and to the land to the south.

This inevitably has brought them into contact not only with other Dinka peoples in what is now South Sudan, but other Arabic-speaking pastoralists from Kordofan and Darfur" in the Sudan.

The history of the area and the identity conflicts between the Africans and Arabs, which the leaders of the area were managing, cut across and linked the racial, ethnic, religious, and cultural divides of the region with global implications. The British in the Anglo-Egyptian Condominium Government focused attention on the Abyei as a bridge between North and South Sudan. And the area was a subject of the US-brokered Abyei Protocol of the 2005 Comprehensive Peace Agreement. The United Nations Interim Security Force in Abyei, UNISFA, is one of the major peacekeeping missions the UN Security Council is closely monitoring and regulating. The assassination of our brother, the Paramount Chief of the Ngok Dinka, by the Misseriya Arabs in 2004 received international attention and condemnation, including by the Security Council. Abyei has the potential to be a point of peaceful coexistence and cooperation between neighboring communities, or a point of confrontation whose implications can extend to the countries and the region, reaching deep into Africa and the Middle East.

A soon to be published book, *Abyei Between the Two Sudans,* has this to say about the strategic importance of the area:

"Abyei of the Ngok Dinka is currently contested between the Republics of Sudan and South Sudan. The land has been invaded twice by the Sudanese army since the signing of the 2005 Comprehensive Peace Agreement (CPA) between the Sudan Government and the Sudan People's Liberation Movement and its Army, SPLM/A. After the last invasion in 2011, Sudan was persuaded to withdraw its troops and the United Nations Interim Security Force for Abyei, UNISFA, was established to provide interim protection for the population, which it now does, albeit with limitations in the mandate and territorial coverage. The CPA grants the people of Abyei dual citizenship pending the resolution of the final status."

The authors of the book make the case that Abyei is indeed part and parcel of South Sudan, as demonstrated by the role the Ngok Dinka have played in promoting the cause of the South nationally, regionally, and internationally, and specifically in the wars of liberation in which they distinguished themselves for their bravery, discipline, and unwavering commitment to the national cause of the South. The book also observes that although Abyei is currently contested, it has historically served, and could still serve, as a constructive "Bridge" of peace, reconciliation, and cooperation between the two border communities, extending to their respective two neighboring countries, Sudan and South Sudan.

When I was the Permanent Representative of South Sudan to the United Nations, my colleague, the Permanent Representative of the United Kingdom, used to say that he had closely followed the conflict between India and Pakistan over Kashmir and that Abyei has all the makings of Kashmir, which should not be allowed to happen. On a more positive note, my father used to highlight the strategic position of Abyei by describing himself as the needle and thread that stitched the North and the South into a United Sudan. And Uncle Deng Makuei (Abot) likened Abyei to the eye which, though so small, sees so much. In some of my writings, I have reversed this to say that although Abyei is such a small area, the eyes of the world are now focused on it.

For a variety of reasons, including the strategic importance of Abyei in the region, and from the perspective of African history, ethnography, and biography, I hope this book will reach a wider audience than merely one of interest to our family and serve a cross-cultural purpose. In a way, it forms a part of my yet to be published, *Invisible Bridge: My Turbulent Journey Through Cultures,* which aims at a broad global audience. In a world in which races, religions, and cultures meet, co-exist, and interact, it is important to understand what each one brings into the process of mutual influence. Since we cannot expect everything from our background to be understood, appreciated, and accepted by people with whom we come in contact, this inevitably requires strategic selectivity. It then becomes a question of clarifying for ourselves and others what we consider to be of vital importance, not only to our own sense of identity and dignity, but also to our contribution to the pluralistic context. It is this which justifies the demand for recognition and respect for our identity and culturally oriented behavior from those with whom we relate across the racial and cultural divides. The process need not be consciously calculated or articulated; it is almost inherent and deeply ingrained in our upbringing, although the degree of realization will differ from one individual to another. As I explain in my book, *Talking It Out: Stories In Negotiating Human Relations,* even my approach to diplomacy was not a function of applying formally learned professional code, but of practicing deeply ingrained values that continue to guide one, whether in personal relations within one's own community or country, or cross-culturally and internationally, including in diplomacy which ultimately rests on interpersonal relations.

To the extent that this book represents a personal account of a family and community in transition, interacting with the outside world, and being impacted upon by powers beyond their control, it is a story of cross-cultural communication, accommodation and influence. It is also a story of change and continuity, and the degree to which my background, including events that occurred before I was born, have influenced my attitude and response to new situations. Whether consciously or spontaneously, inside the pluralistic context of my country or abroad, the means by which I remain connected to my background, wherever I have gone and lived, whatever I have done, and the dynamic process through which I have related to both ends of the transition, is what I have called *Invisible Bridge.*

The Western reader should be warned that precision in the factual details is secondary to the larger objective of value-oriented communication. Some inconsistencies in the various versions of the same story is part of the competitiveness and the principle of relevancy which are vital to storytelling among the Dinka. Their literature, or history, is a dynamic social process with a living or functional purpose. I hope the reader will find this volume both entertaining and informative on the Dinka and their world, a world that has now widened far beyond the wildest dream of our forefathers.

But while our ancestors have long perished as physical entities, their moral presence and significance have been continued through successive generations of descendants and their words remain a source of wisdom and inspiration even to some of us, the so-called modernized Dinka. This is the essence of the concept *Koc e nhom*—"Standing the head of a dead man upright"—a notion of genetic and spiritual immortality, described by Professor Harold Lasswell in his introduction to my book, *Tradition and Modernization: A Challenge for Law Among the Dinka of the Sudan,* as the myth of permanent identity and influence. "Man dies and passes on"—said my maternal uncle, Ngor Mijok, whom I interviewed in Khartoum in the mid-1970s, *but he leaves behind a progeny to continue the name. The word of the son of man, the way I am now talking, will be recognized. It will go on and on, never letting the name disappear. So, to you Mading, those are the words that remain. I have now passed them on to you.*

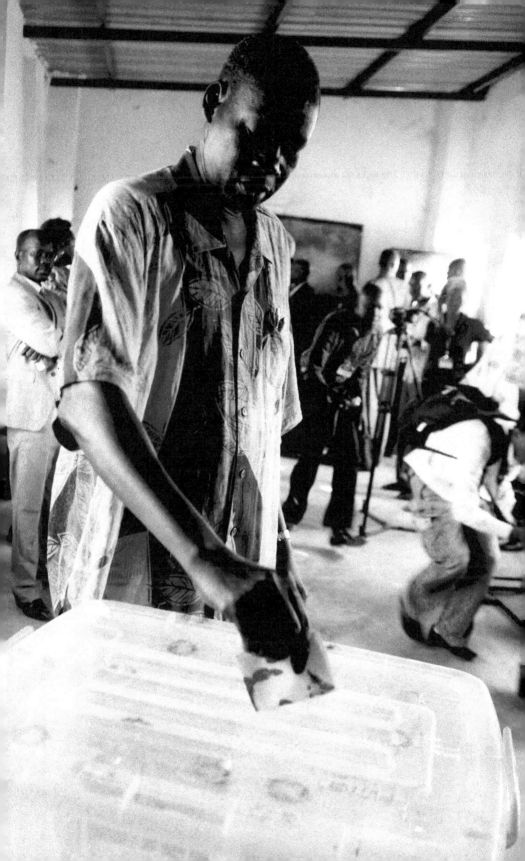

Two

Heritage In Crisis

The Dinka are a congeries of some twenty-five mutually autonomous groups. They are by far the largest ethnic group in South Sudan, as they also were in the pre-partition Sudan. The Ngok Dinka of Abyei, the group from which I come and on which this book focuses, occupies a bridging, but now contested, area between the Sudan and South Sudan.

Their administrative affiliation in the North first occurred under my great grandfather, Chief Arob Biong, who sought protection for his people through his Northern connections. This association was reaffirmed by the British colonial administration and upheld by successive Ngok Paramount Chiefs, my grandfather Kwol Arob and my father Deng Majok. The peace agreements that ended the two Sudanese civil wars (1955—1972 and 1983—2005) between the North and the South gave the Ngok Dinka the right to decide whether to remain in the North or revert back to the South. These provisions were not honored, and the area remains contested. The Ngok Dinka, however, consider themselves and are widely recognized as an integral part and parcel of South Sudan, and, more specifically, as northern gatekeepers for their fellow Dinkas to the South, with whom they share intense pride in their ethnic identity and cultural heritage.

I conducted my first interviews with prominent Dinka Chiefs in the South at the first anniversary of the Addis Ababa Agreement in Juba in March 1973. The interviews comprehensively covered Dinka world view beginning with the myths of creation, origins of divine leadership, earliest migrations, contacts with the outside world leading to the present, analysis of the current relations with the Arabs, and a vision into the future, specifically whether the country was headed toward integration or partition. Two books came out of those interviews. The first, *Dinka Cosmology*, reproduced the translation of the interviews verbatim. The second, *Africans of Two Worlds: The Dinka in Afro-Arab Sudan*, was based on an analysis of the interviews following the same themes.

My interviews with the Ngok Dinka Chiefs and elders were conducted in the 70s and 80s. The first set of interviews followed the same themes as the ones with the Dinka Chiefs in the South. And some of the materials from the Ngok interviews were included in *Africans of Two Worlds*. The provision of the Addis Ababa Agreement on Abyei had not been implemented and the area was still tense. The educated youth from Abyei were agitating for Abyei joining the South, which was in turn being met with repressive measures by the central government and its security forces. A local rebellion erupted in Abyei which would eventually trigger the second civil war. Abyei political elite, most of whom were family members, were rounded up and arrested. The Government declared that they would be charged and tried for treason. Building on the policies our forefathers had adopted for managing our sensitive borders, I had proposed an alternative approach that would grant Abyei an autonomous administrative status and develop it socially and economically as a North-South Bridge and a model for national unity and integration. That proposal proved to be very controversial among the Ngok Dinka and was opposed by the young educated political class. Now detained and threatened to be tried for treason, they were more responsive, though still discreetly opposed, to my initiative. However, I was able to negotiate them out of detention.

The second set of interviews in the mid-70s and 80s were part of a research for my book on my father, *The Man Called Deng Majok: A Biography of Power, Polygyny and Change*. Some of those interviews were conducted by my relatives, mostly university students, and were focused on the story of my father, and his approach to the role of Abyei between North and South, which had been pivotal to Abyei continuing to be administered in the North. Despite his decision to remain in the North, Father continued to be a towering leader in the South, especially among the Dinka traditional leaders. When I interviewed the Dinka Chiefs in the South, one of them asked me whether I was interviewing them as the son of Deng Majok or as Representative of the central government. If I was talking to them as the son of Deng Majok, they would talk to me openly without reservation. If I was speaking as a member of the central government, then something would be left out of our conversation. Of course, I assured them that I was talking to them in my personal capacity and not as representative of the Government.

My conversations with elders in both the South and among the Ngok Dinka not only reinforced my profound admiration for Dinka culture and oral literature, but also revealed the crisis of change which the Dinka are currently undergoing and which is seriously threatening their heritage and indigenous knowledge.

Chol Adija, an elder from the Ngok Dinka, and a close associate of my father, vividly highlighted the problem to me. He began with a general reference to the political crisis in the area and the opportunity to consult with me on the situation.

Mading, now that the country of your father has been destroyed by war and politics, as it is, what do you say? A person does not find you often to talk to you. So, if we have now found you, we should ask you about the affairs of the country.

He then focused on the issue of his immediate concern, the lack of constructive consultations between the young educated class and their illiterate elders.

Our educated youth have pushed us aside, saying that there is nothing we know. Even when we try to talk to them about the important affairs of the country, they dismiss us saying that there is nothing we know. How can there be nothing we know when we are their fathers? Were they not begotten by us?

Chol Adija argued that education was initially envisaged by the elders who sent their children to school as a source of knowledge that would complement their indigenous knowledge and not discard it as part of illiteracy and ignorance:

When we sent them to school, we thought that they would learn new things to add to what we, their elders, would pass on to them. We hoped they would first listen to our words and then add to them the words of modern education. But now it is said that there is nothing we know. This has really saddened our hearts very much.

41

He, however, ended on the hopeful note that insinuated understanding and appreciation for what I was doing as a source of hope and an exception to the behavior he was complaining about.

But we will look around. There will be one or two among you whose hearts will remain alive to the words of their elders, people who will continue to listen to what their elders tell them. That is why I am glad that we are talking to you and why I am asking you what you think about what is happening in Abyei.

My response to Chol Adija was essentially to agree with him, and to reassure him that my interviewing them meant that the cause was not entirely lost, as he had indeed indicated. *Uncle*—I said,

there are many things I would like to discuss with you people, things that are of interest to me personally, but are also related to what you have just said about the attitude of our young people.

I alluded to the fact that I had proposed measures for addressing the crisis situation in Abyei that built on the wisdom of our forefathers in managing relations between the communities on our sensitive border.

You might have already heard of my views on Abyei. As you have just said, ideas do not grow in a vacuum; they reflect knowledge accumulated over time from elders and the words passed down by generations of forefathers, going back to even more distant ancestors. What a man thinks should be a combination of his own ideas with what he has heard from all those before him, including his father and the forefathers before him. The question of Abyei is not new. Our great-grandfather, Kwol Arob, faced it; our grandfather, Arob Biong, faced it; and our own father, Deng Majok, also faced it. We have to understand and consider how they managed the situation and what lesson we can draw from their experience.

I then proceeded to explain my position on Abyei, building on the policies and strategies which both my grandfather and my father had pursued, and which ensured the security of the area and gave Abyei the benefits and strategic importance as a conciliatory Bridge between the African South and the Arab North of the Sudan. Then I turned to my main theme:

What you said about how the educated youth look at their elders and how the Dinka at the time of our forefathers were in the forefront are matters that are very much on my mind. My concern made me talk with the Dinka chiefs of the South, prominent chiefs like Geir Thiik (Giirdit) and Arol Kachwol and Makuei Bilkuei—many chiefs, I talked with them. And what I wanted from them was their knowledge about the affairs of our land, beginning with the time man was created, up to the present day, and how they saw the world ahead; those were the things I discussed with them. So, I would like to ask you some questions.

I went on to discuss how modern education is undermining our traditional knowledge and related cultural values:

Our people seem to think that education means that once you go to school, you must turn away from the traditional ways of your people. To them, an educated child is one who knows the Arab ways and the European ways, but not the Dinka ways, because it is said that the Dinka are a backward people who cannot write.

I explained that education is essentially passing on to younger generations the ways and means by which their society functioned in the past and is functioning today. I drew a distinction between knowledge in literate societies and oral knowledge in pre-literate societies like that of the Dinka.

In the literate world, what is read in books is what exists in society. It is how people live that is put in books so that people coming, generation after generation, find it written down. But in our traditional society, people without writing and reading, it is the elders who are the custodians of the words of the country. When a child is born and as he grows up into adulthood, he learns from his elders. What in the Western world is written down to be read in books is, among the Dinka, told by fathers and elders to their children so that a child grows up knowing the affairs of the land, past and present.

I gave my own personal experience, the reorientation we received in education away from our traditional culture, and my own personal awakening that led me to studying and recording Dinka law, history, and culture generally.

When I saw that my education was not showing me the affairs of the Dinka, I asked myself as I studied law, why is it that our Dinka laws are not being taught? Why is it that we learn only the laws of the English and the laws of the Americans, and the laws of the Muslims, and the laws of other peoples? Why do we come to school to study other people's laws and not our own laws?

My teachers in Khartoum University—some of them English, some Americans—and others liked my thinking. So, whenever I went home on vacation, they gave me questions to ask so that we could write down Dinka laws. That is what produced the book I showed you before—*Tradition and Modernization: A Challenge for Law Among the Dinka of the Sudan*. When I went to England and on to America, I found that the ways of our Black African people were, for the first time, being looked for, written down, and taught.

I addressed the diminishing population of our knowledgeable elders: *The people who know the ancient words of the past are getting fewer and fewer; education is changing the minds of our people. Only a few remaining elders know the traditional ways of the Dinka.*

I then elaborated on what I had been doing to address the crisis: *So, what I have been doing is to gather as much information as possible from here. I am still working on the information I have already gathered. And these are things which, one day, even if years become a hundred, the children of our children and their descendants will read them and say—'In the past, this is the way those people lived, and this is the way their ancestors were.' Even for the people who will call themselves educated in the future, it is these materials which will be the subject of education. The man who knows this will be a man who will be known and called educated. An educated man will be the man who knows the words of the past and the way new things have added themselves to the ways of the past, up to this day.*

I went on to explain the radical changes our society is undergoing and how views on critical issues affecting the country have become sharply divided. I said I chose elders and chiefs to record and capture their knowledge and views on issues, because in our Dinka society, an elder like the chief is like a book.

In books you find words of the people of the past. You read what they

44

have written and then add your own words to what you have learned from them. Where there are no books, it is the elders and the chiefs who know the most. It is in the houses of the Chiefs that people meet and whatever is said anywhere comes to the chief. So, for a person who wants the words of the country, the chiefs and respected elders are the ones who know the most.

I reiterated what I had often told our people in the Diaspora about the importance of remaining in contact with their cultural background and related values:

If a person should allow education to make him forget the culture of his people, and their way of life, he would be like a tree without roots. A tree without roots cannot stand or survive. A tree may stand erect, but if it has no roots, it is dead and will sooner or later fall.

These themes in my discussion with the Ngok Dinka elders were in many ways a reiteration of the introductory remarks I had made in my interviews with the Dinka Chiefs. My discussion with Chief Arol Kachuol in Juba, in early 1973, was particularly insightful and deeply moving. I began by telling him my critical perspective on modern education for our Dinka youth:

Our education has not passed on to us the words of our people. Education was meant to take the minds and hearts of the children away from their home into foreign lands. But as the saying goes, each man has his back. This is what has kept the minds and hearts of some of us in our land. Many of our educated youth still believe that education means turning away and forgetting the ways of our people. But there are some among us who believe that such education does not have much to be praised, that education which does not respect the roots of a child is not the right education for growing up. In truth, a part of every educated Dinka believes this, to a certain extent.

I then went on to explain my experience with the Dinka I meet abroad, and with whom I discuss the affairs of our people and country. I said that in those discussions, I quickly find out that education has not altogether succeeded in erasing their tradition and cultural values.

So, even though we have travelled extensively and have gone to distant lands and have grown up to be men away from home, it is still said that so and so is from country so and so, that he is from family so and so, and that his roots are there! This has not left our hearts. Much of what I have done abroad relates to the Dinka. I have written books which are concerned with the ways of the Dinka. This book, 'The Dinka of the Sudan,' for instance, I wrote while I was in America in order to show the ways of the Dinka to the outside world.

I said that we used to hear the names of the prominent chiefs of various Dinka tribes and that I did not expect that God would one day give me the opportunity to meet them and discuss the important affairs of our people and our country. I explained that I wanted to discuss with them many issues: how our people lived in traditional society, how we came in contact with other people, such as the Arabs of Northern Sudan, how the English came and went, how the events of the more recent years have affected our people, and how they viewed the future of our country. And of course, I told them that they could add to the list of issues whatever else they wanted to discuss or any message they wanted to convey to their young educated children.

This talk of ours, if it goes well, can produce things that should be recorded to be read in the future. These are the things that will be taught to our children in the future. Our children and the children of our children and their children and many more generations to come will read them and say—'Chief so and so once said this and that.' What is important is that we should talk like one people; a person should say the words of his heart. When I go to write them down, if I find anything that I believe should not be said publicly, anything a chief does not want to be made public, I shall keep it to myself; it will not be heard. What I find useful to say, I shall write down and make available for people to read. So, ours is a conversation of one family—a conversation between a man and his son. You may now begin.

This is what Chief Arol Kachwol said in response and I quote it at length because I believe it summarizes important aspects of Dinka worldview:

Your words are true, Mading. The world has been lived in for a long time. It is God who changes the world by giving successive generations their turns. For instance, our ancestors, who have now disappeared, the way their world began and the way they lived, they held the horns of their life.

Then God changed things; things changed until they reached us, and they will continue to change. When God comes to change your world, it will be through you and your wife. You will sleep together and bear a child. When that happens, you should know that God has passed on to your children, born by your wife, the things with which you lived your life. For instance, your father, Deng Majok, if he had lived without a child until his death, his would have been the kind of life that continues only as a tale. But if he bore a big son like you who can be spoken of—'This is Mading, son of Deng' —then even if a person never met your father and he hears that you are the son of Deng in the same way he had heard of your father, he will meet through you your father whom he never met.

So, the world goes on by the will of God. God who created people and who changes things. Take you, for example, the beginning of your fame was when you were chosen to go to school and learn. Here you are, you have gone far. You have left behind the country in which your mother was married. But you were chosen by your father to go and learn the words of other peoples.

Chief Arol then introduced the important issue of mixed marriages and implications of relations across tribal or racial divisions:

In your search for knowledge, things happened. For instance, where is this girl, your wife, from? Is she not from America? And you have brought her back to your country. If you bear a child together now, in that child will combine the words of her country and the words of your country. It is as though God has given her to Deng, your father.

So, the way we see it, God has brought peace and reconciliation into your hearts. None of you is to hate the race of the other. Even if a man was a slave or descended from a slave, and he marries into a family, he becomes a relative; he becomes a member of the family. Even our brothers, who were taken away as slaves, by now they have probably found their circles and have combined with other peoples to create their

47

own kinships. So, if a man has secured a wife, as you have married, it is for him to bear his own blood and to bear the blood of his wife's kin. That's the way it goes. Tomorrow, the people of that tribe or the people of that race, God will take them and mix them with the people of that race. They too will bear their own races through their children. When that happens, whatever hostility might have been between people, should no longer be allowed to continue. Relationship kills those troubles and begins the new way of kinship...Man is one single word with God.

Dinka religion promises no heaven after death, only continuity through the living, even though some form of continued existence after death is recognized as a projection of this world into the next. Social continuity can be achieved through various forms of procreation by proxy. According to a custom known as 'levirate' among anthropologists, a man cohabits with a junior widow of his father or other relative to beget children to the name of the dead man. And in what anthropologists call "ghost marriage," a man marries a wife for a deceased relative and begets children with that woman to the name of the dead man.

But to the Dinka, continuity is best achieved through one's own biological children, being the nearest to one's self:

Your father died—said Arol Kachwol to me—and when he died, even if he had not given you his words, he left you a life. His words went with him, but they also remained in you. Even though your father was mourned when he died, today, seeing you, there is no reason to mourn your father anymore. Whatever words died with him, one can now see that they have also remained and continued to live in you.

The Dinka consider procreation to be more than a function of biology; it involves the social climate of family relations. The desired results are achieved when harmony and happiness prevail in the family, especially between husband and wife. *A father gives his heart to his son if there is happiness between him and his wife*—said Chief Ayeny Aleu, whom I also interviewed in Juba in early 1973.

Heredity is a matter of happiness. When a man enters his mother's womb through his father's urine (sperm), it is happiness between his father and mother which gives him his father's good blood. The father passes on to the son his best qualities if he is happy at the moment of his sleeping with the mother. If your father had quarreled with your mother, you would not have entered your mother's womb with the qualities you have now.

For instance, if my wife tells me a bad thing and I blindly go to bed with her, the child I will beget will never get my qualities. And as you sit here now, it is because of the good food your mother cooked for your father and the good words they said to one another that you came out just like your father. That is why Deng Kwol begot you so straight with his qualities.

The cooperation required in procreation goes beyond the parents and the unity and harmony of the living members of the family. God is seen as playing a pivotal role in the creation of every individual, one of the reasons why the Dinka see in every person the divine attributes of God's work. Ayeny Aleu expressed it with a colorful vividness:

Where God created people, I do not really know. It is very difficult to imagine in one's mind. But he did create people. And he did not leave us; the Creator did not leave us. Why? There is one thing which makes me believe that the Spirit that created us was good and is near. For instance, your mother was married and what she did with your father was a game; they were playing a game of pleasure. And that game has now become Mading.

So, you see, can we really say that the Creator has gone away? He is here and he is good. Here is Mading, and it all began with a game between your father and your mother, between Deng Kwol and your mother. Here you have emerged as Mading and you have satisfied all of us. So, you see why we are happy.

These are central elements of Dinka social order. Every society has fundamental norms which provide the inner logic of the system and determine the basic principles that guide behavior. Three principles are central to the Dinka value system. The first is the concept which I have already introduced, *Koch e nom* (or *nhom*), "Standing the head of a dead man upright"—a form of immortality which, as I noted, Harold Lasswell, in his introduction to *Tradition and Modernization*, termed "The myth of permanent identity and influence." But among the Dinka, this is more than the word myth usually connotes; it aims at ensuring the continued presence and participation of every individual after death. It accounts for the practice of what anthropologists call *levirate*, which requires that a child-bearing widow lives with a relative of the dead man to continue bearing children to the name of her dead husband. The concept also obligates the relatives of a man who dies before marrying to marry a wife for his spirit or ghost to beget children in the name of the dead man. Anthropologists call this 'ghost marriage.' While *koch e nom* theoretically applies to every person, it is more related to men because of the dominance of the patriarchal lineage system.

Another principle which is fundamental to the Dinka value system is *cieng*, a concept of ideal human relations aimed at unity, harmony, and conciliatory management of differences. *Cieng* has a wide range of interrelated meanings, including custom, law, behavior, conduct, and way of life. *Cieng* is both prescriptive, what ought to be, and descriptive, what in fact happens. It is supposed to be inherently good, unless qualified as bad. It is sometimes specified as *cieng e baai*, and *baai* means home, village, community, tribe or country. *Cieng* is therefore specific to a social unit and inclusive to expanding circles, ultimately embracing humanity.

Ironically, *cieng* can also mean to dominate, but implying benevolent control. Built into *cieng* are fundamental principles of what we might refer to as human rights. But the Dinka believe that *cieng* should cover respect not only for humans as God's creatures, whatever their race, culture, or religion, but also non-human creatures of God. It requires being in harmony, not only with humanity, but with nature. As one elder put it to me, one must respect even birds that fly in the sky, the fish in the river, the trees and all that do not speak; they also have the dignity of being creatures of God. Despising them risks divine wrath that might be disastrous for the wrongdoer. "Even your precious things that you so carefully guard and protect will be destroyed."

The paradox is that while *cieng* prescribes peaceful persuasive means for resolving differences and is strongly against the use of violence, violence was a frequent feature of what are often referred to as the warrior Nilotic tribes, including the Dinka and the Nuer. This was largely due to the division of roles that made chiefs and elders the peacemakers, and organized young men into warrior age sets whose identity and dignity rested in being warriors, supported by their female counterpart age-sets, to defend society against external aggression, a role they exaggerated by going to war at the slightest provocation. As will be evidenced in this book, this is often in defiance of the chiefs and elders.

Another fundamental concept among the Dinka is *dheeng,* which can best be translated as dignity. This is a concept which covers such elements as physical appearance, the esthetics of beauty, and artistic expression in song and dance. It also covers proper conduct in relationship to others, which includes observing the ideals of *cieng.* One can have *dheeng,* and be respected as *adheng,* which can best be translated as a gentleman (the concept also applies to women), either by virtue of the status one is born into or which one acquires by merit. One can be an *adheng* because of wealth, but that must be connected with generosity or benevolent attitude toward others. Otherwise, one may be rich, and an *adheng* by Welty, and yet be known as *ayur,* the opposite of *adheng,* if he is miserly or ungenerous.

These moral values apply to power and leadership. When a person assumes control of the community, the tribe or the country, he is said to *dom baai,* and *baai,* as I said, covers home and expands up to the tribe and the country. *Dom* also applies to physical seizing or holding of cattle. But *dom* is not merely physical control; it implies pacification and ensuring peace, security, and order. The next requirement is *guier baai,* which means improving the situation by solving any problems that existed before assuming control. Two concepts relate more directly to physical control and exercise of authority to ensure stability of the improved situation. One is *mac baai,* which internally means to tie or bind, a term normally used to mean tying cow to a peg with a rope. *Mac* also refers to family or kin. The other word is *muk baai,* which means 'keeping,' a word that also applies to cattle

51

and to nurturing, for instance a child, and implies stability. These values are circular and mutually reinforcing. To have *mac* or *muk baai* is also to have *dom baai,* back to the normative meaning of authoritative control.

To be a successful leader requires living up to these values. The word for a chief, *beny,* also means rich, generous, and benevolent. All these principles and the values associated with them tend to agglutinate and carry benefits with responsibilities. They must all be born in mind when discussing qualifications for leadership among the Dinka. In many ways, Deng Majok, my father, excelled by the standards of all these values.

Kathryn Teter Ludwig and Lawrence Augustus Ludwig, parents of Dorothy Deng

Left:
Francis Mading Deng and Dorothy Ludwig Deng wedding picture.

Next spread, left page:
Acok, wife of Deng Majok and mother of Francis Mading Deng

Next spread, right page:
Deng Majok (left), Bishop (right)

Acok, mother of Francis, and
her grandson David Kwol with
cousins in Abyei, 2009

Next spread, left page, top:
Family Photo. Daniel Jok,
David Kwol and Dennis Biong
(back row)
Francis Mading, Dorothy and
Donald Deng (front row)

Next spread, left page, bottom:
Family Photo. Donald Deng,
David kwol and Daniel Jok
(back row). Dorothy, Dennis
Biong and Francis Mading Deng
(front row)

Teter-Ludwig-Deng Family
Reunion, East Stroudsburg, PA

Next spread, right page, top:
David and Elizabeth's wedding:
bride and groom with relatives
from Abyei, 2012

Next spread, right page, bottom:
Four sons of Dorothy and Francis:
Daniel Jok, Donald Deng, David
kwol, Dennis Biong, 2012

Three

A Family Of Multitudes

The attributes for which my father, Chief Deng Majok, was known, and the Dinka Ngok, the cultural values associated with leadership more generally, more or less represent the pillars of the family and the society in which I was born and raised. Obviously, most of the values described are aspirational, providing guiding principles rather than actually achieved or even fully achieved objectives. But what I observed of my father and what I heard of my grandfather, these leaders epitomized models of virtuous leadership by Dinka ideals of leadership. Perhaps my grandfather was more the ideal traditional leader, while my father reinforced those ideals with the modern tools of state coercion, which paradoxically compromised the moral and spiritual ideals of traditional authority, but made his leadership more effective in enforcing law and order, and therefore peace, security, and stability in his tribe.

But let me start the story from the beginning, my birth into what (to the best of my knowledge) would become the largest family in the Sudan, probably in Africa, and arguably in the world. In accordance with the Dinka practice for a first born in those days, I was born at Maker, the home of my maternal grandparents, several miles from Noong, my father's traditional home. No one knows the precise date of my birth, but historical coincidences and my mother's recollections suggest that I was born in the autumn of 1938. Despite the wishes of my maternal grandfather, Mijok Duor, that I be named Mading after the bull he and the elders of his clan had sacrificed and prayed to for her to beget a son for her first born, when, as a baby, I was taken to my father's home, I was given the name Arob—after my great grandfather, Arob Biong. On hearing that, grandfather Mijok was infuriated. He went to Noong one early morning and called for a meeting with my father and Uncle Deng Makuei. He said to them:

All I wanted from the marriage of my daughter was that Head [of Deng Majok] that drove away the cattle from my daughter's engagement and imposed his will on me to marry my daughter. And I appealed to God for divine justice. If God has responded to my prayers by giving me my Mading, how could you think of naming him Arob Biong? Never ever call this Mading of mine by any other name. Father later spoke to his family and said, he does not want to hear the child called Arob anymore. He will be Mading.

In accordance with Dinka practice for a first born, I went to my maternal relatives at the weaning age of about three years. My time among my maternal relatives was perhaps the happiest part of my childhood. I was in the center of everything and everyone, and I received as much love as there can be. I remember days when I would sit with my grandfather just playing or conversing, listening to his wisdom and religious intonation as he invoked his clan spirits or responded to the sounds of the totemic animals of his clan. We would sit and eat together in a combination of ages, which my observation among the Dinka has found to be very rare. From my grandmother, Ayak, I received an intensified version of a mother's love, and, among the Dinka, a mother's love is almost unqualified. My grandmother seemed to me the most tender loving person there was.

My father was generally against his children living with their maternal relatives. He made concessions only in favor of first-borns and apparently meant that to be for brief periods. On one occasion, he asked me to go home with him. Instead of responding to him, I turned to my maternal relatives and demanded that whatever my father had come for be granted or else I would leave with him. This technique worked. My father understood my preference. With a smile, he allowed me to stay.

I really loved it among my maternal relatives. Leaving was rather difficult. With time, however, my father's objection increased and even when he did not come in person, we received the message through my mother's frequent visits. Father became adamant that I should return home without further delay. I went.

Although I loved being with my maternal relatives, I found Noong very exciting, to us the most beautiful place on earth. And indeed,

Noong appeared to be the center of this world, a meeting point of many welcomed guests. Uncle Arob, Father's younger brother, was to express these sentiments in a song:

In our clan, we do not cheapen our words
We hold the place we have held
Since man emerged from the Byre of Creation;
Our Noong booms like a marketplace
Anticipated with confidence by travelers.
God has created all kinds of men,
Some he has created to attract guests.
My brother, Deng, the Crested Crane,
Once said: 'What is given goes around,
And the big thing swallowed is wasted'.

Noong was more than a meeting place; it was a village belonging to a family of multitudes. Let me tell an open secret which I learned much later. When my father was in his youth, he had relations with a girl who, with the Dinka flexible use of kinship terms, was a daughter of his maternal uncle. I do not know the precise degree of the blood ties, but they surely fell within the prohibited degrees. Among the Dinka, these are very wide, and the prohibition is very strict.

My father's wrong was a serious violation of the Dinka moral code, but the curse he received was wonderful in his own judgement. The curse was—*Deng, son of my sister, no disease will come your way. Your only disease will be women. It is they who will cause your death.* In other words, my father was cursed to love women and to die in their pursuit. He loved them, and, although he died of liver cancer, the Dinka claim that women caused his death.

As soon as he started marrying, one marriage followed another. Nyanboldit, the Senior Nyanbol, was the first, followed shortly afterwards by Nyanbol Amor. Almost at the same time, he was involved with Kuei Deng. My mother followed at a time he was already engaged to Aker Tiel from a prominent Twic family. Nyanbol Deng came next, followed by Tiet Aguar. Then he took Nyanawai from an

65

engagement to another man.

The next, Amel, deserves special mention because she introduced a modern Sudanese way of life into the family. When she was born, her family had migrated into a Northern town. She, of course, spoke Dinka and was also fluent in Arabic. She also had an Arab name, Hamdi, although I never knew whether she had converted to Islam. Amel was very short for a Dinka, rather stout, and almost Arab-like in her brown color of skin and mannerism. In her form of dress, cooking and housekeeping, she was a "sophisticated" Arabized woman.

Knowing that much influence depended on meeting both Arab and Dinka standards and being himself a model for selective change, Father saw a great deal of merit in Amel. Although she never begot a child, he made her a right-hand woman, furnished her with all necessary modern household equipment: china, cutlery, aluminum cooking pots and utensils, pewter and glassware, silver or aluminum trays, and other newly introduced objects, which were considered luxury items in that context.

Above all, Father made Amel an educator for the rest of his family. Within a short time, Amel influenced the family in a way that turned many more into modern homemakers and educators of new ones yet to come. It was generally felt, and Father often acknowledged, that Amel had much to do with his becoming Paramount Chief. In most ways, Father's younger wives and, to a lesser extent, the older ones, became members of a self-sustaining system in which every newcomer quickly learned the techniques which ultimately went back to Amel: cooking, manner of dress, which included frocks and sari-type *toub* and veil, braiding of the hair, and Arab harem-like pattern of behavior.

The line of newcomers never stopped until my father's death well into his late seventies or early eighties. When I returned home from weaning around 1943, my father had about fifteen wives. When he died in 1969, he had been married close to two hundred wives from nearly all corners of Ngok Dinka land and the neighboring tribes, from whom he had about four hundred children. The Dinka consider it necessary for a Chief to have many wives. It is in part a political strategy. My grandfather had about thirty wives. My father obviously broke the record. The main criticism against him as a leader came from his excessive marriages, and most of the problems he had, private and public, were in one way or another connected with marriages. Many people, from whom he took girls they had intended to marry and to whom they were sometimes already engaged, complained to higher authorities. Political opponents alleged corruption behind his ability to afford so many marriages. His wives, at least the younger ones, wore relatively expensive clothes. And his family was relatively well fed with food for which ingredients had to be bought. There were clearly arguments for whoever wanted to stain my father's name on account of his marriages.

But polygyny is also an investment of more material value than political support. A man shares in the bride wealth of the female relatives of his wife, and in the case of a Chief, the circle is wide, and the share is gladly and promptly given. Marriages also produce daughters who in turn bring wealth through marriages, and the daughters of Chiefs are the most expensive. They may not always be the most beautiful, but there is much of that too, since their mothers are carefully selected for reasons which include beauty. Furthermore, the Chief does not pay for his marriages alone, for the collection of bride wealth is usually made by a wide circle of relatives and friends. In the case of Chiefs, this circle is particularly wide. It is true that many ceased to help as marriages continue, but it is also true that many new sources gladly emerge. So, from the point of view of the Dinka economy, my father's marriages were also lucrative. Father had the greatest number of cattle in the tribe; cattle accrued almost daily.

The family was divided into three main groups called "Houses" headed by the top three wives: Nyanbol Arob (Nyanboldit), Nyanbol Amor, and Kwei (Kwen Deng). Aker Tiel assisted Nyanboldit, while my mother assisted Nyanbol Amor. Kwei was assisted by Amou who was married at the time Father decided to have a branch of the family at Abyei, to which he transferred most of his junior wives and appointed the three middle wives, Amel, Nyanawai, and Amou, to represent the seniors in the leadership of the groups. Amel represented Nyanboldit, Nyanawai represented Nyanbol Amor, and Amou represented Kwei.

The structure and stratification of the family was relative to time and place. Initially, wives like my mother were junior at Noong in relation to the Big Three. But later, with more marriages, and with other villages established, they became among the most senior. Amel, Nyanawai, and Amou became the Head Wives of the three family groupings at Abyei. As another village was established at Nainai, more junior wives were appointed to head the groups there. In due course, even those junior wives became senior in relation to other more junior wives in the even newer villages that Father was to establish. The segmentation process and the relativity of seniority continued with the expansion of the family size and settlements.

Father exercised much of his control over the family through the leading wives. Many conflicts between the wives were investigated and settled by them. These may be extensions of children's quarrels, disagreement over domestic assignments, or minor arguments fanned by deeper sentiments of rivalry and jealousy over the husband and his distribution of family resources. Senior wives wielded considerable authority and commanded great respect. Junior wives addressed them as "Mothers," but gave them greater rituals of respect than Dinka children show their mothers.

In certain matters, each wife could go directly to my father, but in most cases, their demands were channeled through their leaders, who also represented my father to them. There was a cardinal rule against jealousy and stringent measures were taken to suppress it. But loathed as jealousy was among the Dinka and particularly in our family, it is recognized as an inevitable aspect of polygyny. Success in repressing jealousies is only a matter of degree. In view of the size of our family, this degree was impressively low, but jealousies nonetheless persisted, especially between the leaders of the houses.

My close companions were Bol, the third child and second son of Nyanboldit, and Kwol, the third child and first son of Nyanbol Amor. There were two older brothers, Chan, the second child and first son of Nyanboldit, and Arob, the first child of Kwei. For some reason, maybe age difference, my early memories do not bring Chan and Arob into focus. As for Bol and Kwol, we were about the same age. Bol and I were born the same month, and although we eventually ascertained that he was older, for a long time, neither our father nor our mothers could tell us exactly which one of us came first. Kwol was a little younger than us, but that made no difference.

We were acculturated to live up to the values of family solidarity and loyalty to my father. This was not really a change since those values had been inculcated in me among my maternal relations. But the transition from identifying with the maternal kin to becoming integrated into the paternal line was not so easy. Among the maternal relatives, one is called by the mother's name as son of the mother. I was Mading d'Achok among my maternal relatives. Among my paternal kin, I was to be Mading de Deng. A boy is tested early in life to answer the question whose son he is: "Whose Mading are you?" was the question. The answer should have been an unequivocal—*I am Mading de Deng*. It is said that I used to hesitate by saying—*I am Mading de Ngadang*—*Ngadang* being a word that alludes to a name one has forgotten or is uncertain about. That meant being torn between calling myself Mading d'Achok and Mading de Deng. Identifying with the father is the first step to being taught to list the line of your ancestors to the founding father of the clan, which was not really required of the maternal lineage.

It was now evident to me that I enjoyed among my paternal relatives general appreciation similar to what I had enjoyed among my maternal relatives. I was particularly fond of attending Father's court and interacting with the court members and other attendants. Although Father was not explicit about his attitude, it was obvious that he took pride in my performance and in the lavish praise I received. People in my father's court would send me on any one of many errands. There came a time when my mother was so concerned about the danger of my being bewitched that she told me to stop my displays at court.

But I had already reached the point where I felt that, according to Dinka values, a mother's advice was not to be taken seriously to avoid being perceived as *menh e tik,* "the son of a woman," in the man's world of the Dinka. My mother knew that on the whole my formula was correct. She loved me and believed in me so much that she was not going to let her controls block my way. At the same time, she knew that I loved her so much that whatever I did externally against her was not a qualification to my love, but an assertion of how best I thought our common goal could be achieved. I think this was the most important understanding between my mother and me.

There was something quite unique about my mother, which is impossible to describe. Although she was just over six feet tall, in the context of the Dinka, she did not strike me as particularly tall; I saw her as average. Within the modest limits of traditional life of the time, my mother was very meticulous about her appearance and was always well groomed. The mere sight of her gave me a great sense of pride, joy and security. But as I got to know my mother, it was not the physical aspect that I grew to admire so much as her wisdom, discretion, courtesy, generosity and charm. She had great success with people; intelligent, prudent and well spoken, she won admiration from all circles. Her persuasiveness also made her a peacemaker in the family. I grew up hearing a great deal of praise for her, not only among elders, but also from my brothers, relatives and other associates of my generation.

Perhaps the most beautiful words I ever heard about my mother came from my father much later in my life. And they were the most beautiful because they came from him. I was then attending University. The two of us sat in a man-to-man candid discussion of our father-son relationship that I had initiated. When I think back now, I am amazed that I was so daring. To reassure me of his approval of me, my father surprised me by bringing my mother into the picture. He said that among the Dinka, a father's attitude toward his child is in significant part related to his view of the child's mother. He spoke in lavish praise of my mother and concluded with the words,

She is like a first wife to me. When I am away and Achok is present at home with Nyanboldit, I do not worry. I trust that she will keep things under control. Even if Nyanboldit is away and Achok is present, I feel I

have a first wife present.

This was most unlike my father, for he was not one to be so lavish in his praise.

As for me, I could never praise my mother sufficiently. Whenever I was away at school, especially after reaching adulthood, I would feel regretful that I never revealed my feelings for, and to, her. I feared she might have doubts. Some of my European female friends who got to know of her through me would urge me to let my mother know how much I loved her. But somehow, I always assured myself that she knew exactly how much I loved her, and I knew how much she loved me. We did not need to say it in words. Even when we disagreed, our mutual love was never in doubt. In talking about my mother, the way I am now doing, I am making an exception for the imperatives of this book, for I would never have dreamed of openly expressing such deep sentiments of love and affection for her; it is very UN-Dinka.

Although there was a recognized special bond between mother and child, family solidarity was an overriding value which I meticulously observed. Whatever polygynous "jealousy" meant, we were conditioned to avoid it, and I was determined to reject it. I also hoped it would not be shown to me. Generally, it was not. My father's wives took us all as their own sons and we felt worthy of their approval. Dinka culture teaches one to conceal love and affection for one's own mother but demonstrate them to stepmothers as a means of reinforcing family unity and solidarity. Love for the mother was a recognized function of the heart, while love for the father was a function of the mind. And that meant seeing him as the symbol of family unity and solidarity.

But father was probably more feared and revered than loved. Personally, I was simply scared of my father. He had one of the most excruciating tongues I had ever heard, and this was common knowledge at home and in the tribe. He would not hesitate to insult anyone in front of the crowds that constantly surrounded him. But Father's most important power of control over both his family and his tribe was the force of his personality, reinforced by his physical appearance. He was about six feet three inches tall, slim but not unduly thin. Like an Arab sultan, he wore long robes and a turban. Only once did I see him in western clothes: a dark suit, a shirt, a tie, and a hat. His face was rather long, and his features were sharp. On his upper lip was a scar said to be the result of a fight with a lion in defense of his younger brother Arob. Rather than disfigure his face, it added character to it, almost looking like nature's final touch. The face itself was stern and determined, but by no means cruel. His intelligence glowed and the power of his eyes penetrated. He was very particular about his appearance, and it was total in its impact. I have still to meet a man who left no question whatsoever about his superiority, even among his administrative superiors, as my father did.

My father's wives feared and respected him. He was not just a husband; he was the Chief and they referred to him as such. Occasionally, the senior wives called him by his name. Junior wives would run into hiding whenever he was heard to approach. They would never eat in his presence. When they talked to him, they always covered their faces and looked away. They never looked straight into his face. My feelings and thoughts about my father consolidated themselves with time and they continued to be obsessive to me until his death. For years after his death, I had nightly dreams of my father, healthy and in full control, sickly and dying, and alternating between life and death. The more I knew him, the more I feared him, admired him, and adored him. I felt insecure about how much he loved me and that itself imposed a confusing qualification on my love for him. Whether I loved him more than I feared him or feared him more than I loved him is something I still ponder. He seemed to me so far beyond any human being that he was hardly human to be judged by normal standards.

What made me accept the formality between us was my early realization that love and affection for the father in Dinka society were largely objective. One loved one's father if one lived up to the ideals of the family. By meeting that challenge, one could count on the objective love of a wide circle of relatives and associates. I was confident that, excepting doubts about my father, I was loved by a wide circle of my father's relatives and admired by the many strangers I encountered at home. Although I had doubts about the mutuality of feeling between my father and me, I observed him keenly and took him as the model of what I should be in the future. But I realized that I was only a small addition to a long line of ancestral giants going back to Jok, the founder of our clan Pajok, whose names we were taught to memorize from early childhood. I did not know then the importance of my maternal lineage, although I knew them as virtuous people and loved them very much.

Four

Legends of the Forefathers

The roots of my paternal line go very deep into Dinka history—according to mythology, back to the time of creation. To be sure, the line contains only eleven well-known generations, including my own, with several more vaguely traceable beyond Jok, the founder of our clan Pajok. But mythology has it that Jok was the "Breaker-Through"—*Athurkok*—who opened the gates of the Byre of Creation so that his people, the Dinka, could exit into freedom.

Dinka myths of creation go deeper into man's existence and bear surprisingly close resemblance to the stories of the Bible. Garang, the first man to be molded from clay, and Abuk, his wife, who was made from his rib, are sometimes referred to by their biblical names as Adam and Hawa (Eve), which obviously indicates an age-old contact between the peoples of the Nile Valley.

For me, one of the most creative and daring ideas of John Garang, the Leader of the Sudan People's Liberation Movement and Army (SPLM/A) was tracing our roots to the ancient Kingdom and civilization of Kush, a case of reconstructing identity to boost self-perception and confidence in state and nation-building. Dr. Lual A. Deng, in his book, *The Power of Creative Thinking: The Ideas of John Garang,* wrote:

"A people without a traceable cultural heritage would not have
a body of knowledge to create commonwealth and sustainable
legacies for their future generations. In this respect, throwing away
the rich legacy of the Kushites, as some elements in South Sudan
propose, would be an act of self-denial, and social suicide. Our
very being is our heritage bequeathed to us over five thousand years
since the time of Kush/Cush kingdom. Dr. John's conviction is
evidence-based belief, for Biblical sources and archeological findings
support it (8)."

After citing the Genesis and archeological research that confirm that Kush/Cush was the first recorded kingdom to be established in sub-Saharan Africa, the author observed—"Because of our lazy thinking, we have not been able to dig deeper into our history. But Dr. John did that" (Ibid). He then proceeded to quote sources establishing Kush as a Black Kingdom that wielded considerable tools of power—military and governance—though "without having a system of writing, an extensive bureaucracy, or numerous urban centers." Alleging that historians have mislabeled Kush as a vassal of the state of Egypt, the author went on to write:

"So, the challenge is for our historians to join hands with world-renowned archeologists in their quest to dig deep into the Kushite system of governance, for the ugly face of racism and prejudice concealed this reality (9)."

This reconstruction of identity, a pervasive aspect of John Garang's promotion of his New Sudan vision, was one which I initially viewed with skepticism as too contrived. But I grew to understand, recognize and appreciate it as a creative mythology of identity formation. I do not use the word "myth" to connote lack of reality, but as a concept which has become well established in the social sciences to mean frequently occurring or recurring ideas and practices. "A community myth is comprised of identifications, demands and expectations" (McDougall and Lasswell, *Law, Science and Policy,* 1964, quoted in Francis Mading Deng, *Tradition and Modernization,* Yale, 1971 p.23). This mythical shaping of identity mirrors in many respects the way the Arab-Islamic identity was shaped.

My own work on this specific aspect of the evolution of identities in the Sudan was informed by extensive interviews with Dinka Chiefs and elders in Juba in 1973 during the first anniversary of the Addis Ababa Agreement, the results of which were published in two books, *Dinka Cosmology* and *Africans of Two Worlds: The Dinka in Afro-Arab Sudan.* The views of the elders I interviewed indicated the connection to the Biblical and Koranic scriptures and religious practices which have also been documented by anthropologists. Centuries of intervening hostilities have however overshadowed this connection. Perhaps for the same reason, I don't think this revivalist reconstruction of bridging identity resonates with most South Sudanese. This is, however, not a reason to stop the scientific search for knowledge on the issue.

Dating the origin of our family to the time of creation is a metaphor which revitalizes Dinka belief that God has a hand in the creation of every individual. The values associated with God's involvement become particularly pronounced in the case of divine leaders as God's chosen sons in a given community, at a given moment of time, and under a particular set of critical circumstances. Jok was evidently the product of such circumstances.

Bulabek Malith, a close member of our clan, said,

When we came from the Byre of Creation, there was an elder called Jok, who is our Founding Father. He was the man who led the people. He is now known as Jok Athurkok. And why he is so known is because he was the man who broke through the Byre of Creation. It is what Jok left behind that I am going to relate to you. Jok said that when he was in the lead, God put him to many terrifying tests to prove that he was the leader of the people. After he passed all those tests, God said—'I will make you lead the people.' That is why God put him ahead to lead the Black people.

Bulabek then introduced the idea of the sacred spears, explaining that God gave Jok the spears for the protection of all Black people. Longar is then introduced as a co-leader:

Jok said to his people that God had told him that a man called Longar would lead the people with him. 'Longar will lead, and you, Jok, will follow the people to protect them from behind. You will protect the people from a plague which will follow them, a plague which, if it reaches people, will never leave them again, it will always destroy your people.' Jok named the plague; he said it was the cyclone. Cyclones would come and he would stop them.

Longar was in the lead when he found a woman called Ayak who stopped the people on the way. She said to Longar—'You cannot pass.' So, all the Black people stopped because the woman had blocked their way. People who were being protected by Jok in the back stopped going forward. So Jok went through the crowds to see what had stopped the people from going forward. He found this woman who had sat in the path.

Jok said—'Longar, why have you stopped?' Longar said—'This woman has refused to let us pass.'–What does she say?' 'She says—"If anybody steps on my flour, it will be bad for the person."' Jok went ahead and stepped on the flour of the woman and nothing bad happened. That allowed the people to pass. Then Jok told Longar to go ahead and lead the way.

The story is continued by Loth Adija, a member of a different clan from another section of the Ngok tribe:

While Longar was leading, people came to a wide river. It was such a big river that people could not cross. They were stopped by people in the river who said—'You cannot cross.' People were afraid. So Longar went back to Jok and said—'The way is blocked. And our people cannot settle in this barren land. We must cross the river.' Jok said—'What stops the people from crossing?' Longar said—'There are people in the river who say—"If you step into the river, we will kill you."'

So Jok said—'I will go and look into that.' Then he went. And when he arrived, the people in the river re-appeared and said—'If you come into the river, you will see disaster with your own eyes.' Jok said—'What if I offer you cattle, will you let my people cross?' They said—'We do not want cattle.' – 'What if I give you sheep and goats?' They said—'We do not want them either.' Then he said—'If you insist, I have only one daughter, but I can give her to you to save my people.' The girl's name was Achai. With the mention of the daughter, the river people submerged into the water without saying anything more to Jok. That was taken as their having accepted his offer. So Jok returned to his people and said—'My people, we are going to cross the river.'

He then took bracelets off people's arms, white beads and other ornaments to decorate his daughter Achai. He then took Achai by the hand and they waded into the river as he sang the hymns. He was carrying the sacred spears pointing backward to indicate to the people in the river that he had no aggressive intentions. Holding his daughter's arm, they walked deeper and deeper into the water. When they reached the deepest point where the water reached the girl's head, she submerged and disappeared. The moment she disappeared, the water separated; one part flowed in one direction and the other part flowed in the opposite direction. There was suddenly dry land for the people to cross. That is how the Dinka crossed that great river and came to the land we now occupy.

The people in the river are sometimes described as white and on horse backs. But any attempt to explain this as probably connected to the slave raids and Achai given into slavery to redeem her people is resisted by our people. The people in the river are regarded as having been spirits and the sacrifice of Achai and the opening of the waters a miracle associated with divine leadership. Achai has now been immortalized as a spirit in the river to which annual offerings are made and is one of the ancestral spirits people pray to for redemption whenever needed.

Achai's sacrifice and the parting of the waters for people to cross bears obvious resemblance to the story of the Old Testament and Moses leading his people across the Red Sea. After the people had crossed to the other side of the river, Longar contested Jok's leadership.

He wanted to win the chieftainship—said Bulabek Malith.

What our ancestor said is that Longar wanted to test him. Longar had a bull of the color pattern Mangar. He sharpened the horns of that bull. Whenever the cattle were released to graze, he would stain the horns of his bull with blood and encouraged him to fight with other bulls. And whenever his bull fought with other bulls, he won and killed those bulls. That way, he was finishing off the bulls of the cattle-camp. Jok had a bull of Mijok color whose horns were widespread. He was a peaceful bull.

Jok's bull, Mijok, behaved like a chief. He did not mix with cattle. He would graze alone and go back to the cattle-byre on his own. Although he was peaceful, he was feared and respected by the other bulls. Longar's bull, Mangar, had subdued all the bulls in the herds, except for Jok's bull, Mijok. Longar began to brag that his bull would challenge Jok's bull to fight him. He said—'I am taking Mangar to confront that bull, Mijok, which people consider the chief. We will settle this contest over the leadership through our bulls.' So, he took his bull, Mangar, to confront Mijok inside the cattle-byre. Mangar advanced toward the byre. Mijok looked out and bellowed. Jok then said to his bull—'Mijok, here is a deadly beast which has been killing the bulls; he is being brought to fight you. He is coming to kill you.'

As Mijok heard that, he walked to the door of the cattle-byre and extended his front quarters outside the byre while his hind quarters remained inside. He waited there as Mangar advanced. They no longer had time to work up their anger. They met. Mijok quickly pierced his horn through the nape of Mangar's neck. Mangar fell in a heap in front of the byre and died. Longar said—'What has Mijok done to my bulls?' People said—'He has put him to an instant death.' That is how the saying came—'The bull of Jok wins his wars with part of his body inside the byre; Mijok of the son of God.'

Chan Dau, the chief of a section and a close associate of my father had a song in which he recalled this myth of the fight of bulls in competition of leadership, linking my father's powers to those of his ancestor's bull:

Deng, Crested Crane
Nothing happens and disappears forever;
Everything goes and returns.
What your ancestor Jok once said
That Jok wins his fights sitting in his cattle-bye
Has come back to us;
That is why you win your wars
Sitting on your throne
And tribes cry out—'Mijok is coming;
He will destroy us.'
Son of Yor, do not even try,
This is a Deng to be avoided like an electric eel
He destroys his foes.

Jok's genealogy has continued in leadership through the observance of the rule of primogeniture by which the most senior son of the most senior wife succeeds. The circumstances may sometimes be complicated enough to permit a latitude of choice among the sons of the Chief. There is always a way to find the best qualified person and

80

then justify the choice to conform with the traditional requirements. In their descending order, Jok's genealogy includes: Bulabek, Dongbek, Kwoldit, Monydhang, Allor, Biong, Arob, Kwol, and Deng Majok, my father. The positions of these individuals in the oral history of the Dinka vary significantly. Some are known only as names and hardly any major events are associated with their leadership. Some of them are men whose times were calm, peaceful, and uneventful. Others led their people through hard times and their prominence was in direct proportion to the problems they had to overcome. For example, Kwoldit's leadership coincided with one of the most difficult periods in Dinka history, the nineteenth century upheavals in which "the world was spoiled" by slave-raiders and hostile tribes. A faction of the tribe, including a regiment of militant young men, had moved northwards and come into contact with the invading forces from the North. Dongbek, Kwoldit's father, had remained behind. *We met with the Arabs and people were fighting*—said Bulabek Malith:

People held a meeting. All the nine sections of the Ngok Dinka met and decided to send their young men back. Young men of the age-set called Kiec (the Bees), were sent. Elders said to them—'Go back and fetch a descendant of Jok to come and provide leadership in this difficult war.' So Kiec age-set returned to fetch the great-grandson of Jok, the son of Dongbek. Dongbek blessed his son, Kwoldit, gave him the sacred spears of his ancestors, and sent him off to lead the tribe. As they carried him away, they sang a hymn which the Ngok still sing during the inauguration of their Paramount Chief:

'Kiec, this is the light to brighten your way.'
Dongbek honored us with Kwol,
'May Kwol give you the life of my father, Bulabek.'
In the land of Bulabek we had no Chief to guide our way,
No Chief to arrange our words.
'Kiec, this is the light to brighten your way.'

According to Dau Agok, an elder from Abyor section:

Kwol came and said—'How is this war being fought?' The people said—'The Arabs strike us with their swords.' He said—'Make shields from softwood and the day your shields and clubs are ready, let me know.'

The tribe proceeded to make the shields and clubs. When they were done, they said to him—'Chief Kwoldit, the shields and the clubs are all made!' He said—'Carry me tomorrow morning while I hold the sacred spears of my ancestors. Take me to the battlefront where the Arabs are.'

The next morning, he was carried to the battlefront. When they reached the front, he said—'Put me down.' They put him down. He took the spears and pointed them in the direction of the Arabs four times. Then he took the axe and hit a tree and said—'Now proceed to battle. But when you meet them, do not be the first to charge. Let them first charge at you. God will grant you victory.' That was what happened. When the Arabs tried to hit with their swords, the swords got stuck on the wooden shields. That was how the war was won. And that was how the river Kiir remained with us.

It is Kwol who made it possible for us to hold our country up to this day—said Bulabek Malith.

The coming of Kwol is what saved our people. Kwol begot his son, Monydhang, during the war with the Arabs. His father told him—'Keep this spear and use it against the enemy, but never point it at the Black man. God gave us this spear to be the guardian of all the Black people. If you fight with the Arab, point it at the Arab; he is your enemy. But the Black peoples are not your enemies.'

Not much is said about the next three leaders—Monydhang, Alor, and Biong—beyond the mere mention of their leadership, where they died, and where they were buried. Biong's period was the beginning of another critical phase in the history of the Dinka. The wars with the invaders from the North resumed and intensified. The Turko-Egyptian rule had extended itself into the Sudan in 1821 when Mohammed Ali Pasha, an Albanian Representative of the Ottoman Empire in Egypt, invaded the country. His main objective was to obtain Negro slaves, some of whom he intended to use as soldiers in his army.

It is generally accepted that slavery in one form or another prevailed along the Nile Valley for as far back as recorded history. For most of that time, it is also generally accepted that the Negroid tribes in the South were the consistent victims of slave raids. However, their own determined resistance and natural barriers protected many of the pastoral peoples from any deep penetration by slave-raiders. Consequently, it was not until the Turko-Egyptian government opened the Bahr El-Ghazal and Equatoria provinces and established relatively more security from outside invaders that the trade became well established.

It was, however, no easy feat for the Turko-Egyptian rule to establish itself in the South, and it was not until the 1870s that they could claim any degree of control. In the process of trying to establish itself, the Turko-Egyptian government carried out punitive expeditions throughout the tribes. Although the invaders encountered strong and determined resistance, the victim tribes suffered enormously. Chiefs were slain, their people killed, cattle seized, crops taken or burned down, and houses destroyed.

In addition to official government raids for slaves, there were private bands, some of which were led by Arab tribal leaders who saw in the trade an opportunity not only for bounty but also for extending their dominion. Biong Allor personally led the resistance of his people, and although a Divine Chief is normally supposed to perform war rituals and remain at home to pray for victory, the situation reached levels such that he got physically involved in battle.

Our ancestor, Biong, fought and fought while carrying a baby on his back—said Uncle Deng Makuei (Abot).

That baby died on his back while he was fighting. It was a critical situation. In a critical situation, everyone fights. But if it is not so critical, the Chief can remain to perform ritual functions and pray for peace or victory, depending on whether this was an internal war between the sections of his own tribe, or a war with a foreign aggressor.

Arob, Biong's successor, also took the brunt of the wars. He is said to have sacrificed his son to save his people, although it is not clear what form that sacrifice took. Songs about the sacrifice speak of 'giving up his son,' 'cutting his throat,' or simply 'breaking his son's back.' Father's youngest brother, Arob, addressed the issue in one of his songs:

Disaster came
(Arob went to the Government through Nuerland)
Nuerland was the land of his Fathers;

The territory of the Arabs stopped at Deinga (Muglad).
Something is now encroaching into our land
Ali, the leader of the Brown People
Is now wearing the Tassels of the Country
He is encroaching into the land of Arob;
But he will meet with ancient events
When one man ate the ribs of a donkey
And endured the pain of bad things;

And cut the throat of his son
To save the land of his father;
Arob cut off his son
And saved the land of the Ngok.

Arob is also said to have worked to overcome the crisis confronting his people through diplomatic and administrative contacts with Arab leaders to the North. The first point of conflict as well as resolution was with the Rezeigat Arabs of Darfur Province in Western Sudan. *The Rezeigat captured our people and destroyed our country*—said Chol Piok.
Arob Biong was taken to Twichland for protection. Whenever a
country is destroyed and people conclude that it is a disaster which
cannot be overcome, the Chief must be taken and hidden in safety
somewhere. Allor Ajing (The Deputy Paramount Chief) was also taken
to Nuerland.
And when the country was brought back to order, it was because of

one man called Dau Kiir. Even today, you will hear his name chanted: 'Dau Kiir, Dau Kiir.' It was he who saved our country. He could run faster than a horse; he was with another man called Chol Atem. They could outrun Arab horses until the horses would stop and just gaze at them. They were the only people who remained on our River Kiir. The wife of Dau Kiir was with them. They would leave her in a hole which a crocodile had abandoned and had dried up. And then they would go to hunt. They would spend the day away and return in the evening. One day, the Arabs saw the woman where she was hiding. They captured her while the men were away. When the men returned in the evening and did not find her, Dau said—'Chol, son of my Father, you go where you may find people to stay with, whether they are Twich or Nuer. I must go after my wife. With my wife gone, I no longer value life.'

The Rezeigat Arabs, now known as the people of Ibrahim Musa Madibo, had captured the land. They established a station at Gongmou from which they would attack and attack. They were right there at Gongmou, near Akechnhial on the River Kiir. That is where they established their station. Dau Kiir, searching for his wife, went to the Arab camp. As he approached, the police guarding the Chief wanted to shoot him. But Madibo said—'No, do not shoot him. What about the thing that brought him here? This tall man let us see why he chose to come on his own!' And Dau was known to have killed Arabs in exceptionally large numbers.

Dau is reported to have approached a large shady tree under which Madibo sat with his assembled crowd. To indicate peaceful intent, he held his spears in a lowered position and placed them on the ground at a distance. He approached the assembly empty-handed and sat at the edge of the shade. Chol Piok's narration continued:

Madibo then asked him—'Who are you?' 'I am Dau'—he said. 'Dau, son of whom?' 'Dau, son of Kiir.' 'So, you are Dau, the son of Kiir, the man who is said to be killing off the Arabs. Is it you truly?' Dau said—'Yes, it is me.' 'Now that you have come here, are you not going to die?' 'That is exactly what I want'—said Dau. 'How can I remain alive alone when all our people of the Ngok have died?' Madibo then

85

*said—'Tell me why you came! What do you want?' Dau said—'I am
after my wife who was captured last night.'*

*Madibo then turned to his police and asked them—'Was a woman
captured and brought here yesterday?' The police said—'Yes.' 'Where is
she?'—he asked. 'She is at the other end of the settlement'—they said.
'Fetch her now!'—he ordered. So, they went and brought the woman.
Her neck was loaded with a yoke to which both her hands were tied.
She was brought, being pulled. As soon as she saw Dau, she jumped
on him. The weight of the yoke and the chains threw him down. Dau
reacted with the same passion. Madibo then said—'Save him! She is
killing him. Pull them apart.' Then he said—'Take off the yoke and
the chains.' They were taken off. 'Take the woman and wash her to
be clean.' She was taken and washed. Then he said to Dau—'Go and
wash.' Dau went and washed.*

*Madibo left them alone that night. The following morning, he said—
'Dau, are you the son of the Chief? Dau said—'No, I am not!' 'But
where are the Chiefs?—asked Madibo. Dau said—'The Chiefs are
there. Arob is there. And Allor is there in Nuerland.' 'And who is the
Paramount Chief?'—asked Madibo. 'Arob is the Paramount Chief'—
said Dau. Madibo then said—'Is he near?' 'Yes, he is near!'—said
Dau. 'Then you will fetch him'—declared Madibo. 'You go with your
wife and come back with him. Otherwise, I will give you the authority
to represent your people since the Chiefs have gone into hiding.' Dau
said—'No! Our people do not do it that way.' So Madibo gave him a
gown and told him—'You go and fetch the Chief.'*

*That is how Arob was fetched. When Dau went, Pajok clan refused:
The few people of Pajok who had remained with the Chief refused to
let him go. They were afraid for his safety. They said—'He cannot go.'
But Arob said—'What nonsense! Even if I should be slaughtered, will
someone else not be found to take my place? I must go.' So, his brothers
went with him, people like Miyan Biong. With them also was a
woman called Aluel-Dol, the grandmother of Achwil Wun-Biong. She
said—'How can the son of my brother risk getting killed in my absence?
I must go and be slaughtered together with him.' So, she ran after the
men. They left and went to the Arab camp.*

86

That is how Madibo gave Arob Biong back his authority and gave
him the robe of honor. He then said—'You Arob, I will now leave in
peace. As you have come and we have met, none of your people will be
captured again. You will make a home in a place like Nyinchuor. You
will also make a station at Anyanga Diil so that anyone escaping there
can find that station. And make another station at Agany Achueng so
that anyone escaping from the South can come and find that station.'
Relations with the Rezeigat were thus normalized and Madibo, the
Chief of the Rezeigat, saw to it that the people of Arob were not raided,
and if captured, were returned.
In the war of Mabil—said Chol Piok—*the father of Ajuong Tiel was*
captured and was later rescued and brought back. Chol Piok listed
those who were the intermediaries with Madibo. They included
Agoth Akuei, Akuei Allor, Bulabek Biong and Kweth, the father of
Arob. These were the people who would go and gather those who
had been captured. They were the people familiar with the Arabs.
They would go to Madibo and Madibo would send the police to go
and look for the captured people. The people would be brought to
him and he would then send them to my great grandfather, Chief
Arob Biong. Madibo is said to have gone beyond that to ensure compensation for the people of Arob Biong who could not be redeemed.
That compensation came from raids further South, some of whom
were freed and returned to their people and some of whom were
integrated into his family as relatives.
That was how your (adopted) great uncles were captured and brought
and given to your great grandfather, Arob Biong. Among them were
people like Arob Anyonker, and Mioriik, and Koor. That is how they
were brought into your family.
While relations with the Rezeigat Arabs were normalized, relations
with the Missiriya Homr immediately to the North were still ambivalent, involving friendship with some Arab leaders and hostility
with others.
The man called Azoza was the Chief of the Homr Arabs—said Chol
Piok.
He came running for safety into the country of Arob Biong—Arobdit.

87

Arobdit then seated him by his side. These Homr Arabs had been completely destroyed and dispersed into the wilderness. They even used to chew hides. When it rained, they would throw into the rain the hides of dead animals that they had gathered from the forest and then take the hair off them and eat them. They used to wear leather aprons similar to the ones our women used to wear. They also used to sleep in the ashes of burned cow dung.

When the Arabs were destroyed by famine—said Uncle Deng Makuei (Abot),

Our grandfather allotted the people of Aziz, Azoza's brother, the land from Rialnok up to Antel. He settled them there. And he took the people of Azoza and settled them with him at Mithiang. He accommodated some of the Arabs at a place called Dheen. Others he placed at Gung-Bial. And settled yet others at Gong-Mou.

Arob and Azoza took the oath of friendship. And Arob then told his people—'*I do not want a single person throughout the tribe to take anything wrongfully from an Arab.' The Arabs stayed there through the hard period into the new year. They survived well and then returned home.*

Ibrahim El Hussein, a descendant of Chief Azoza, was to tell me the story from the Arab perspective:

We are relatives of Arob, the son of Biong from the days of our ancestor Azoza. It was a friendship witnessed by Biong himself; it was also witnessed by our ancestor Mugaddam, the Uncle of Azoza.

This is how the friendship began. Azoza was traveling with his cattle. He entered Dinkaland. There was a man by the name of Dut Anyar from Anyiel who was a very strong man. When Azoza entered Dinkaland, Dut Anyar captured Arab cattle. Arob Biong had spiritual powers which had totally dominated Dinkaland. Even Dut Anyar was frightened of him. Arob sent for Azoza. Azoza called upon his brothers to join him and they all went to Arob, the son of Biong. They said— '*We are no longer after our captured cattle; we have abandoned them. What we want is friendship and brotherhood. We want that the path between us be clear and that we live together as cousins.'*

Arob and Azoza are said to have carried out a ritual by which they feed their blood to become relatives. Ibrahim El Hussein continued his Accor of the events:

Arob, the son of Biong, spilt his blood and my grandfather licked it. And Azoza spilt his blood and Arob, the son of Biong, licked it. They became relatives. Drums were beaten to celebrate the occasion. Whenever their daughters were married, our fathers would receive their share of cattle as relatives. This was passed on to Kwol, the son of Arob. Our fathers too became men and had children. They remained together. Our fathers gave them gifts of horses and they continued to give our fathers cattle from the marriages of their daughters. It was a well-known relationship.

It should be noted that racial, religious, and cultural differences did not interfere with the relationship. Then began the Mahdist Movement of 1882, ending in the death of General Gordon and the overthrow of the Turko-Egyptian rule in 1885. That is when religion began to emerge as a divisive factor. But even then, Ngok Dinka leadership continued to play a bridging role between the Arab Muslim North and the then "pagan" South.

Uncle Deng Abot related the story:

The Mahdi sent word from El Odeiya, saying—'There is a Great Chief called Arob whose name I heard while I was still far away. I would like him to come and meet with me.' Many chiefs had gone to visit the Mahdi and had been killed. Each Chief would go, and he would have his throat cut through. For two years, the people of Ngok prevented Arob from going to the Mahdi. They argued—'How can you go where people are killed? It is Khalifa Abdullahi who cuts people's throats even before they reach the Mahdi.' But Arob eventually decided to go. He found the Mahdi at El Obeiya. The Homr Arabs had then come as far as Deenga (Muglad). On the way, a Chief called Nyango advised Arob against going to the Mahdi. But Arob said—'No, Nyango, I will not go back without seeing the Mahdi. People are not all alike. You will see me return safely to my country.' So, he went and met with the Mahdi.

Ibrahim El Hussein continued:

When the Mahdi came, our fathers acted as escorts to Arob Biong to meet him. They went to a village near Babanusa called Jamameet. They spent the rainy season there. Then in October, our ancestors took Arob to the Mahdi. He went to declare his allegiance in a place called Um-Harras. The Mahdi said—'From this day, your name will be Abdel Rauf, instead of Arob.' He initiated him with prayers and gave him a sword. Arob then returned home.

Arob's delegation included his Deputy, Allor Ajing, the Chief of Mannyuar tribe from Dhiendior clan. It is said that the two joined the Mahdi in prayer. After the prayers, Allor Ajing is said to have asked Arob whether he saw God as they prayed. Arob responded by saying that he did not see God—*but let us leave matters as they are.*

Although having prayed with the Mahdi is acknowledged, Arob's alleged initiation into Islam is hardly ever mentioned in the oral traditions of the Dinka except for the assertion that he had gone to Jenna, the Arabic word for Muslim Paradise. Certainly, his supposed adoption of the Islamic name, Abdel Rauf, is totally unheard of in our family. But the Dinka did, at least initially, acknowledge the religious power of the Mahdi as the Guided One, and even assimilated the idea into their own religion. It was believed that Deng, otherwise known by the praise name as Dengdit, The Great Deng, a powerful spirit among all Dinkas, had descended upon the Arab, Mohammed Ahmed, who then became known as the Mahdi, and to the Dinka, as the son of Deng. The Dinka composed this hymn about the Mahdi:

It is Mahdi, the son of Deng
To whom we ants pray on earth, our Deng,
We invoke the clan-divinity along with Deng.
The ant-men have been miserable for eight years.
What hurt us in the past?
What the Creator from above spoke of
It is to Mahdi, the son of Deng, we ants below pray, our Deng.

Indeed, Arob went to the Mahdi in search of peace and justice as a man of God. While relations with the leading families of the Rezeigat and the Homr were cordial, there was still considerable traffic in slavery from enterprising Mahdists and other Arab traders, with the broad-based participation of adventurous Arab tribesmen.

What our grandfather did not like—said Bulabek Malith,

Was the position of all the Black peoples. It was the way people were treated, all the Black people. That was what my Grandfather did not like. The Arabs used to steal people. When our Grandfather, Arob, came to the North, it was when Dengdit had fallen on the Mahdi. That was what brought our grandfather, Arob. When he left from home, people said Arob Biong went to Jenna (Heaven). I heard this from our elders; I heard it said by our fathers and our grandfathers.

When our Grandfather Arob came (to the North), he found the people trapped inside a big fence on the other side (Omdurman). That wall inside which the Black people were imprisoned is still there to this day. Those were the people who had been captured and brought from the South by the Arabs. The Arabs would sell them as slaves.

That is why Arob went to see the Mahdi. And when they met me, Arob said to him—'All the Black people here in captivity are my people. I am the head of all the Black people. I am their leader. I am the man who speaks for them all. I have people in our area, our neighbors, who steal my people.'

According to popular myth, the Mahdi challenged Arob in different ways to prove his claim to the leadership of the Black people. In the words of Chol Adija,

The Mahdi said—'Are they truly your own people?' 'Yes, they are my own people'—Arob responded. 'Are they your people for whom you would be willing to sacrifice by going through some bad things to attest to your claim?'

Arob asked—'What kind of bad things?' 'Something to drink.' 'Yes, I would drink it.' He then put something into water, beat it up, and gave it to Arob to drink. Arob drank it. He was then given all his people; the girls and the young men who had been captured.

I have always interpreted this story as a reflection of Arob being given food or drink that was unfamiliar to the Dinka and therefore seen as "bad." It is indeed sometimes said that Arob was made to eat donkey meat, which some dramatize as the afterbirth of a donkey.

According to Bulabek Malith:

Mahdi then said to Arob—'You will now return to lead your people and the Arabs will do no more harm to your people. None of your people.'

He gave him a piece of earth, a spear, and a sword, and said—'You now go back home and lead your people with justice. Let a man without cattle be helped by those with more. Let cattle be divided; let a man with five cows give away two cows to assist the needy.'

On the way back, an old man called Maleng Deng, who was a son of Arob's paternal aunt, worked against the Mahdi's plan. The Mahdi on whom the Spirit of Dengdit had fallen had warned Arob—'If you do not divide the cattle to provide for the poor, destruction will fall upon your country; an epidemic disease will go and kill masses of your cattle.'

When they returned, Arob returned, Arob's cousin, the elder called Maleng Deng threw away the piece of earth which the Mahdi had given him. Maleng Deng also refused to have the cattle divided. That is what destroyed our cattle. As the Mahdi had foreseen, disease came and killed large numbers of our cattle. And the sacred spear which the Mahdi had given Arob was also discarded by Maleng Deng and did not reach our land.

It is said that upon his return, Arob built a large fence in which he accommodated those he had rescued and sent word to all the neighboring tribes, including the Rek, the Twich and the Nuer, saying—*Let people come to identify their people.* People went and identified their people and took them back to their areas. The area where Arob kept the free slaves is still known as Mitrok, "Building a Fence"— just outside Abyei town.

The Mahdist rule was overthrown by the Anglo-Egyptian reconquest in 1898. But the British had not yet established law and order throughout the country. The slavers were still rampaging and plundering in the West and the South. Arob died in 1905 and was succeeded by his son, Kwol, my grandfather. Kwol was still very young when he assumed leadership of the tribe. Ali Julla, who had been a prominent veteran of the Mahdist wars, was now back in the land of the Homr and was instated as Chief, replacing the family of Azoza.

Hostilities between the Dinka and factions of the Homr Arabs became aggravated under the leadership of Ali Julla. Sporadic raids by the Arabs increased.

Ali Julla went and started to engage in the old thievery, stealing children from our area—said Chol Piok.

Rezeigat had long stopped; they had accepted peace. But the Homr went on stealing. If they found a gentleman cutting grass, they would seize him and tie him up. Women were no longer permitted to go and cut grass alone; they would be accompanied by men to provide them with protection as they cut the grass for thatching huts. Women who wanted to go and fetch firewood were also accompanied. Arab horsemen would all be waiting in hiding to catch them.

They captured a man called Monyjur at a place called Athau—said Deng Abot—*and they captured Agok; and they captured the wife of Kiir, and four other women; they took them all, there at Leche. We were then at our home on the River Kir.*

Arab attacks extended southwards destroying the Rek Dinka—added Chol Piok.

Kwol said—'Should our people go through this suffering again?' Have the Arabs truly brought back their old aggression? Have they again brought back what my father had ended?' Kwol decided to take his complaint to the new British administration. But first, he had to equip himself with gifts of ivory.

But hunting elephants with spears was no easy feat. It could indeed be downright dangerous. Spiritual protection was needed. *When the cattle moved to the pastures of the toc*—Dau Agok related the story of the risky hunting for elephants with spiritual blessing—

people went to a person called Riek de Malong, and to Riek, son of Chol de Kon, and to Wol Ajot-Nok. Kwol said to them—'Gentlemen, please charm the elephants for people to hunt. We need elephant tusks to take with us: we must go to see the Government.'

Three elephants were then killed. Abyor carried the tusks of those elephants. People passed through Nuerland and Paan-Aruw. Kwol's Uncle, Miyan Biong, was prevented from traveling because he was ill. But he said—'The son of my brother is still young and does not know

*the Arab way of talking. I have to go to this case of Ali.' People said—
'But what about the illness you are suffering from?' But Miyan would
not be persuaded. 'Even if I should die, I will have died pursuing the
duties of my ancestral leadership'*—he insisted.

The Missiriya Arabs did not want the Ngok Dinka to have access
to the Government in Khartoum and were prepared to block their
passage. *Kwol left to go to the Government*—said Choi Piok.
*The Arabs heard of his plans and began to threaten—'Where does the
slave think he can pass? We shall slaughter him and his men should
they come this way. If they go by way of Kadugli, we shall also slaughter
them. And if they go by way of Rezeigat, we shall also slaughter them.'
They sent scouts to all those areas where they thought Arob and his men
might pass. People did not know what to do. At the beginning of the
summer, Kwol called his people and said—'My people, I am leaving. If
we get destroyed, do not follow us. But I must go and look into the roots
of this problem.'*

To avoid being intercepted by the Arabs, Arob took a much longer
detour through the South which had its own risks but is now being presented as evidence of the Ngok identification with the South.
Chol Piok continued his account of Arob's trip to Khartoum:
*They had selected a number of noblemen to accompany him. With them
was an elder called Milang Nyach. They passed through Nuer country.
They reached Tharngop. And there they took the way through Nuer
country. The Nuer nearly killed them. They were only saved by Milang
Nyach. He had a friend among the Jekeny Nuer in the area which is
now Bentiu. The Nuer had refused to give the group a canoe to cross
with. Instead, they said—'If we have truly found Kwol Arob, then he is
dead. This very day, he will die.' People stood bewildered, not knowing
what to do.
Milang then walked along the river until he came to a shallow spot.
There, he crossed to the other side. And he hurried to his Nuer friends.
When they saw him, they said—'O! O! is it really you Milang?' He
said—'Yes!' They said—'What makes you travel during the rainy
season?' He said—'I am travelling with Chief Kwol Arob. But they
have been stopped on the other side by people who say they want to*

slaughter them.' No more was said. Members of that Nuer section got up. Each man grabbed his shield and dusted it. They grabbed their spears and ran to the riverside. As soon as they got there, people who were holding the canoe quickly apologized and said—'We never knew they were your friends. We truly did not know.'

So, they were taken across the river. Two bulls were slaughtered in their honor. On the sixth day, they were canoed across to Panaruw. That was how Kwol crossed and then went to Kadugli. And when they reached Kadugli, Miyan Biong suddenly died. He died at Kadugli. They buried him and continued on. Then they went to El Odeiya.

Kwol then explained the whole situation to the Government. He said— 'How can it be that the country is in peace, and my area remains the only one still under destruction? The person called Ali has made himself the Government. Children, women, and even adult men cannot walk in peace. If a man is not killed, he is captured and tied up and taken away. A woman too would be caught, tied up and carried away. A child too would be picked up and taken away.'

And indeed, it was a bad situation. Even if a child had to go to an area near the village, he must be accompanied by a man carrying spears. No man would go to converse with neighbors. Members of each village would remain around to guard their houses. You would remain ready with your brother, holding your spears, and should the Arabs find you, then you must fight to defend yourselves. Kwol Arob gave a full account of all the things Ali was doing in the area.

Ali Julla was summoned and severely reprimanded and made to commit himself to stop the raids on the Dinka. Indeed, Arob and his companions returned through Missiriya land without any more threats. That is how Kwol saved the land—concluded Chol Piok. "That is the peace that remained until we grew up."

According to Dinka oral history, Ngok Dinka Leadership was then given seniority by the British administration over their Arab counterpart. According to Deng Abot, the British said—*Kwol, the Arabs will now be in your hands. Ali will consult with you. If he has a case he cannot settle, he will refer it to you. You are the one with the oath-ashes. You see, we used to administer our Dinka oath to the Arabs. Even I, Deng, I*

have administered Dinka oath to the Arabs, when we were at Wubeny.
The Arabs later developed their ways of killing people with the oracles of
their religious men like the Fakis. But they used to be sworn on Dinka
oath of ashes. My son, I am telling you the whole truth, leaving aside any
words of lies. My father continued to control the Arabs that way.
When Ali Julla became an old man, his son, Nimir, took over the
Chieftainship. But he died soon after he had assumed power. His son,
Babo, was still a very small boy. Chieftainship was nearly taken from
him. Then Ali Julla, now a very old man, pleaded for my father's
support for his grandson. With my father were elders like Deng Nyac,
Mijakdit, Kwol Marieu, and Allor Mathii. My father's people said—
'There is no more to be said. Even though Babo is a child, let him
succeed his father!'

Babo Nimir spoke on the circumstances of his succeeding his father:
My father became Chief in 1918 and died in 1924 on the 13th of
January. Out of the whole of 1924, he lived only 13 days. I was 13
years old. The tribe, the Ajaiyra, heard about it and met at Abyei to
select his successor. Chief Kwol of the Ngok Dinka and Chief El Haj
Ajbar of the Falaiyta were there. The District Commissioner also
attended. They went as far as Abyei and met with the whole tribe. I
was under the Tamarind tree at Abyei, sitting in a tent. Chief Kwol
had sent my grandfather a container of honey. I took the fruit of the
Tamarind tree, poured some water on it, and added honey to it. As I
was drinking the water with the tamarind fruit and honey, I heard
the voices of the people discussing. They were assembled in front of the
District Commissioner.

The people all agreed that the Chieftainship be given to the son of
Nimir. Nazir Kwol said—'I support the word of the tribe. Nimir died
while his son was still small. But I heard him praise his son a great
deal. And therefore, I support the idea that he should succeed his father
as the Chief. And with the will of God I hope he will grow up to be a
leader like his father.' Those were the words of Nazir Kwol. Nazir Kwol
and Nazir El Haj Ajbar united and said that the son of Nimir should
succeed his father. They chose me and then appointed a regent.
As I was so young, only thirteen years old, I do not consider their choice

*to have been directed toward me; it was, in effect, a choice for my
father because of what the people had seen in him: his personality, his
treatment of the people, and the way he had run the affairs of the tribe.
I was not known. I was like the chick of an ostrich. When people see the
chick of an ostrich, they wonder whether it is going to be a male or a
female. No one can tell. They claim that the legs of the male are a little
bigger, but no one can really tell. I was still unknown. No one could
tell whether I would be a good leader or a bad leader. Only my father's
work made the tribe unite and say that his successor should be his son.*

To the Dinka, Kwol Arob was the determining factor in the out-
come, and, presumably because of his age, was recognized as the
leading personality among both the Arabs and the Dinka. K.D.D.
Henderson, who was the British District Commissioner in the area
in the late twenties and early thirties, later told me that *the Government regarded Babo's position as Nazir of the Homr as more important than Kwol's, but it recognized Kwol's wisdom and hoped that Babo
would learn from him, as he did.* This degree of recognition for Kwol
was enough to make the Dinka see an even greater profile for Kwol.
Deng Abot's recollection:

*Arabs remained under my father's control until he died. I used to look
into Arab cases and administer Dinka oath at the home of (the Arab)
Abo, whenever my father was away. That was the situation.*

*And when Babo was given the robe of honor at Leu, that was when
he grew up into seniority. I had told Deng Majok—'Deng Majok,
Babo must not come to be honored in our land. If it is a question of
our witnessing the ceremony, we can go and watch in Muglad.' But
Deng Majok suppressed my point of view. Babo became senior to him,
although none was to look into the appeals from the other's court. But
my father used to hear the appeals from Arab courts.*

The Arab elder, Ibrahim El Hussein, who applies the courtesy title of
Father to Kwol Arob, observed: *Our father Kwol became the Chief in
the whole of this area. He established peace in the area and would attend
tribal assemblies with the Chiefs of other tribes. It was a sweet period in
the history of our people.*

Chief Kwol Arob was placed in charge of all the neighboring tribes of the Dinka, including the Ngok, the Twich, and the Ruweng, from whom he continued to collect taxes and hear appeals. This continued to be the case for a good part of the British rule. Later, part of the Twich broke off under the leadership of Rian. The partition was at least sanctioned, if not initiated, by the British on the grounds that the area was far too large for the administration of one Chief. Later, at the time of Kwol Arob, the other tribes were also taken away from the jurisdiction of Ngok leadership on the same grounds.

Chol Adija gives an account of these partitions, presenting them as breakaways by the Chiefs of the areas concerned:

Taxes used to be paid in grain and bulls to be slaughtered. When taxes began to be levied in cash, Rian said—'You, Arob, you will now remain under El Obeid (Kordofan Province) and I shall pay my taxes to Wau (Bahr el-Ghazal Province).' Arob said—'So you are dividing the country?' Rian said—'Yes, I am dividing the country.' That is how the country separated. Arob remained with Ruweng and the Twich of Kuac. We continued to come here to El Obeid until Arob died, when the Chieftainship remained with Kwol. The Kuac and the Ruweng were later separated from us at Tharngop meeting. Lang took Kuac and Monytuil took Ruweng. It was the Government which then gave those areas to them. Kwol was left conspicuously alone in the North.

The role our family has played in promoting peace at the border through their connections with Arab tribes and with the successive administrations in the North is widely acknowledged, even among the Dinka of the South.

In the words of Chief Monyroor Rian of the Twich Dinka:

Arabs used to come and capture people, it was Arob Biong who would go and redeem them. He worked on redeeming Black people to the point that he drank filth in order to save his people. And he continued to play a vitally important role of leadership at the border. If our people were captured by the Arabs, he would go and redeem us. That is how the Ngok and the Arabs got to know one another. Kwol then succeeded to the Chieftainship of his father and did the same.

Many Dinkas didn't know what was going on—said Chief Giir Thiik (also Giir Kiro or Giirdit) of the Rek Apuk Dinka.

*We didn't know anything. Only the Ngok knew the Arabs. And even
the fact that there are Dinkas today—people are here because of your
family. It was your great-grandfather and your grandfather who
saved the people. It was they who saved the people. The Mahdi came
to liberate the people from the Turks. That was what we heard from
the North. Word came that the Mahdi was liberating the people. So,
contributions of remaining cattle and sheep and goats would be made
and sent to the Mahdi through your great-grandfather. Then your
great-grandfather would pass them on. It would be my father here
gathering things from his tribe, sending them to your great-grandfather.
Yor Mayar on his side, would bring his contributions to your great-
grandfather. Mawien Ariik would come from the side of Luach. And
someone called Akol Arob would come from the Kongoor side. All those
Chiefs would gather and meet with your great grandfather.*

As Giirdit's account indicates, Arob's, and later Kwol's, influence was
in no small measure due to their ability to collect sizeable contributions from the whole of Dinkaland and channel them through the
controlling authority in the center.

*Bulls used to be contributed by the Twich and the Ruweng and leaders
would then come to El Odeiya led by Kwol Arob*—Chol Piok recalled.
*And it was the same way with Arobdit further back. When the
Government came and sat at Abyei, things would then be collected from
all over the area to be brought to Abyei. Bulls would be brought from
the Twich; grain would be contributed from the Twich; and it would
all be heaped up and gathered in really large quantities.*

Chief Giirdit elaborated on the extent to which the Chiefs of all
of Dinkaland cooperated toward the common goal of their people's
welfare with our grandfather as their coordinator, what might be
called a confederation of Dinka tribes:

*Son of Deng, there were great men who were keeping this country.
There was your grandfather, Kwol Arob, the son of Arob Biong; there
were people like Allor Ajing; there were people like Bol Nyuol, and
people like Chom in Twichland; and in Apuk, there was Thiik. They
were the people who would go and meet with your grandfather Kwol.
There were also people like Yor Maker and people like Mawien Ariik.*

*It was the big things of the country and how they would run their
country that they would meet and talk about; such things as how people
should relate to each other on the borders. Those were the ways of those
big leaders of the past. And what is now said that—there is this and
that—is all a lie. There was Chieftainship in the past. Chieftainship is
not a new thing. Chieftainship is an ancient thing; it is not a thing of
today. A country is lived in because of a Chief.*

Ironically, the close contacts and cooperation that used to exist between the prominent Chiefs of Dinkaland became increasingly erod-
ed as the tribal leaders became dependent on the Central for the
administration and security of their tribes. Tribes became identified
with new administrative units, Provinces and Districts. Although pe-
riodic meetings were held between the leaders of the various tribes
or provinces, an element of separation emerged where autonomous
factions had previously viewed themselves as part of one Dinka people or nation.

The demarcation of provincial borders and the identification of tribal
groups with those borders made the Dinka tribes in the South feel
the need for the Ngok Dinka to join the Province of Bahr el-Ghazal,
where most of the Dinka with whom they had maintained close ties
had been affiliated. The British, who favored the idea of the Ngok
joining the South, encouraged the Southern Chiefs to persuade
Chief Kwol Arob to join them.

Chief Giirdit later recalled the discussion between them and Chief
Kwol:

*Your grandfather was brought by the Government—your grandfather,
the Kwoldit, son of Arob. And he said—'You, Kwol, you have become
like an Arab—but you are a Dinka. I would like you to unite with
the other Dinka and become the District of Gogrial.' Your grandfather
refused.*

Kwol Arob was not undiplomatic with his fellow Dinka Chiefs. After
refusing to join the South, he pulled Giirdit aside and spoke to him:

*We went and stood a distance away. Then he said to me—Son of my
father, what you tell me, it is not that I do not know it. The Arab is a
thief. Even though I am with him, I know he is a thief. If I were to pull*

100

away from him, he would destroy my things. So please leave me. And if my people increase one day and they know the way things are done and know that they are one people with you, they will come. No one forgets where he belongs. I will come. But if I were to come to you now and speak toward Wau, he would spoil my things behind my back. Even the land, which is mine, he might say—'It is my land.'

Kwol maintained this balanced position between North and South until the end of his days. Kwol's image remains towering in the memory of his people and his neighboring leaders to the North and the South. As I grew up, the songs about him used to move me deeply as evidence of how loved by his people he must have been:

Adau, daughter of Ken, cried in dismay:
'Black Stork, what will hurt you in this land,
A land kept in order by Kwol without favor?'
The case will be seen by Kwol, a Chief without bias.
The word of the market goes to Kwol
And the case of a cow goes to Kwol;
O Kwol, keep the people of your father
And lead them to the people of the world.
My Pied One, the Ground Horn-Bill
I love the Black Shade of Mijok of my Father
I love it as much as I love our Chief
I love our Chief who is holding our land.
My Pied One, if no disaster befalls our land
People will point at our Camp because of you.
I will never leave you
Whatever people may say about you
Because of those horns, I love you
I love you as much as I love our Chief
I love our Chief who is holding our land.

And indeed, from what I heard as I grew up, Kwol was a Chief of great virtues and extraordinary charisma. *Kwol's charisma was due to the word of God behind his leadership*—said Monylwak Row.

He had the authority of God behind him. He was a man created with a cool heart; a man of gentle personality. Kwol was a chief by the authority of God. He succeeded to the Chieftainship which had descended down the lineage of Arob Biong.

Kwol's charisma was such as you have never heard of—added Chol Piok—*a charisma which if he were seen approaching and singing his hymns, even if it were a battle that had lined itself up and ready to rage, it will pull apart and people would leave. The battle would end.*

K.D.D. Henderson was later to remark:

When we visited the Bahr el-Ghazal, it always seemed to me that Kwol, as a leader of men and a diplomat, was a head and shoulder above men like Monywir Rihan and Bol Choi. Only Gir Kiro merited comparison with Kwol. In Western Kordofan, only Ali Abu Dukka at El Odeiya was comparable.

The way Kwol Arob performed made the whole area happy with him—said Chief Lang Juk of the Twich Dinka.

He was a good person in every respect. He was a God-fearing man, and he was very generous. He helped any needy person. He loved everybody. He loved the Twich, the Rek, the Ruweng, the Nuer and all the other tribes, even the far away Agar. He was a great leader, heard of all over; he was a great leader.

Although the legends of the clan concentrate on the male members of the lineage, the Dinka recognize that the roles of their female partners are pivotal, even though they may not be overtly pronounced. Very often, foremothers are exalted in songs in which they are projected in high esteem. In this song by Nyandeng Kiir, who was a renowned singer, the wife of Mijak (popularly known as Mijangthii, the Junior Mijak), one of the senior sons of Chief Kuol Arob, praises several wives and mothers of the leaders: Adau, married by Allor for his son Biong and begot Arob; Awuor, married by Biong for his son Arob and begot Kuol; and Nyanaghar (shortened as Aghar), married by Arob for his son Kuol and begot Deng Majok. The names may get confusing, but it is the father who goes after a wife for his son who begets the successor to the throne of leadership:

This began with our Ancestor Allor
When he went after Adau, the daughter of clan Payii
The Mother of Arob Jok-Yar;
Adau is the daughter of Clan Payii
She is the daughter of Clan Payii;
The Clan of Biong won her with the tongue.
The Great Family of our Ancestor Allor began with Adau.
Biong Wak-Beek then left
He went and brought Awor, the daughter of Nyiel-Anook
The daughter of the Clan of Ajon-Rial,
The Mother of Kuol Mijok,
The Clan of Biong won her with the tongue.
Then Arob Miyar (The White Bull), son of Biong left
He went and brought Aghaar, the daughter of Jak-Apiok,
Our Mother Aghaar,
Our Mother Aghaar with the weight of The Rock
Mother Aghaar.

The focus then shifts back to the men in the lineage, seeing the power of the women in the qualities of the sons they begot:

Aghaar begot Deng of Marial Colour, mighty like the Bird Twot,
Marial, the Crested Crane, is like Twot in Clan Pajok
The Mighty is Twot in the Clan of Biong
The Great Clan of Jok Athurkok.
Marial is like Twot.
The Great Awet lies on words as though on a sleeping skin
Marial is the Sacred Shade under which people all gather
People all gather around Marial Ajok.

The theme then reverts back to the legendary deeds of the founder of the clan from whom all the leaders in the line derive their authority and legitimacy:

Marial, you will carry the weight of your Ancestor Jok
The man who broke through the Seal of detention

Allowing his people to break out into freedom;
People flowed into freedom like the waters of flood.
Then they stopped at a river they could not cross;
There was no way the people could cross.
The powers in the sky connected with the powers on Earth
They united and blocked the way.
God and the Earth united and blocked the way.

Here, a competition for leadership which persists to this day between the Clan Pajok led by Jok and the Clan Dhiendior led by Longer, ironically sometimes presented as Jok's relative, is introduced to highlight Jok's victory over Longar:

The Leader sitting on the throne,
The man called Longar Jiel could not manage;
Longar Jiel, the leader on the throne, failed to lead.
Our Ancestor Jok took over the Leadership
The Elder stepped forward and took the lead;
He went and spoke to the Powers of the Earth
And then took his daughter Achai
And offered her to the Spirits of the River
The waters of the River then pulled apart
People all flocked to the other side of the River
They all walked on dry land across the River.
The legacy of the mythical competition is then brought into the dynamics
of the contemporary power relations;

People always invoke the Spirits of their Ancestors
Our people till invoke the Elder called Jok
The Elder Jok of the Colour Mijok
The Man who paved the path to freedom.
O people, who showed our people the Way to Freedom?
Was it not our Ancestor Jok who led the Way to Freedom?
Even if people should make competing claims,
Even if people should continue to make noises like mosquitos

104

We will not worry about those claims
Even if they complain against what the Clan of Biong has done.
O people, who was the Man who unlocked the Prison Door?
The Prison Door of the Creator, who unlocked it?
Was it not Jok Athurkok, the One who broke through?
Who unlocked the Prison in which the people were detained?
Who unlocked the Prison of the Creator?
Was it not Jok?
Without Jok, people would still be in a cage,
They would still be prisoners.
Father Mijok, O Father Mijok,
Your weight is still around.
Your weight has not diminished.
From our Ancestor who emerged from the Byre of Creation
Down to our Father with his age-set, the Koryom.
Our Father came and sat in his cattle Bye and chanted
'I speared dead the Electric Eel in the Clan of Biong'
Who will dispute his claim?
Who among the gentlemen of Koryom Age-Set can dispute that fact?
Can anyone say that the Electric Eel was not killed by the Clan of Biong
Or is it the weight of our Clan that is doubted?
Great Decorated One, your family still carries its original weight
The weight is still as heavy as the Rock
Our Grandfather carried the weight of the son of Jok
Deng the Crested Crane is carrying the weight of the son of Jok
The Crested Crane carries the weight of our Ancestor Jok-Yar Arob.

Remarkably, what was envisaged as a power dynamic at the local level is projected to the Souther and indeed national level, signifying the strategic role the Ngok Dinka of Abyei has historically played in their strategic border area between the North and the South.

Deng hold the Land of your father with might.
Even the land of the Sudan is yours;
Yes, Marial, Sudan is yours;

And the Ngok of Lual Yak is yours;
Marial, they are all yours.

Five

Feuding Over Power

The story of how my father succeeded his father is an extraordinary drama of rivalry and conflict between father and son. My father not only forced his father out of government power, but also claimed and obtained the inheritance of the Sacred Spears, which represented the Divine Authority of the traditional leadership and which his father had willed to his other son, Deng Abot (also known as Deng Makuei) in his dying declaration. But this drama has deep roots in my father's maternal background, and more specifically, in the story of his father's marriage to his mother Nyanaghar.

Nyanaghar's great-great-grandmother, Awut, was from a non-Dinka tribe sometimes called Beggi. It is not clear whether they were Arab, African, or a mixture, even though they are sometimes described by the Dinka as "Arab." They occupied part of the land the Ngok now occupy, stretching northwards. The Ngok and the Beggi used to fight and seize captives who were taken as slaves. But the Dinka practice was to adopt and assimilate such captives as family members to the point where their outside origin became quickly obscured. If female, slaves were considered "daughters" or "sisters" by their "masters" who would then marry them off with cattle as they would any female relative.

Apparently, Awut was the daughter of a Beggi Chief and was honored as such even in her captivity. Patal Biliw gave this account of Awut and her impressive destiny:

The people called the Beggi inhabited this area before the Ngok. Awut was the daughter of an important Beggi chief. She was captured by my ancestor, Pajook. That is how she became known as Awut, daughter of Pajook. Awut was then married to a chief from the Dhiendior clan, Bagat. He paid a bride-price of a hundred cows. Bagat begot Ajuong. Ajuong begot Deng. Deng begot Abuk. Abuk begot Nyanaghar, the mother of your father, Deng Majok.

My ancestor Pajook blessed Awut and said—'Awut, my daughter, your

descendants will one day take the central position in the leadership
of this land. But if you should ill-treat my children, that will be your
curse. If my children should ill-treat you that will be their curse.' To this
day, we of the clan of Awut, we say nothing offensive to one another.
The ancestry of Deng Majok is here at Anyiel—said Chol Piok. He
continues:
His maternal grandmother was Abuk, daughter of Deng. Abuk went
and gave birth to Nyanaghar in Diil. Nyanaghar was then married.
Arob Biong, your great-grandfather, released the cattle for her marriage
to your grandfather, Kwol Arob. And you, Mading, son of my brother,
let me tell you the whole truth; there is nothing to be hidden.
Chol Piok then gave the details of Nyanaghar's marriage to Kwol
Arob for his dead brother in a ghost marriage. That is the root of the
anomalies of seniority that would eventually feature in the dispute
over succession to the chieftainship.
Nyanaghar was the first to be betrothed. But she was married to Kwol's
dead brother, not to Kwol himself. As you know, we have our Dinka
customs, according to which, a family marries a wife for a relative
who dies before marrying. Nyanaghar was betrothed to be the wife
of Arob's son who had died before he married. Kwol Arob was to be a
proxy husband of Nyanaghar for his deceased brother. But Nyanaghar
strongly rejected the marriage on the grounds that she would not be wife
to a dead man. The matter was discussed at great length. But she would
not be persuaded.
Nyanaghar's strong-mindedness is presented as a positive attribute,
when normally it would be criticized as unbecoming. That positive
assessment seems to be a justification for the same attributes in her
son, Deng Majok, who, like his mother, also became tough minded.
Such behavior is normally criticized in a child; and indeed, Deng's
father Chief Kwol Arob would criticize his son for having inherited
his mother's qualities, which would in turn aggravate Deng Majok.
Chol Piok presents these contradictions:
Your grandmother's head was very strong. And that is the character
which our people like from women. If you marry a strong woman, a
woman with a head, a woman with a heart, a brave woman, then you

have married well. That is what our grandfathers used to say, that it is the brave woman who bears a brave son. And with a brave son, when evil appears, as it has now appeared (in the wars between the Dinka and the Arabs of May and June 1977, between the Ngok and the Missiriya), he does not care for his own life, he cares for the lives of his people.

What follows, the contest over Nyanaghar, and her initially favoring another man over Kwol Arob, would become a bone of contention between Deng Majok and his father, and in many ways the source of his insecurity in the father-son relationship.

When Arob Biong paid the cattle for the marriage of your father's mother, she was then being courted by a man called Malual Adol from Mannyuar, the father of Makuach Adol. Your grandmother refused Kwol and said—'Kwol, I am not going to be the wife of procreation for a dead man. If you want me, then first marry another woman for your dead brother.' She eloped with Malual Adol while your grandfather's cattle had already been paid. Kwol withdrew his cattle. Only one black cow remained.

The mother of Deng Makuei was subsequently married. She accepted to be Kwol's proxy wife for the dead man. Then Kwol Arob's ancestral spirits went and made Nyanaghar's body swell in the family of Malual Adol. It swelled so much that she could hardly go through the door of the hut. The doors of the hut used to be smaller than they are today. That is when she was taken back and offered to Kwol Arob. Dhiendior, the clan of Ajuong, went and took her back from the family of Malual Adol, saying—'Will the daughter of our daughter die for a reason that is so clear? Malual Adol, what will you do if she should die? Are you going to compensate for her death?' They took her back. She was then taken to the family of Arob Biong, Kwol's father.

Uncle Deng Abot stresses his father's initial reluctance to have Nyanaghar back. In fact, his account makes his own mother come across as the first choice of Kwol for his own wife, not a fallback wife of Kwol Arob's dead brother, as the account of Chol Piok, and many others would have it:

When your grandmother eloped with another man, people gave up.

117

They left her for the home she had chosen. But in those days, the spirits were much closer to man than they are today. Our clan spirits followed Nyanaghar. She was later brought after my mother had been married and brought home. Nangahar had been crippled by our Clan Spirit called Ring—The Flesh. So, she was brought with a cow of atonement to appease my father. People then worked on my father, persuading him to accept her. But father refused, saying—'This is a woman about whom I was bewitched with rejection, while I was a young man, singing with dheeng (dignity) over my ox in the cattle-camp. She is a woman for whom I was afflicted by witchcraft to be insulted with rejection. Although another girl had already been designated for me, (Deng Makuei meaning his own mother), I wanted to marry her (Nyanaghar) also and have both women as my wives. But since she rejected me and went off with another man, I no longer want her.' But in those days, words used to meet and harmonize. Father's uncles all assembled and persuaded him to accept her. He had both women as his wives.

The next critical issue was which of the two wives would beget a son as a first born to be the Heir to the throne of chieftainship. But this also depended on which of them was in fact the first wife. The blessing and prayers of the elders from Anyiel section of the Ngok Dinka, the maternal relatives of Nyanaghar, would indicate the initial direction matters were taking. *Then Anyiel came*—said Chol Piok. *Anyiel came bringing with them a rounded spear, and a bladed spear, and a billy goat. Those things were brought for blessing the two wives. They were asked to come out. The blessing rites were then performed. The rounded spear (which symbolizes a son) was placed on the right shoulder of Deng Majok's mother and the bladed spear (which symbolizes a girl) was made to rest on the shoulders of Deng Abot's mother. Then they were sprayed with the sacred Ashes. Arobdit asked—'Why are you doing it that way? Is this not the Senior Wife?' They said—'No! Our blessing is the way it is.'*
Deng Majok was then born to Nyanaghar and the girl named Agorot was born to Abiong; she was later followed by Deng Makuei. Deng Majok was born a boy in fulfillment of the rounded spear which

his mother had been made to hold to beget a boy. People had said—
'Nyanaghar should be the first to have a son. And Abiong should first
have a daughter.' That was that. No more disputes arose from that
situation. The cattle for Nyanaghar's marriage were then sent.

Patal Biliu was even more explicit about the intentions of the elders
from Anyiel who were actually also Kwol Arob's maternal relatives:
When the two wives were blessed, Anyiel came with a lamb; a sleeping
skin was laid on the ground. The mother of Deng Majok was seated
on Kwol Arob's left side; the mother of Deng Makuei was seated on his
right side. Anyiel then came singing their hymns and bringing with
them their sacrificial lamb. They changed the seating of the women.
They placed Abiong on the left and Nyanaghar on the right. Then they
grounded in front of Abiong the bladed spear which symbolizes a girl.
And they grounded in front of Nyanaghar the pointed fishing spear
which symbolizes a boy. Arob Biong said—'Why are you doing it that
way?' They said—'That is the woman who will bear the Chief; this is
the woman who will bear the Chief; Nyanaghar is the one who will
bear the chief.' The issue was debated until their word was accepted
and the lamb was slaughtered in sacrifice. When the women gave
birth, Abiong gave birth to Agorot and Nyanaghar gave birth to Deng
Majok. That was how the issue of succession to Chieftainship was first
introduced.

But as Monyluak Row points out—*Kwol then began to say that the*
girl he married after Nyanaghar had rejected him was his first wife. This
was disturbing to Deng's heart, but as he was still a child, he nursed the
grievance without saying anything about it.

Chol Piok too concedes that what really embittered Kwol Arob
against Deng Majok was his mother's initial rejection of him: *That*
was what continued to hurt in the heart of Kwol Arob. He would say—
'The child whose mother rejected me with bitter hostility, how could he
succeed to my throne?'

I chose to pursue the matter with Chol: *What about my father, as he*
grew up, was he bothered by the fact that his father felt some prejudice
against him because of what had happened between his father and his
mother? Did he think about it? Did it pain him? He responded: *How*

119

could it not pain him? Kwol used to say it to him all the time. He would insult him for it. He would say—'Is it your mother's conduct, when she rejected me for another man, that has given you this strong head!?' That would hurt your father very much.

Kwol Arob's relations with Nyanaghar are generally acknowledged as having continued to be ambivalent. They were quite reciprocal in conjugal love and affection, but also turbulent and subject to fights; the consensus on Nyanaghar's tough-headedness to the end must not be forgotten. The co-wives themselves seem to have been quite cordial and harmonious in their relationship with one another.

Uncle Deng Makuei offered an insight that is more reflective of the Dinka negative view about a mother's influence over a son. While some sources view Nyanaghar's hotheadedness as having given Deng Majok the positive attribute of courage and tough mindedness, Deng Makuei presents a picture in which Deng Majok was criticized by their father for having inherited his mother's qualities:

My son, from the time we were born, your grandmother's hut and my mothers were always next to one another. The distance between them was like where we were before and this spot on which we are now. My mother's hut would be here, and your grandmother's hut would be close there. Until she died, Nyanaghar was never separated from my mother for a distance as far as outside this house. But Nyanaghar was a brave fighter. She and my father got into a great deal of terrifying fights. And when Deng Majok also became a fighter, jumping here and there, my father saw him as though he had acquired his mother's ways. Are children sometimes not rebuked in the name of their mothers?

The story of my father's childhood was told to me by his maternal cousin, Jipur Tiel, the chief of Anyiel section. Jipur began with Nyanaghar's background, going back to her mother, Abuk, from Anyiel's leading family of Tiel Deng.

Your father's mother's mother, Abuk, was the sister of Tiel Deng. She was married by Kiir Bar. She went and gave birth to her daughter, Nyanaghar. Nyanaghar then went and gave birth to your father, Deng. When Deng was weaned, he was not taken to his mother's parents' family, the family of Kiir Bar. My grandfather, Tiel, said—'The son of

Nyanaghar Abuk is not to be weaned by Abuk while I am alive. He will be weaned with me. He is the son of my sister's daughter.' So, your father was taken and weaned there.

Jipur then went into the details of Father's weaning period and the characteristics he reflected from his early childhood. *He was an untouchable child. He feared no elder and feared no child. And if an elder did him wrong, he would never leave the matter. It is said that he started this attitude from the time he was still a small child.*

It is ironic that what would normally be criticized in a child is being praised. *Even when he provoked people into anger, my grandfather, Tiel, would say—'He is not to be touched'. He is the one who has inherited my grandfather's character. He is in the image of my grandfather, Ajuong. And he is in the image of my father, Deng Ajuong.*

Here, the Dinka norm of always viewing their ancestors positively, and turning what would normally be seen as negative into a positive, comes into focus.

My father was a man who never listened to anybody. The word of his own head was all he cared about. Deng Majok will be like my father one day. People said about my grandfather Deng Ajuong that he was obstinate.

Interestingly enough, what is praised as a positive legacy by the maternal kin is condemned by the paternal kin and denied as not their legacy, but that of the maternal kin.

Your clan, Pajok, used to deny your father by saying—'This head of his is not our kind; it is the head of Deng Ajuong.' Until your father died, that was the case.

Surprisingly, the claim of Father's maternal relatives that his character comes from them is extended to me:

And even your own determined heart, you Mading, that is the way it is being viewed. People say—'He is the breed of the lineage of Deng Ajuong. They are formidable. Their feud never ends.' That is what there is to this day.

Father acquired a nickname which he later turned into the praise name Majok during his weaning period. He acquired a puppy dog, which the family owned. The puppy was fed on the milk of a cow

121

that had been specially set aside.

Deng had his separate gourd of milk. But he would take his gourd of milk and insist on sharing milk with the dog. People would try to stop him, but he would end up drinking some of the milk and the dog would drink part of the milk. Tiel then said—'Leave him alone! He should be called Deng Majoh: Deng, the Doggish. The heart that makes him do this, will one day manifest itself.'

The Rek and Twich Dinka, believing that Majok was the Ngok Din-ka for Majok, the metaphoric color name of a Pied Bull allocated to the first son of the first wife in the family, began to call my father Deng Majok. Father then formally adopted it as his officially known name in the country, although the Ngok Dinka continued to refer to him as Deng Majoh.

After giving birth to three boys (Deng Majok, Biong Mading, Arob) and three girls (Ayan, Awor, and Abul), Nyanaghar died, her children still quite young. Abiong cared for all the children, hers and Nyanaghar's, with great love and affection, hardly distinguishing between them and indeed as though they were all her own children. Deng Majok and Deng Makuei grew up as though they were full siblings, friends, and close companions. Their next set of siblings, Biong Mading and Allor Maker, were also close friends. Whenever any two got into conflict, the other two would join their half-brothers against their full brothers. The usual polygamous tensions were thus countervailed between them.

Deng Majok is said to have been exceptionally brave. Initiated at a strikingly young age, he faced with remarkable courage the ordeal of scarring the forehead that makes one graduate from the status of a boy, *dhol*, to the highly respected status of *adheng*, a "gentleman." As the oldest son of the Chief, it was thought wise that Deng Majok should lead his age-set and be the first to undergo the operation, even though he was technically still too young to be initiated.

According to Chol Piok,

The issue was debated with some people arguing that he was too young to go through the pain of initiation. Showing any sign of fear or pain during the operation is a disgrace no family would want to risk. Chief

122

Kwol Arob however wanted his son initiated. When he lay down for the operation, people were afraid that he might cry. Of course, he did not. Then followed the customary mock-fights between the warrior age-sets, *biok*, an institutionalized competition for dominance between the outgoing senior age-set and the emerging self-assertive junior warriors. As Chol Piok explained it:

There is something you people missed in this tribe, something called biok, in which members of the older age-set would challenge the upcoming younger age-set by attempting to beat them and getting into a fight. Your father would never run. He never ran. Even when children used to play in the cattle camp, when a senior age-group would beat the younger group with branches of trees, he never ran to show his feet to someone else. It never happened. He would be beaten until people would give up and leave him alone. And he would dart spears at people.

Father is said to have extended that courage into tribal wars that he, later in life, as Chief, would be instrumental in preventing, and eventually in totally eliminating in his tribe. Chol Piok elaborated on Deng Majok's earlier eagerness to join the fight in intertribal wars. *When the battle of Aguet-Tor was fought, he was still very young and Kwol Arob prevented him from going into battle. Deng cried and cried for not being allowed to go to battle. But Kwol said to the people who were restraining him physically—'If you let him go and he gets killed, I do not know how you people will escape from me.' So, he was physically restrained from going to battle.*

Paradoxically, Deng Majok is said to have combined his physical courage and tough-mindedness with reasoning and a disposition toward resolution and reconciliation: *When he was still a child, your father was very hot-tempered*—said Pagwot Deng.

But he was also a man who reasoned well with words. His was the hot temper of a man who could also speak well! He would not overlook anything that touched on him; he would pursue the matter to the end. But he was also for good relations. Even when he fought with a child, he would insist that they sit and eat together. He did not believe in nursing grievances into continuing bitterness. He believed that people should fight and eat together, leaving aside the conflict. That was the way he behaved.

From his early days, Deng Majok distinguished himself for generosity, wisdom and ability with words. Chol Piok elaborated:

The character of Deng Majok that you saw started when he was a small boy. He never changed his character as he grew up. He would quarrel with his father to the point where everyone would know that they had quarreled and that Kwol was angry with his son. Then at night, he would come with a cow and say—'Father, I have appeased you with this cow.' His maternal relatives were a family of great wealth. Whenever he wanted anything from them, it was given to him that same day. So, he would appease his father and their quarrel would end. That is the way they lived. And he would quarrel with his father because his father had a tendency to suppress the rights of his mother's side of the family. That he would not accept.

His hospitality, as many aspects of Father's life story sounds more like a fiction than fact:

When people gathered in the court of your grandfather into the evening, and as they would begin to leave, Deng Majok would be standing by, watching the condition of the people. He was still just a little boy not yet initiated. If he saw a person looking weak and seemingly unfit to travel, he would stop him and seat him. He would give him accommodation and feed him. And the next morning, he would again give him food, and only then would he leave him to travel. That is the way he did things.

Your father began to impose himself when he became of age—said my father's cousin, Ajuong Deng, the Chief Anyiel tribe. His generosity comes across as grossly exaggerated and seems to have been a well-planned strategy for winning recognition and eventually power.

When he realized that his relations with his father were strained, and that his father's preference seemed to be for his other son, Deng Abot, he withdrew. Deng Abot was not a person of initiative. But your father had a great deal of initiative. He developed an attitude whereby, whenever he saw an Arab, even if he were passing some distance away, he would invite him and entertain him well. Whenever he saw a Dinka traveler, even if he were passing a distance away, he would invite him and entertain him. Food was always in abundance. Milk was always available. He himself was never inclined to eating. He would call a person and offer him what he had. During the lean period before the harvest, he would be equally generous.

His generosity extended to making tobacco available. Smoking the pipe used to be popular among the Dinka, and tobacco was a valued commodity:

When he realized that tobacco was in great demand, he would buy and keep it, even though he never smoked. Whenever he saw a person craving tobacco, he would go and get tobacco and offer it to him. If he saw a person passing through at a distance, he would go and invite him. That was what made your father become so popular with the public. Every visitor would leave chanting his name: 'Deng Majok, Deng Majok.' People would say—'This boy, even though he is without a mother, is the leader.'

Marriage and having wives to offer hospitality is said to have been a pivotal point in his campaign for leadership:

He went on that way until he married. Then came the disaster for his enemies. Even before he married, he was nearly always the host for the food that came from the house of Deng Abot's mother. People would say—'We ate in the house of Deng Majok.' And Deng Abot would be there all the same. That was the way your father became popular to the Arabs and to the Dinka. When the issue of Chieftainship was raised, your father's reputation made everyone unite behind him. That was the strength of Deng Majok. And that was how he became popular to the public.

Initially, grandfather Kwol maintained a rather ambiguous attitude toward the two brothers. While favoring the eventual succession of Deng Makuei as the presumed son of the senior wife, he raised them as political equals and even appointed them both as his deputies with equal status. Grandfather Kwol seemed particularly ambivalent toward my father. Accounts of their relationship are conflicting. My father himself was convinced that his father did not love him. He would portray his part of the father-son relationship to us, his children, as one of constant attempts to please his father, but with constant rebuffs. All in all, Father saw himself as a son disfavored by his father. He had a popular saying, which my mother often cited to me, that a person loved by God was far better off than a person favored by his father; the assumption being that he himself was loved by God more than by his father.

On the other hand, it is said that my grandfather saw a great deal of administrative and diplomatic competence in my father, of which he made use. This was especially the case in his dealings with the Chiefs of other tribes and with the Government. Whenever Central Authorities came for administrative rounds or my grandfather went on state visits outside the tribe, he always took my father with him. Some people argue that despite his apparent attitude to the contrary, my grandfather loved my father even more than he did Deng Abot, but that is a viewpoint which is hard to defend.

When my father was a young man and his great uncle, Bulabek Biong, lay dying, he asked him about his status on the issue of succession to Chieftainship. Achwil Bulabek, the dying man's son, who later became my father's right-hand man and the chief of Abyor subtribe, was present. He recounted the scene to me:

When my father was dying, what made your father become the Chief happened. I witnessed and I shall now tell you with my own tongue what I saw and heard. Deng Majok had heard of the seriousness of my father's illness and that he was near death. He came to my father and said—'Grandfather (Great Uncle), I have come because I have sadly heard that you are dying. It is with pain in my heart that I must ask for your opinion. Our people have their own traditions. It is said that the people of our clan do not compete over Chieftainship; that if Chieftainship is contested, it will cause death. That is why I want to ask you. Here we are both under our father. Our father is of course still strong. But the spirit of death does not distinguish between children and elders. If it chooses a child, that child will die. If it chooses one's father and he dies, then the son is expected to step in the position of his father. What I want is the truth. Here we are both deputies to our father on equal bases. What should I do if the question of succession arises in the future?'

126

My father then said—'You Deng, I am going to tell you the truth. I am not going to live any longer. And I am not going to leave you with a word that might lead you to a curse of death. I have nothing more to gain from trying to win your friendship so that people can argue that Bulabek has become a friend of Deng Mujok. Let me tell you that it was to your mother's wedding (as Kwol's first marriage) that we all went; we no go to his second marriage, the wedding of (Deng Makuei's mother) Abiong. That was performed by your grandfather Arob and his sibling brother. But all the four of us half-brothers went to your mother's wedding. When our marriage to your mother was rejected, our ancestral spirits followed her until she was brought back to us. That was something the sons of one man did together. So, on succession to Chieftainship, if the people of the tribe should oppose your becoming Chief, then, you leave it. But if the tribe should choose you to be the Chief, then accept it willingly. You will not have even a headache if qualification is the seniority of the mother. Your mother is the senior wife. So, no illness will befall you on the grounds of seniority. And now, give me your hand.'

Carrying a man and raising him up toward the sky or taking his right hand and driving it high up, is part of the ritual of installing a chief. *Deng extended his right hand. My father held it. Then he raised it up three times. Bol, the son of my mother, was there, and Miyan, the son of my father, was there. They were witnesses. Deng shed tears; he cried over his dying Great Uncle. When Chieftainship was later contested, that was what we disputed with Abyor section. That is why to this day, they say that it was I who gave Deng Majok the Chieftainship.*

Morally reinforced and with Achwil Bulabek as his witness and supporter, my father worked diligently to secure the Chieftainship. *He had already started his campaign with his generosity*—said Chol Piok. *It is the person who gives that people like. Your father was most generous from the beginning. You know, Mading, this thing called food, in all its different forms, once it attracts a chief above other things, that is a reason for people to dislike that chief. Our people can dislike a chief simply because he likes food. Conversely, whatever a chief does wrong, if he is hospitable and generous, he is most likely to be loved.*

127

Politeness and deferential treatment of people are among the attributes associated with leadership and for which Father is also credited: *From the time he was a child to the time he grew up, and throughout his life, your father, Deng Majok, never showed disrespect even to a single elder. In fact, he never showed disrespect to any person. Until he grew up and married, he never slighted anybody, whether the person was from his own Abyor section or from another tribe, for that matter, whatever the background of the person. But why he was loved so much is because he had managed everything very well indeed. He abandoned fighting, and even if a person wronged him, he would get his right through the Government.*

The more my father's popularity rose, the more Grandfather Kwol Arob became concerned and the more he tried to influence the central government authorities to ensure Deng Abot's appointment as a First Deputy and eventual successor to Chieftainship. Deng Majok used his friendship with Babo Nimir, the Paramount Chief of the Missiriya Baggara Arabs who had pronounced influence on the British Administrators, not only to promote his own rise, but to force his father out of power. Babo was to intimate to me many years later the history of their friendship and how my father pursued his political ambitions:

I used to hear from the people that Kwol Arob had two sons. One was Deng Abot, and the other was Deng Majok, both young men. The other brothers, people like Arob and Biong and Allor Maker, were not mentioned. Those were younger brothers. The sons of Kwol who would come to the meetings at Abyei whenever authorities went, were those two, Deng Majok and Deng Abot. It was only after my father's death that I became close to Deng Majok; that was after I became the Head of the tribe. Deng was, of course, older than me, but we became very, very close friends. He would come to see me in our dry season settlements, whether at Leu or Ngol or at Nugara. We would sit and chat. He would come with his followers. We would stay together for three or four or five days. At that time, the Nazir (Chief) was still Kwol; Deng was not yet the Nazir.

His name began to rise: 'Deng Majok! Deng Majok! He is a man who shows great deference for the people. He loves all his people and all the people of the tribe love him.'

He became far ahead of Deng Abot in his popularity, even though according to the traditions of divine leadership among the Dinka, Deng Abot was said to be the one entitled to succeed his father.

Our Father Kwol Arob and our Father Mijak (Mijangdit, Kwol Arob's cousin) said that Deng Abot was the one entitled to succeed because his mother was the first wife. But because of our love for Deng Majok and because of his own merits, we investigated the situation to find justification for his succession.

In other words, once Babo Nimir and the supporters decided that Deng Majok should succeed to the Chieftainship, they wanted to establish his legitimacy on the basis of Dinka customs governing succession. Babo Nimir explained their approach with impressive candor:

We wanted to avoid imposing Deng Majok on the tribe without a sound basis. We investigated and discovered that Deng Majok's mother had been the first to be betrothed to Kwol but had initially refused to marry Kwol. When she refused so adamantly, the cattle which Kwol had paid for her were returned, but one cow was left behind with the girl's father. Kwol took the cattle and paid them to the relatives of Deng Abot's mother. Deng Abot's mother was married and brought home. So, Deng Abot's mother came first and was considered as the first wife. But according to Dinka religious ideas, the girl who had first been betrothed had not been freed, because the one cow that had remained behind maintained a bond with her. That single cow was a symbol of the marriage. The rope had not been cut.

Once they got the justification they needed, Deng Majok's supporters embarked on a vigorous campaign on his behalf:

When we heard this, we called Jipur Allor (of Dhiendior clan) and asked him. Jipur confirmed this fact to me and to Rahma El-Ferie (Rahma Nyok, the interpreter who was a Muslim, but ethnically and culturally an Arabized Dinka). Then we met the British District Commissioner and explained to him that Deng Majok was the true leader and that he would be the one to inherit the Sacred Spears, the symbols of authority. His mother had been the first to be married and although the cattle had been returned, that one cow which had remained had maintained the bond of marriage.

Babo Nimir explained that he and Deng Majok had also entered into a bond of relationship. *Deng and I had taken an oath of brotherhood; we agreed to be brothers and took an oath to that effect.* It is quite remarkable that the racial, ethnic, religious and cultural differences between the two did not create a barrier between them.

I wondered whether they were counseled by an elder or if they had thought of the pact by themselves.

No elder counseled us. It was we alone who thought of it. He and I would sit and converse with the people. Then we would have dinner, the people would disperse, and he and I would sit conversing alone, sometimes until midnight. He would be with me for three days, or four days, and then he would leave.

Whenever I visited Abyei, the same thing would happen. He would come from the cattle-camp to visit me in Abyei. We would be together for five days and six days, sitting and conversing.

I asked Babo what their conversations were about:

Our conversations were about leadership. We agreed that Nazir Kwol had become a very old man; that he was more or less no longer able to execute Government instructions one hundred percent. Of course, we were for Deng Majok taking over. Our plans for Deng were what you people in Khartoum here mean when you say—'So and so is being groomed to be this or that.' We were grooming Deng Majok for the day we wanted him to assume the leadership.

Babo's account makes it clear that the conflict between Deng Majok over the issue of succession had become almost public and was sharply dividing the family. It also shows how Babo was the kingmaker with a pivotal influence on the British administrators:

Mijak (Mijangdit) and Nazir Kwol would sometimes come to me and say—'Babo, what's this about Deng Majok? This leadership is not his; it is Deng Abot's. Son, you better stop pushing for Deng Majok. Stop it. It is not his, it is Deng Abot's.' I would say to Kwol—'Father, Deng Majok too is your son. Whether the Chieftainship goes to Deng

Abot or to Deng Majok, you will not have lost anything. In any case,
nothing has happened that you should be concerned about.' Whenever
Deng Majok's name was mentioned, Kwol would say—'Don't mention
him. He is only a Chief for the Arabs; a Chief popular because of his
generosity with food.'

And indeed, the close relationship between Deng Majok and Babo
Nimir was partially a reflection, or a consequence, of Deng Majok's
favored position among the Arabs generally. This in turn reflected
Deng Majok's favorable treatment of the Arabs when they went to
Ngok Dinka territory during their seasonal migration in search of
water and grazing:

Whenever Arabs came to his home, Deng would slaughter animals
for them and show them a great deal of lavish hospitality. Deng
Abot, on the other hand, did not want the Arabs at all. Kwol saw
that Deng Majok had become intimately associated with us and had
become just like any one of us. Whenever the District Commissioners
came, he would join us and we would sit together with the District
Commissioner, while Deng Abot stood some distance away.

They (Kwol Arob and Mijangdit) began to fear that should Kwol not
be there, this man, Deng Majok, would probably assume the chair
of leadership. They never uttered an ugly word. But Mijak and the
Nazir himself, our Father Kwol, would come to me and say—'What
is this? This thing is not Deng Majok's; it is Deng Abot's. How can you
go about trying to do otherwise!? Yours is the Arab position. This is
something that should be done according to our Dinka tradition.
If we disregard our tradition, disaster will befall our tribe. If you ignore
our tradition and promote Deng Majok to seize control of leadership,
destruction will certainly fall on the tribe.' That was what they said.
They feared that, as I was a friend of Deng Majok and as the British
District Commissioners always appreciated my views, I would probably
influence the situation and enable Deng Majok to seize control of
Chieftainship. In fact, when Deng Majok became Chief, we found
what we had hoped for in him. By God, we in our area had not the
slightest doubt that no man who went before Deng Majok would ever
leave feeling injustice. Deng would give him full justice. He would give

a man what we were sure the man would not find with Deng Abot or with Akonon (Chief of Mannyuar section) or with other leaders. With Deng Majok, we felt assured of the protection our people would get whenever they went there.

Achwil Bulabek was later to tell me:

I saw for the first time the genuine friendship which can exist between two sons of Chiefs with your father and Babo Nimir. Their relations were excellent, even with the Government. For instance, when the Deng brothers were aspiring for Chieftainship while their father was still alive, whenever Babo spoke with your grandfather in the reckless way of youth, should Deng intercede, Babo would always concede and leave the matter.

When Deng happened to have enemies, who would conspire against him and even report him to the Government, Babo would have something to say to the Government in defense of Deng Majok. He might say—'This is the man; Deng Majok is the person who will bring unity to our people.'

So, one cannot swear that Babo never helped Deng Majok to become the Chief. Of course, Deng was strong in his own right, and Deng had his own supporters among his people, supporters to whom he was the Chief. For instance, the case we had ultimately about succession, was Babo present? Yet, there was some mutual reinforcement between all these contributions. Babo often mentioned Deng Majok's name with compliments, even to the Government. And they usually travelled in each other's company.

Indeed, Babo himself concluded his account to me on the note that when the issue of succession eventually came up for discussion—*We then moved away from the situation.*

What Deng is said to have planned with Babo—in Matet Ayom's words—*Largely reflected the accusation of Kwol that Babo used to speak favorably of Deng Majok to the British Commissioner and that Rahma Nyok also used to speak favorably of Deng Majok to the District Commissioner. That was how the Commissioner was said to have known Deng Majok to the point where he began to proclaim Deng as the Chief. Even as the Chieftainship was disputed, Deng Abot used to say that it was the work of Babo and Rahma. Besides, Deng Majok became acquainted with the Arabs rather early. And because he was that acquainted with the Arabs, Babo used to stand on the side of Deng Majok. He did not stand on the side of Deng Abot. And he did not stand on the side of Kwol Arob.* Kwol Arob's shortcoming in stopping tribal wars and Deng Majok's demonstrated ability to move with administrative competence tilted the balance in favor of Deng Majok's assumption of power from his father.

Traditionally, a Dinka Chief is a divine leader who must not use force, but mostly persuasion. He may ultimately resort to supernatural sanctions by inflicting a curse on an uncooperative or disobedient subject. Divine prerogative is particularly opposed to spilling blood. A Dinka Chief should not even see blood, nor is he supposed to appear on the battlefield. He is to remain at home, praying for victory if the war is with an enemy, or for peace if the war is between factions of his own tribe. He might draw a line on the ground, placing his sacred spears—the insignia of his office—on the line, praying that those who disobey him suffer defeat.

On the other hand, modern administration required more than the charisma or awe of divine power. The Chief had to resort to a more effective use of state power, and, if need be, employ the police or the security forces of the secular state power. When tribal wars broke out, my grandfather acted in a traditional fashion, which did not impress the British colonial administrators. My father, on the other hand, got physically involved, riding into the battlefront, whipping the warriors as he struggled to disperse the front line. Although he could not stop the raging fight, the British were impressed by his role, giving him an advantage over his father, which was to prove a deadly blow to the old man.

The story is told by those who witnessed the events: *Our tribe exploded in wars*—said Chol Piok, who was intimately involved. *Our people were fighting themselves. Bongo clashed with Achueng at Maker. They fought and many people were killed. When the fight started, Kwol sent me: 'Chol, go to Bongo. You are the one most acceptable to all the warring tribes. Koich (Achueng) are your people.*

133

*No one will kill you. And the Bongo are your maternal kin. No one
will kill you. You go and see the situation, where the warriors will be
this evening, and where they will sleep.'
So, I ran all night. I slept in Bongo. And early in the morning, when
the first cock crowed, what you would call six o'clock, I crossed the
River Nyamora. I scouted all the battlefronts of Bongo at Maker, away
from the river. Then I left. When I reached the pool at Kol Amer,
I met Kwol Arob himself. With him was Mijak (Mijangdit) Kwol
(Chief Kwol's cousin). Mijak was driving a black bull, Michar, which
was to be sacrificed to stop the people from fighting. Kwol then asked
me—'Chol, where are the Bongo?' I said—'Bongo are very near here
at the edge of the woods.' And he said—'Do the Bongo know the person
they ambushed last night?' I said—'No, they do not. Who is he?' Then
he said—'They ambushed Nainai last night. He is now lying inside a
hut with only remnants of life. Go and see him, and then return to the
Bongo.'
Ambushing is strictly forbidden by the customary law of war among
the Dinka. It is not clear how Nainai was attacked, but it clearly
signaled a particularly grave violation which added to the gravity of the
situation.
I went and saw Nainai lying down. He was a striking gentleman,
wearing four ivory bangles on his upper arms and large copper coils
on both his lower arms, the kinds of coils our people used to wear.
And in addition, he had a large string of blue beads wound around
his waistline. He was a huge, brown man. I saw him and returned.
Kwol said—'Tell the Bongo to go away. Let them not wait for the
Koich.' That is how I went. On the way, I met Yom, the section of Chief
Pagwot. They held the right flank. I said to them—'O people of my
mother, do you know that you ambushed a person last night? And I am
not talking about the people you killed in battle yesterday.' They asked—
'Who was ambushed?' I said—'Nainai. So, let me tell you! Kwol Arob
says that you should leave and proceed as far as Wachanguam.' Bongo
got up to leave. Awet section, Adhar section, and Yom section all ran
and took their cattle across to the other side.*
Kwol Arob directed his son Deng Abot to go to Bongo and 'drive'

them away from the confrontation front. The use of the word
'drive' implies that they were moving with their herds of cattle. But
Deng Abot was proved ineffective:

*Kwol said to Deng Makuei—'You run and confront the Bongo! Drive
them away from Wunlou where I understand they have camped. Drive
them as far as Wachanguam.' When Deng Makuei went, he found it
impossible. He could not manage Bongo. The warriors simply boomed
with their war songs and proceeded to tether their cattle in the camp.*

The role of Deng Majok in the effort to prevent the fighting was
contrastingly more effective.

*Deng Majok got up and put a saddle on his grey horse. And he followed
to the confrontation scene. He found Bongo having completely subdued
Deng Makuei, who was about to leave. Deng Majok jumped down
from his horse and proceeded to untie the cattle of Deng Nyach's family
without saying a word. All he said was—'If anyone dares to, let him
spear me in the back.' He proceeded to untie the herds.*

*Deng Nyach then spoke to his people—'You Awet section, what else
can you say? You have heard that the camp of Pagwot has moved.'
And he drove his herds away. Each person from Bongo would see that,
and drive his own cattle away. Deng Majok followed them until they
reached Wachanguam in the middle of the night. And then he returned
the same night.*

That experience apparently gave Deng Majok an edge over his
father and his brother as a more competent leader and agent of law
and order.

*That is how Deng Majok started to shoulder the responsibility of
leadership. He then realized that both Kwol Arob and his son Deng
Makuei had fallen short of governing the country.*

*That battle was eventually stopped. That was the Battle of Maker. It
ended. Then came the Battle of Dokura. That was the battle in which
people like Kwol Deng, the father of Atem-Chol Kwol, and people like
Mathii, were killed. In that battle, many people were killed.*

Nainai, who had been wounded in the Battle of Maker, eventually
died of his wounds and the man who killed him was later identified
as Dur Ayiik. He was tried for murder, found guilty, sentenced to

135

death and executed. That was the first time the death sentence was introduced to the Ngok Dinka, and it would have its own consequences as a trigger for tribal war.

Word came that Dur Ayiik, who had killed Nainai, had been hanged— said Pagwot Deng, Chief of Bongo.

He had been taken away by the Government and was eventually hanged. Dur Ayiik was from Bongo. When the word of his death came, Bongo rose up to attack Achweng. Abyor was allied with Achweng. They intercepted Bongo at Dokura. People struggled to prevent that fight, but all in vain. It broke off the first day. The following day, war cries rose again. And the Battle of Dokura was fought.

Again, Chol Piok was closely involved in that fight:

And it was true, he had dispersed the Koich. Even when the people were eventually killed, it was old men who were killed and not the warriors. A young man from Allei called Yak Bayak pointed his spear at me saying—'Don't you see, Chol wants to disperse our battlefront?' Right at that moment, they boomed with their war songs and continued their way. And I continued. I had only gone a short distance when I met Bagat Allor at the head of the Malual age-set of Mannyuar, singing their war songs. I lowered my spears. And the Malual too suddenly stopped. I told them my message. Bagat simply dismissed me by saying—'Son of Piok, go your way. These matters will be discussed later when people return from the battle.'

So, I went on until I met Deng Akonon. He was leading the warriors of Mithiang age-set, singing their war songs. Then he said to me—'Son of my maternal uncle, have you not met with Jipur?' I said—'Yes, I have met with him.' Again, he said—'And have you not met with Bagat?' I said—'Yes, I have met with him.' Then he said—'Those are the people leading the war. So, there is nothing I can do to prevent it.'

Then I went to Bongo. Again, I gave them the message. But as I talked, young warriors rampaged past me in the opposite direction. They came and found Abyor empty. Turuk age-set of Abyor had left for the cattle-camps. Mijok age-set of Anyiel had gone. Dhierget age-set of Mareng had left. And the Gol age-set of Achueng had also left. All our young warriors had gone away to the cattle-camps. That was the war that

*crept in on old people in Dokura and killed the elders; it killed the
elders in a dreadful way. If Deng Majok had gone instead of me, no one
would have died. Any battle to which Deng Majok would go, no one
would die.*

*One year passed. And when another year came, Abyor planned an
attack. They left. Kwol Arob also left with Mijak Kwol. People had
gone to the home of Dhel, which was well out in the country. It was
an area which no members of another tribe could reach. There they
planned the war. That season continued without incidents as yet.*

*But just about the time new crops were to be reaped, Abyor attacked
Bongo in the middle of the night. It was near those trees known as the
Tamarind Trees of Chan. That was the war of Nainai.*

*In that open area near the Tamarind Trees of Chan is where my cattle-
byre was. My cattle-byre was right there in the area past the Trees of
Chan, where dhunyghuol (Tebaldi tree) is. That was how far the war
front extended. That was the war that was fought. It was fought and
fought and fought, with so many people killed. That was when the Two
Marials were killed—Marial, the son of Mijak, and Marial, the son
of Allor. Bongo overwhelmed Abyor with strength. They chased Abyor
in a manner you have never heard of. They chased Abyor so badly until
Anyiel came. It was Anyiel who held the front. They killed two people
from Alei on one flank. And they chased them. They had crossed the
small creek which you cross before reaching the home of Achwil. They
reached there. And the chasing started in the open plain near the house
of Ajak Deng-kwei. They came passing near my cattle-byre.*

*Deng Majok came and found the battle already raging. Nevertheless, he
was the one who struggled to stop the fighting. He would go to one side
and when people responded to him and separated, the other front would
clash. He struggled alone until he was exhausted. He struggled and
struggled on his horse while the battle was raging. Whenever he saw a
small opening in the battlefront, he would get in. And when the battle
closed in, he would take the horse out of that situation.*

*That is how the fighting went on. It raged and raged with people
killing themselves and killing themselves. Deng would step out, but
then he would see the situation becoming intolerable, with the many*

137

people falling dead and dying. He would again step into battle to make another attempt at separating the people. It was a war which Deng Majok worked extremely hard to prevent. He really struggled a great deal. The man called Minyiel, with whom he had contested his wife, Nyanawai, nearly speared him. Deng was on the horse. When he began to realize what might happen on the flank where Minyiel was, he said—'Jipur Tiel, give me two spears!' So, he was given two spears. He held them together with the reins and pushed the horse through the battle. Even a person like Minyiel, who had such a strong grudge toward him, lashed with his whip.

Had Deng Majok arrived before the battle had started, he would certainly have stopped it. But he found that the battle had already raged, and people had been killed. Dead people remained in front of my cattle-byre. They had been killed and skewered. And then he met Abyor while Abyor was being chased. They met in front of Achwil's home at Nainai. Abyor stopped.

Abyor fought and fell dying. When Deng tried to break the battle, the people were already entangled; there was nothing he could do. But he struggled until he eventually stopped the fight.

The battle was broken when the sun had gone far down late in the afternoon; it had started early in the morning. It stopped at that late hour. Bongo then travelled at night.

Pagwot Deng recalled:

When the fight first started, it was Abyor who first planned the attack. They even told your father at Noong. But your father refused. He said—'Let it not even be known to have been contemplated. Let it not even be heard that Abyor thought of attacking. Let it end within our own circle.' So Abyor stopped. When Deng went and related the matter to his father, Kwol did not call Abyor. He remained silent. Word then leaked within Abyor and even reached Bongo. Even the fact that Deng had related the matter to his father and his father remained silent without calling Abyor to reprimand them was also known to Abyor and Bongo.

Kwol did not ask Abyor—'What do you have against Bongo? Why did you plan to attack Bongo?' He never asked them. That was that. Then

138

Abyor planned another attack and even mobilized at Maker and then moved as far as Mitbaai. It was there that your father stopped them. He had heard of their moves while he was at Noong. So, he ran after them until he caught up with them. He made Abyor return to their homes. He then left for Abyei. Again, he explained everything to his father. His father once again failed to call Abyor and ask them what they had against Bongo. He had now failed twice to check Abyor.

We overlooked all that and remained silent. Then came the following year. Later that year, Bongo made a drum at Minyang-Loor and organized a major dance. Abyor came to the dance of Bongo but refused to dance. Instead, they took their spears and surrounded the dance for no reason at all. They were moving to attack without provocation. When your father came, he gathered Abyor together and went and met with them at a distance away from the dance area. He said to them—'Are you here to dance or to fight? You know my position; I have made it clear to you. If you have a different plan with my father, then that is different. I have told my father all that I had told you on former occasions, but he has done nothing about the situation. He has remained silent. And now you come to surround a tribe that has made its drum and has brought it out for a dance, and you say you want to fight them. Are you going to spear at dancers, including their dancing women and girls!? That cannot be. If you do not want to join the dance, then you better leave now and go back to your homes. If you do not want to leave and return home, then at least stand far away from the dance. You can watch from far away and disperse once the dance ends. That is my word to you. But what you are about to do is something that has never occurred. From the time man was created, I have never heard of a tribe attack another tribe and spear them while they are dancing to their drum. I know of no example of this sort. So, never think of it ever again.'

Abyor listened to his words and accepted them. Then he went and related the situation to your grandfather. Again, he did not call Abyor to question them on the situation. Abyor then rose up determined to attack. They left your father's word aside and attacked, passing by Achwil's village. When they emerged out of the woods leading to the

*open area on the borders of Bongo, the people of Bongo began to emerge
from their huts to face the attack. The battle began. Abyor advanced
until they were halted at Dhunydhuol. They were then pushed back up
to the creek at Achwil's village. They were pushed across the creek. Then
both sides held their front on each side of the creek, and they continued
to fight with the creek between them.*

*Deng Majok went, but it was not a fight he could stop any more. It
met in the morning in his absence, and then he came. He could no
longer stop it. I myself said to him—'You should no longer get involved.
Minyiel, the man with whom you contested a girl, is after you. He even
comes close to the river here looking for you. I told him to go to the
flank of Alei and that if he wanted to kill you, he should wait for you
there and not on our side of the fight.' The battle went out of hand and
became impossible for your father to stop.*

*But when the attack was being planned, your father prevented the
attack several times earlier. Abyor did not tell him of their plan that
last time. So, your father did not know of the attack. It was people like
Deng Mathii who were leading the attack. But people like Mijang
Kwol and Allor and Mahdi knew of the plan. They knew how it
started. It was their war. And could they all have known about it, and
Kwol remain ignorant while they all sat in the same place?*

The following winter, the British District Commissioner came—said
Chol Piok.

*He convened the Assembly and said—'You Kwol Arob, how could
people be killed in such large numbers near your home!? The distance
between Nyinkuach, where the fighting took place, and your own
home, are they not within seeing distance? Where had you gone!?' Kwol
said—'I was sleeping. And when I got there, I found the battle too
advanced and people had already been killed.' He said—'O Kwol! And
how could Deng Majok run all the way from Noong, which is so much
farther away, and he managed to reach the battle and struggled to stop
the fight? Even if you were crawling on your knees, would you not have
reached before Deng Majok?'*

According to Pagwot Deng,

District Commissioner had already begun to question the leaders of

*the tribe discreetly and was told by the people that had Deng been the
Chief, this war would not have been fought. Abyor at first mobilized
itself, but he stopped them and said—'Let nothing be heard about this!'
And he went and informed his father. But his father never questioned
Abyor. Abyor did it again, and he once more stopped them and told his
father. But his father never questioned Abyor. So Abyor kept this last
plan secret from Deng. Is he therefore not a person who can save lives?
Kwol Arob has the virtues of a true Chief, but he has been misguided
by his brothers. So, if Deng has proved himself so able, it would be
worth giving him the chance to try the leadership of the tribe while his
father is still alive.*

Chol Piok continued:

*That winter, about the time the stalks of the second crop were open
to cattle, Kwol was fetched to go to the North. He was called by the
Government. He was taken to Nahud. He was then told—'You, Kwol,
you have failed in stopping wars. The people who died in your hands
are many. And you did nothing to save their lives. In the war of Maker,
many people died. And in the war of Dokura, many people died. The
war of Nainai again killed large numbers of people. You will have to
sit and retire. Your children have matured. They have matured enough
to assume the responsibility. So, you show us which one of your sons you
would want to take over.'*

*The British District Commissioner introduced the matter of succession
in that discreet manner. He said—'Show me the one you believe will
govern the tribe as well as you used to govern it.' Kwol said—'It is Deng
Makuei.' The Commissioner then said—'If Deng Makuei is the one you
have chosen, then you will not return home as yet. We will go to the
area first and ask the people. All your people who are called the people
of Arob Biong, we shall ask them. If they want Deng Makuei, then we
shall accept their word. If they want Deng Majok, we shall accept their
choice.' Had you said to us—'You Government, it is for you to see the
one you think will be able to govern the area, we would have talked; we
would have given you our opinion. But now, we shall not reveal to you
all our thoughts as yet.'*

Kwol Arob was stunned. He did not know what to do. When he

141

realized there was nothing he could do, he said—'I have surrendered. If it is the name of Deng Makuei which will detain me here and prevent me from going to my area, then I have given in. And you Government, you will go and talk to my people in my presence. But although I shall be there, I will not do anything to interfere with the plan. Whatever the people will say will be. If the people say—"It is Deng Makuei," I will have nothing to say; and if the people say—"It is Deng Majok," I will also have nothing to say.'

That is how Kwol was released and allowed to return home. My cattle-byre was there at Dhunydhuol. I heard that Kwol had nearly been arrested but had been released and had just returned. I rose early one morning and went to him. He had just returned from Nahud the day before in the late afternoon. I rose before dawn. I was a young man wearing ivory bangles. His age-mates had not yet even gathered. I found three of them under the tree with Mijak Kwol and Deng Patoc. I rested my spears on the tree. I was still wearing my ivory bangles. Then I called him. I said—'Father of Agorot, there is something I want to talk to you about.' He immediately understood that I was going to ask him about his detention at Nahud. We went inside a small room that had just been built for him; it was a very tiny room. That is where he took his tea in the morning. I asked him about those matters. We spoke. Then I said to him—'The people who reported you to the Government are these: there was Deng Patoc, and Deng Nyac, and Bagat Allor. Those were the people who reported you. The day they discussed you, I was lying down under the tree. They came and sat down. And there were no other people. And then they talked. They said to the District Commissioner that they would like to talk with him without your presence or the presence of any other persons. Then they talked against you while I lay there listening. They thought I was not interested in such matters. They talked and talked. They spoke in Dinka and Rahma interpreted into Arabic. With those enemies around you, why are you intensifying the battlefront with your own son? What is the matter with you? Is Deng Majok not your son? Was he begotten by someone else? Even his mother, did she beget children with someone else before you married her? You, this issue of Deng Majok is really a fault on your side.'

142

*Then he said—'Chol, son of my father, I do not hate him. It is just
that I fear Deng Majok will outwit my people. He will not take care
of the children well.' I said—'And how do you know that? What about
his good treatment of people in general, will he not do the same to your
children?' Deng Majok was then outside sitting under the tree. Then
Kwol said—'I have given in. Will I bring it up again when it was a
major problem for which I was almost detained and kept away from
begetting children in my family!? I have surrendered. They are both my
children.'*

*Then I left. I took my spears and left. I went beyond the creek near
Deng Makuei's house. There, Deng Majok caught up with me. He
said—'You there, wait for me.' Then he said—'What were you talking
to your cousin about?' I explained to him. He laughed. He accompanied
me until he reached Nyinkuac. He returned to the stream in Nyinkuac.
A public meeting was convened under the Court Tree. People then
spoke. And when people talked, all our people of the area, including
elders and court members were assembled. The old men of the tribe
were included too. People like Amor Miorik were included, even though
they did not hold any public position. Another elder from Mannyuar
tribe who was called Kur Alak, a crippled man, was also brought in.
He was an old man. He was brought, carried on a bed. The issue was
then raised. The Commissioner said—'You people, what we have said
with Kwol is this and this. And what brought the matter here is for
you to choose the person you want to be Chief, whether it will be Deng
Makuei or Deng Majok.'*

*An old man called Katdit got up; an elder called Katdit from our
Anyiel tribe. He said—'Deng Makuei is not a Chief. Deng Majok
is the Chief. He is our Chief who will sustain us. It is he who will
keep our tribe in order. As for Deng Makuei, he is not a Chief. Deng
Makuei is a brave man, but a brave man who will never reason. As for
the man called Deng Majok, he is brave, but he combines his bravery
with ability to talk. Deng Makuei's courage knows no words.' People
all joined that opinion. Then the Commissioner turned to Kwol and
said—'Chief, now say your word.' Kwol said—'I have nothing to say. If
this is what the tribe says is their wish, how can I have a separate word.*

143

It will be as the people have spoken. So, you, Deng Makuei, you leave the matter. Let Deng Majok take my place. And you leave the matter. This is something that threatens to destroy us if we contest it.' Deng Makuei got up and left.

Deng Majok was then installed by the tribe as the Chief. As soon as he was instated as Paramount Chief, the District Commissioner asked Deng to conduct the war trials with him. I was there. The District Commissioner said—'Where is the clan-head called Chol Piok!?' People said—'Here he is.' And he said—'Tell us all about the fighting! We understand that you were the person sent when the people refused to obey. Tell us what happened.' I told them all, as I have told you. I said—'The people who started the fight were Jipur Allor and Bagat. These are the things they said. You Bagat, were not these the words you said?' Bagat got angry and said—'Chol Piok, why are you after me? Am I the young men who went to war?' I said—'You were their Chief.' And I went on to mention the rest of the people. I said—'There is Minyiel and there is Yak of Bayak. Those were the people.'

They were arrested and seated separately. Bagat Allor was questioned. But he strongly denied the responsibility; he passionately denied it, saying—'I was only following the warriors.' The Commissioner then said—'And why does Chol say you were ahead of the warriors on a horse? And Jipur too is said to have been ahead of the warriors on a horse? How could a chief be overwhelmed by his warriors while he leads them? A Chief is only overwhelmed when his people disperse and run. You are at fault. And you will be fined like all the rest.'

They were fined. Deng Majok then said—'Commissioner, the person called Minyiel and the person called Yak should both be fined and flogged.' The Commissioner said—'Chief, your opinion is right.' So, they were made to lie down. And that was the beginning of flogging in our area. Each one received twenty lashes.

Deng Majok imposed punishment on his own section, Abyor, and left the Bongo free—said Matet Ayom.

He said—'Abyor was the first to attack Bongo. And if wrongs are equated, wrongdoing will never cease in this land.' So, Abyor was severely punished while Bongo was left free. That was the case that

deterred the people of our land from warring.
When the case was decided—added Monyluak Row,
Deng said—'Bongo have a just cause. Bongo was attacked at home.
They had not even said anything provocative. Yet, they were attacked,
and their people were killed. The fight broke out and many people were
killed on both sides. It is because of Abyor that all these people have lost
their lives. Although Bongo killed more people from Abyor than Abyor
killed from Bongo, they were defending themselves against the attack.
I believe Abyor should be punished as the aggressors. They should be
made to pay a heavy fine of cattle. And they should be made to pay
compensation for the people they killed among the Bongo. Bongo should
only pay compensation for the people of Abyor whom they have killed,
but they should not be made to pay the fine. *That is how Deng ended*
the case and that is how the tribe settled in peace and order. It was
because of your father.
Deng Majok then moved to settle the disputes with our neighbors to the
South—continued Chol Piok.
We left with him and went to Gogrial. In addition to myself, there was
Chan Dau and Chier Agoth and Allor. We went to the Assembly at
Gogrial. And then we went and crossed the land of the Twich until we
went and stopped in Diil. That is when Deng Majok had the Twich
compensated for their grain which had been captured by the Ngok
during a fight with the Twich. Each person's storage container would
be brought and filled with grain. Another container would be brought
and filled. Yet another would be brought and filled. And the person
whose container would be filled would take oath that he had lost that
much during the fighting. He settled the compensations, imposed the
fines, and replaced the lost grain. We returned to our area in Abyei after
people had already seeded their fields. And we had left during the dry
season. We spent three months away.
That is how Deng Majok took over the country. He became established
as the Chief. There was nothing else. Our people became happy.
Everything was then reorganized by Deng Majok and he maintained
it so. Bongo and Abyor, he reconciled them and there were no more
conflicts between them. That is how internal warfare ended in our area.

And that is how our warring with the Twich ended. We then stayed in peace. Deng Majok was the Chief.

A year after my father took over the leadership; he went to the North to receive his insignia of office, a red robe of honor. The Arab elder, Ibrahim El Hussein, describes the scene of his return:

Mahdi and many men from the lineage of Kamil were on our horses to escort him back home. We escorted him with our horses. When we reached Akwong, the Dinka came to meet him. Crowds came booming with songs and blowing their horns. Animals were slaughtered. Cries of joy filled the air. We stopped at Deng's village at Naam (Noong). Your father was wearing the red robe of chieftainship. He slaughtered more cattle for us. His wives prepared plenty of food.

We spent the night there at Naam.

The following day, we escorted him again up to Abyei. His home was on this side of Abyei where you buried him. Kwol Arob was in his home on the other side of Abyei. Kwol used to spend the day under the huge tree in front of his home. We went over in a crowd that filled the shade of the tree. As we approached, we greeted them: 'Peace be upon you!' Kwol refused to greet us back. He was angry over the issue of chieftainship. 'Greetings,' we said again, but he did not respond.

An old man of his age who was in our group said to him—'Kwol, here we are bringing your son to you, how can you not respond to our greeting!?' Then he responded and greeted us. We went back to the cluster of trees near the area where the police station is now located. Deng Majok slaughtered a great number of animals for the festivities. It was a festivity which had no limits. Hospitality was one of his outstanding virtues. That is how Deng took over the chieftainship. He kept the Arabs with one hand and the Dinka with the other hand. He protected the Dinka and he protected the Arabs. He guided the Arabs with words of wisdom as he guided the Dinka. And the Arabs fully accepted his word. The Arabs looked to Babo's chieftainship only when they were back in Arabland. But when they were in Dinkaland, their chief was Deng Majok.

Even after my grandfather had given up on the Chieftainship, he continued to be concerned about the future of his family and in particular his two sons. He confided his concern to Achwil Bulabek, who recounted their conversation to me:

He sent me Maleng Kwol and said—'Let Achwil come early in the morning.' I left very early in the morning—so early that it must have been about five o'clock. I went to Abyei. I found he was still sleeping in his elevated hut. Then he came and found me waiting outside. He used to rise early. He said to me—'Were you sleeping here!?' I said—'No, I came this morning. It was you who sent for me. Is all well?' 'Yes, all is well!' he said. One of his wives then went and brought him some water. He washed his face. Tea was then made and brought. We drank tea. People had begun to gather. There was Mabeng de Kwol and Mijak and Yowe and Malual Adhar—four—and then he and I, we were six all together.

Then we left and went to the police center where the police station is now built. At that time, it was built of small huts. He said—'Why I sent for you, I have been searching in my mind a great deal. You and I began to come into conflict from the time you were not yet initiated into adulthood. When the appointments of Junior Chiefs were discussed, you always took your independent line on anything I said. Whatever I said, you would stand against me and push your own line until you end up winning your argument. That made me dislike you, which is why we often came into conflict. But recently, I have been searching in my mind as I lie down to sleep. I have thought a great deal, and I have found you to have been consistently correct in the positions you have taken. What you used to tell me, I have found today to have been the truth, all of it.'

He began to trace the issues from the time he and I had first come into conflict and said I had been right on all those issues. 'Son of my father, I have come to realize fully that you have a good head. Why I am calling you today is the sake of my children. I do not think it good for a man to wait and then make his will and wishes known as he is dying. Here are my two sons, the Deng brothers. One Deng is a poor speaker. But Deng Majok is clever. Should I die and they have quarrels among themselves, unless you step in between them, they will never live in peace. Even the public will not reconcile them. Even your brother Bol would not help

147

much because he is hot-tempered. He will give his opinion against the person he believes to be in the wrong and if his word is not heeded, he will get impatient, lose his temper, and give up. But with you, you will persuade a person to see his wrong and even if a person disagrees with you, he will think at night until he realizes that what you had said was the truth. So, there are my children!'

I said—'So this is what you wished to say to me!?' He said—'Yes!' I said—'Have you at last truly accepted me!?' He said—'I have wholly accepted you!' I said—'Kwol Arob, a man grows old and eventually dies. He is then praised by people after his death. You will be glorified after your death when people will say—'This is our beloved land of our Great Chief Kwol Arob.' But I want to tell you now that I myself will not praise you. I want to tell you this while you are still here with us.

'And why I will not praise you—you have allowed our people to be divided and scattered. You have allowed Rian to take the Twich of Kwac. Twich Kwac belonged to our ancestors. The burial of our ancestor Allor was attended by the Twich. Our uncle Arob came with cows of tribute from the Twich. That was where the Bull, Maker, came from, the Maker for which you were known when people would say—'Maker of Kwol Arob.' Is that not true?' He said—'Yes, it is!' I said—'These are the people you abandoned to Rian, a man who used to accompany Arob de Biong as his servant. How could such a person take our people, the Twich, and annex them to Wau. I dislike you for that.

'The second point concerns the Ruweng. Why they are called Allor is because they were the people of our ancestor, Allor. You have also abandoned them to Monyjok de Michar and Kon Awuyak, the father of Choi Kwol and Mayeng d'Ador. How could you abandon our people to them? Just because they came with hats, you got frightened by the hats and abandoned our people to the Nuer while it was you, Kwol Arob, who gave Kur Kwot his Chieftainship. You said—'Kur will be my representative here because the distance is too long. He will settle problems here, and I shall only come to resolve serious matters.' Now you have simply given them away.

'Thirdly, the Government has now registered Ngol in the map as part of Arabland according to your own declaration. Because of your dispute

with Monycol—because of one man, Monycol Monytuung—you said to the Government that Ngol was not part of Dinkaland. You did so simply to stop that one man from settling there. That one man called Monycol! What if you continued to imprison him as you had been doing anyway? Would that not have achieved your objective? Now, you have alerted the eyes of God to Ngol by having it set on fire three times. Monycol would go and build his home there and Kwol would have the houses burned down, saying to the Government that he did not want any of his people to build there because it was not part of his land. He said the tribe should settle together in one area and not spread out. Ngol has always been part of our ancestral land. But you have now abandoned it. That is why the Arabs so arrogantly rush to Ngol during the dry season.

'Because of these three things whereby you have forced our people to become contained in a tight area like a pot when people should settle and procreate over a wide and free territory, because of these, I will never praise you Kwol.' Then he said—'That is precisely what I mean and that is why I called you. Son of my father, when a man tells the truth, it cannot be obscured. You are telling the truth.' I said—'As we are now, you will leave us in grave danger. If people were to relive in their graves and hear and observe what happens on earth, you would hear what I have said come true.' Later, when we fought with the Arabs, I recalled this to your father. I said—'Deng Majok, was this not what I had told your father?'

Achwil's blame of Kwol for the manner in which he had conducted his foreign affairs did not address the concerns of Kwol Arob for the future of his country, and specifically the relations between his two sons. One of the issues still pending and soon to surface as a hotly contested issue was succession to the Sacred Spears after Kwol's death. After all, the Sacred Spears were the core of the Chief's legitimacy and effectiveness among the Ngok Dinka.

Six

Contest for the Sacred Spears

My grandfather did not live long after he had been stripped of power. It is obvious that he began to see the end in sight. Deng Majok was already asserting his leadership at home and in intertribal affairs. But in the Dinka view of things, succession to his leadership was not yet complete as long as he still possessed the Sacred Spears in which real power was believed to rest. As had been increasingly the case, Achwil Bulabek was to play a critical role in the developments.

The following year—continued Achwil—*Your father came to the North and was given his robe of Chieftainship. He became a fully fletched Nazir (Chief). That was the year your grandfather became ill. There was to be an inter-tribal assembly in Tongliet. Deng was then the man in charge of the tribe. The Sacred Spears were still in the possession of your grandfather. When we went to Tongliet, Deng Majok said to the Government that leadership and the Sacred Spears were never separated in Dinka tradition. He called Jipur Allor and the matter was explained to the British District Commissioner. Mr. Owen was then the Commissioner. He called the people to assemble. There was Jipur and Deng Majok and Deng Abot and Choi Dut and Miyan Arob and myself, Achwil Bulabek. The chairs were then taken to a spot near the bridge, a bridge like this one. The matter was then raised.*

It was argued that the spears should be given to Deng Majok. The Government said that they should be given to Deng but that the Government would welcome comments from those present at the meeting. I spoke and said—'*You District Commissioner, if we saw a man walking on that bridge as we are sitting here and we saw a man go and try to take the spears by force from the owner, which of the two would you defend?' He said*—'*I would protect the owner of the spears.'*

Then I said—'*Then why would you want the spears of Kwol Arob to be taken by force when he is still alive!? Can your word be a word of justice?' He said*—'*what then do you say on the matter?' I said*—'*If it were my judgment, I would say that he should be allowed to keep his spears until he dies.' He said—'and what after his death!?' I said—'The spears should then go to Deng Majok. That is the day they will cease to be Kwol's and become Deng's. But if we take the spears from him now, it will be as though he were dead. It will even hasten his death.' He said—'The case will end in accordance with the opinion of Achwil. I shall leave tomorrow morning, but the Assistant Commissioner will remain. And you Achwil, will come with me. You will tell Kwol yourself. Is he not your brother?' I said—'Yes, he is my brother.' He said—'Then you should be the one to tell him.'*

The next morning, we went into his car. I said—'I would like Chol Dut to accompany me. He will be my witness.' So, we left in the morning while the assembly was still in session. They had met for three days, but there was yet another day to go. We drove until we reached Abyei. When we arrived at Abyei, we found Kwol's illness had become critical. As soon as I got out of the car, I was told of the situation. That is when my brother, Bol, and I quarreled. I found him there and with him was Deng Akonon. Bol said to me—'This message of yours which you bring with reckless urgency will never come true!'

That same evening, Kwol worsened so much that people ran to alert the tribe and gather the cattle for funeral sacrifices and rituals. The Deng brothers were still at the Assembly in Tongliet. Some people had been sent to them, but our paths had crossed. Word had gone to them: 'Your father is critically ill!'

On receiving the news, the District Commissioner told them that they could take his car once a minor repair had been done. He himself could then be fetched the following day. Deng Makuei would not wait. He jumped onto his horse and raced to Abyei.

My father later followed by car. According to Achwil Bulabek,

As they arrived, Deng rushed to his bedside and before he died, he uttered to them his dying will. But he had already made his dying will to others before they came. In that, he bequeathed to them two sets of shoes symbolic of succession in Dinka tradition. He gave Deng Majok modern shoes which symbolize succession to Government power, while he gave Deng Makuei traditional Dinka shoes to symbolize succession to divine traditional authority. He said to Deng Makuei—'This is your

path, the path of our ancient traditions including the Sacred Spears,
and Deng Majok's path is that of the Government.'

Chol Piok, who was still with my father and Deng Makuei in Tongliet, narrates the developments there:

Kwol had been ill for some time, but he had begun to improve. And
after the people had gone to Tongliet, he suddenly got worse at night.
The person who was sent said—'The Chief will not survive the night.'
Deng turned to the Chiefs and said—'I must leave. I cannot stay to the
end of the Assembly. My father is dying.'

That is how we returned. The following morning, Deng went by the
Commissioner's car, and we travelled on horses. I was on my Miyom,
which was brown with a white spot on the head. He was a remarkable
horse. Those who had remained with us included Chan Dau and of
course Deng Majok and that small man called Allei Monyjur who
was a servant. We kept our horses going. At about the time cattle were
unpegged to graze, we came to Mitrok.

Deng also arrived at the same time by car. He jumped down from the
car and entered the hut where his father lay. He approached his father
and said—'Father, are you dying?' And his father said—'Is it you,
Majoh?' His voice was no longer audible. He caught Deng Majok's
head and placed Deng's ear close to his mouth. What he actually said to
Deng, I did not hear. And Deng has never said it to this day. As soon as
Deng raised his head from his father, his father passed away. He died.
The grave was then marked. People began to dig. The grave was dug
and dug and dug. Then he was placed into the grave. You know the
Dinka way; as the dead Chief is placed in the grave, the new chief must
be installed at the same time. No moment is allowed to lapse without
a Chief. But, Abyor had already agreed on a secret plan unknown to
the other tribes. They caught Deng Makuei and installed him. They
brushed Deng Majok aside so that he was no longer the Chief; Deng
Makuei was then the Chief.

Achwil Bulabek elaborated on the dramatic developments that followed, especially the role the section Abyor, of which he was the
Chief (*Omda*), played:

Kwol died in the early morning, the tribe began to assemble. The cattle were then driven to Abyei. I myself went and brought Abyor to Abyei. Mitrok was filled with people. The grave was then dug. Even as the grave was being dug, people were conspiring that Deng Makuei should be the heir to Chieftainship. But whenever I joined any meeting, people became silent. And when I moved to another gathering, people became silent. That was the plot made by Abyor. The whole of Abyor had gathered including women. As the body was being lowered into the grave, people stampeded for Deng Makuei. Matiok Malek, the grandfather of Bol, ran with the crowd and pushed me aside almost knocking me to the ground. As he pushed me, he chanted—'These were the words we used to seal up in mud containers, but we shall now openly place them in straw containers!' He said this as he proceeded. Then he returned again and pushed me the same way. And he went on insulting me through his chants. They seized Deng Makuei and lifted him, ritually acclaiming him the Chief.

Deng Majok sat at a distance with his brother Arob and myself. Then all the people left to bathe in the river (according to tradition). We bathed separately from the rest of the people. After we bathed, we proceeded straight to Abyei. The District Commissioner had arrived and had set the following day for the discussion of succession. Then I left that evening for my home. Of course, according to custom, nobody should milk the cows or cook food or eat during the whole of that day and night. I proceeded to my home at Nainai. I went to my cattle-camp and gave instructions according to our Dinka custom for mourning the Chief that all the lactating cows should spend the night with their milk—they must not be milked.

The following morning, I said to them—'You may now milk the cows and boil the ghee for offerings on the grave of the Chief.' Then I left. Abyor had scattered back into their homes. But in the morning, a group formed and came after me. They caught up with me on the way in that area near Pagwot's home. They said—'Achwil, will you not be forced to accept the will of Abyor, now that people have decided to bring their choice for Deng Makuei to the Government?' I stopped and stood facing the people who were following behind me. I said—'You, this entire tribe of Abyor, is there anyone among you who is braver than me?' They said—'No! There is no one.' I said—'And even with spoken words, is there anyone among you, the entire Abyor, who is a better speaker than me?' 'No,' they also responded. 'And is there anyone among you who is a better speaker than Deng Majok?' Again, the response was 'No.' 'Today, Deng will hold one flank and I shall hold the other flank and the Commissioner will be in the center of the battlefield.' We debated without agreeing. So, we proceeded together to Abyei.'

What emerges is a situation in which the British District Commissioner comes across as the dominant authority, but not knowledgeable about the customs and appears like a pawn in the Dinka war of wires. Achwil Bulabek continued with his account:

The Senior Commissioner who had come with us had left immediately, but the other Commissioner who had remained at the Assembly came shortly afterwards. His arrival coincided with Kwol's death. He even attended the burial and then returned to his rest house. The following day, the matter of succession was discussed. When the Assembly was convened, Abyor all gathered, including women. They filled the shade of the Court-Tree and extended as far as the river. The whole of Abyor was there. The Commissioner then asked—'What do you, Abyor, say? Who should be the Chief?' They said—'We are opposed to Deng Majok's succession!' He then lined up the people and asked them one by one. When he had questioned some thirty persons, he said—'That will be enough.' The overwhelming number of Abyor wanted Deng Makuei to be the Chief. Then he turned to Jipur Allor (the Deputy Paramount Chief) and said—'Now that Abyor has obviously rejected Deng Majok, what do you say?' Jipur said—'I am confounded!'

It should be recalled that together, Babo Nimir, Rahma Nyok and Jipur Allor were the people who promoted Deng Majok for succession. He was also from Nhiendior clan, who were the rivals of Pajok. And his Section of Mannyuar led the anti-Abyor alliance with Bongo against Abyor in tribal wars.

Achwil Bulabek continued:

The District Commissioner then turned to me. I was sitting all alone; separate from Abyor who were all lined up. He said—'You are the Chief of Abyor and therefore their leader. What is your opinion?' I held

155

*my hands in opposite directions and said—'You see how far apart my
hands are!? That is how far apart my position is from the position of
Abyor.' He said—'In what way?' I said—'When Kwol died, was he
still the Chief?' He said—'No!' I said—'And who was therefore the
Chief?' He said—'Deng Majok was.' I said—'And did Deng Majok
kill a person last night to be disqualified for Chieftainship? How could
this same Deng be clothed with the robe of Chieftainship this year and
during the same year you come to question people about the same Deng?
And it was you, the Government, who placed him there. Is a Chief not
deposed because he has committed an offense? And is Chieftainship not
contested when a Chief dies, leaving the position vacant? Had Kwol
died still holding his position as the Chief, the matter would then be
discussed and the one wanted by the people would then succeed him.
But Deng Majok assumed the Chieftainship while Kwol was still alive.
How can you come now and question us again on the same issue!?'*
Achwil Bulabek then proceeded to tell the conversation Deng Majok
had with Achwil's dying father about the principles of succession to
Chieftainship:

*'But let me tell you something! You hear it said that Deng Makuei is
the elder son. He is not. Deng Majok is the eldest son. Before my father
died, Deng Majok sought his expert opinion. When he obtained his
opinion my brothers Bol and Miyan were there. Only Biong, who is our
older brother, was absent. My father took Deng's right hand and raised
it up and said—'Chieftainship will not give you even a headache.'
So, you better ask Bol and leave aside all these people who have been
talking. They know nothing. I am more informed than these elders you
were questioning. These spears are always handed down to the person
who assumes the Chieftainship. So, ask Bol—'Did your father say so
or did he not?' My father and Kwol's father are sons of the same father.
Arob, the father of Kwol, is the son of Biong and my father, Bulabek, is
also the son of Biong.'*

*The District Commissioner listened and then turned to Bol and
said—'Bol, did you hear what Achwil has just said or did you not hear
it?' Bol remained silent. 'Bol, it is you I am asking!' He remained silent.
'Bol!' Achwil said—'Sir, he will never deny it. That is why he will not*

answer. If he answers you and denies it, let him swear on our Sacred Spears.' The Commissioner then turned to Jippur and asked—'How should we resolve this matter? It is now clear that you Abyor are in the wrong. So, you Jipur, sentence them.'

Jipur said 'They should be fined 100 cows.' The Commissioner wrote that down. He finalized the decision. Then I got up and said—'You Commissioner, what dispute have you had with the cattle when you came into Dinkaland? Did you ever call the cattle and talk to them?' He said—'No!' I said—'Then why are you after cattle when the people who are causing trouble for you are right here in front of you? Who are the offenders, is it the cattle or people? Abyor is a tribe with a great deal of wealth. The cattle you are now demanding for fine will be provided by noble women, whose husbands are dead. They will call on these women and say to each—'Woman, this is the reason for your membership in this tribe. A challenge has emerged.'

The District Commissioner comes across as not only naïve and inept, but almost juvenile, and yet, he was the decisive authority. A more nuanced interpretation is that this scene indicates the operational manifestation of indirect rule by which the British remotely ran the country and maintained law and order throughout the vast country of nearly one million miles with minimum human and material resources from the central government. The District Commissioner asked Achwil Bulabek,

'And what would you do!?' I said—'Although you have written down your judgment, I do not agree with it; cattle have nothing to do with this. Arrest the people responsible and leave the cattle.' He said—'And who are the people?' I said—'There is my brother, Bol. If you really want the matter to end, there is Bol, the son of my mother. And there is (Mijak) Mijangdit. These are the people carrying Abyor on their heads. It is they who pull Abyor along with them. It is Bol who divides Abyor and gives them courage. I then added other names: people like Biong Mijak and Malual Chol and his father and Matiok Malek. All those people, including people like Miyan Arob and Bulabek Deng Awak. That was why they were all arrested and taken away to jail in the North. They all got arrested and imprisoned. Mijangdit said—'O Bol,

*son of my father, people do not get exterminated in two days; let us go.'
That was how those people were arrested and imprisoned. Deng Majok
said to me—'Achwil, I am going to beg you for two or three people.
And please do not insist. First, leave Mijangdit out; Mijak is second to
our father in seniority. Now that my father is dead, even if Mijak has
come to dislike me as he now dislikes me, I cannot extend my hands
to touch him. Release him with his son, Biong. Perhaps you can save
Biong with a payment or fine, the cows which were mentioned before.
Please, son of my grandfather, release them. Of the four hundred cows
mentioned earlier, two hundred will be blood-compensation and two
hundred will be fine.' I almost got angry with him, but he pleaded with
me. He requested Biong with his father. Malual Chol and Chol Guiny
remained in jail. So, I went to collect the fine. I collected the entire fine.
That was how Deng Majok came into Chieftainship and remained in
Chieftainship.*

Chol Piok's account focuses on the issue of the spears:

*The Commissioner said—'Now, right this moment, the Sacred Spears
must be brought. Where are they?' They said—'The Spears are in the
same hut in which Kwol died.' He said—'Let them be brought at once.'
When people tried to be evasive, he called for the police and said—'If I
go myself to fetch the spears, that village where they are and even that
part of Abyei close to it will not look good afterwards. I will have it all
destroyed with guns.' Mahdi Arob (Kwol's half-brother) then got up and
made his famous statement—'My Roaring Leopard Bull! The country
has been captured. Deng Thokloi, son of my Father, we cannot allow
the Government to fetch our Sacred Spears. Let us fetch them ourselves.
Let us give them to the Government ourselves. And then we will see
what he will do with them!'*

*So, they went and brought the spears. The spears were then placed in
front of the Government. The sacred skin on which they always rested
was also brought. The skin was laid down in front of the Government
and the spears placed on it.*

*Then the Commissioner said—'All of you present, is there anyone who
still wants Deng Makuei as the Chief?' He would pick each person from
the group and ask him. And when all denied in fear, including those he*

had detained, he then took the Sacred Spears and placed them in Deng Majok's hands. Deng Majok took them. They were now his and he carried them away to his home.

Deng Makuei was then detained and banished to Nahud. He spent a year there. Although he was put in prison, it is said that he was kept in a separate area from the rest of the prisoners. People were not permitted to visit him. Only his wife who had been taken with him was allowed to stay with him. He was eventually permitted to return after a stern warning by the District Commissioner.

Chol Piok gave this account:

The District Commissioner said to Deng Makuei—'Let me not hear a single word from you any more about Chieftainship. You have lost even the position of the Deputy Chief that you held.' Deng Makuei surrendered. He was returned and seated in his house. He became an ordinary man. Two years passed. And when a successor to Deng Makuei was sought, people said it should go to Nyok (Deng Makuei's younger brother). But Deng Majok refused. He said—'Nyok has his job as a teacher. Let him continue in that position. Let us return Deng Makuei to his previous position.' The Commissioner said—'But if we put him back into that position, will he not do the same thing he did before?' Deng Majok said—'No, he will not. Let us at least give him a chance. If we now deny him any position, his heart will break. So, let us place him under me.' That is how Deng Makuei was placed under Deng Majok. It was Deng Majok himself who requested it. The Government was against his being reinstated. They feared that he would start another trouble. That is how it was. Nothing else was said. They never quarreled about anything again.

Uncle Deng Makuei later gave me this version of the contest for power and the Sacred Spears:

Deng Majok had started the problem with Father's illness. People kept coming to my father to report: 'This is what Deng Majok is saying with Babo; and this is what Deng is saying with Rahma.' That was when my father said to me—'You, Deng Makuei, as we hear it rumored, the Spears might be taken from you by force. If they are taken by force, do not contest the Chieftainship in court. If you do, you would be

*the son of a woman.' That much my father told me; I cannot hide it
from you, son of my brother. Father said—'If you should go to court
for Chieftainship, you would be the son of a woman. Let the Spears
go; one day, they will fall down by themselves. If our Chieftainship is
not an ancestral heritage, but a personal achievement of Deng, son of
Nyanaghar, leave them to fall on their own.'*

It is difficult to understand why Kwol Arob preferred that the Spears
eventually fall by themselves rather than be contested by Deng
Makuei. The only possible interpretation is that it was some form
of a curse that Deng Majok's succession was not legitimate by the
criteria of Dinka moral code and that divine justice would eventually
prevail and Deng Majok would fail. I do not think that my father
was oblivious to that point. During the last days of his life, he sought
my legal opinion on whether Deng Makuei could claim the Chieftainship after his death. I assured him that according to the law of
succession, Chieftainship would go to one of his sons.

Deng Makuei's account makes it clear, without being explicit, that
Deng Majok's succession was imposed on the tribe and not the free
will of the people:

*When Father died, we buried him and sacrificed our bulls on his grave.
Then we were confronted with the District Commissioner, and Jipur
and Rahma. We went under the Court Tree. But Deng and I never
talked; we did not confront one another in front of the public. Deng
had already established his case with the District Commissioner.
When it was announced that Deng Majok was the Chief, our people
all dispersed, leaving them alone under the tree. So, I got up and went
after the people. I said—'You people, come, listen to my words. I am
the one to whom you belong. Please, stop! It is all ours together. It is
the authority of our father, the one and only Kwol.' That was when
one elder from Mannyuar, a man of our father's generation, responded
to my word and said—'O people, let me tell you, if Deng has spoken
the way he has, I am sure he does not want a lengthy discussion on the
issue! Deng knows more than we do. Let the matter come to rest!' That
was how the tribe then settled down.
Then the District Commissioner said to me—'Deng (Makuei), you go*

and bring the Spears.' That is when I said—'I will never hold them with this hand of my father. If you want to take them by force, then do so. I will never ask you why.' The District Commissioner saddled his horse and rode for the Spears. That is when our Uncle Mahdi Arob ran and caught up with him in the area which is now the airstrip. Mahdi said to him—'Go back; I will fetch them myself.' So, it was Mahdi who fetched them from the hut and brought them into court. Your father then got hold of the Spears. I sat there only watching. Is it not over now? The issue of the Spears was always discussed even when your father was alive, but I never said any more about it; I never commented on it again. Even when your father's family sacrifices bulls for the Spears, I never attend the ceremony. I remember my father's words and try to protect myself. I keep my distance for self-protection from my father's word.

Uncle Nyok, Deng Abot's sibling, was later to compose a song, obviously directed against my father, which included the lines:

The Spears possessed by Kwol,
Were not stolen,
They were bequeathed to him,
Son of Madibo, they were bequeathed to him.
Great Chief, Bol Nyuol,
And you, Allor Ajing
And you Father, son of Arob
Father, The Almighty
The Foreign Ruler is destroying your land.
The man who ate the ribs of the donkey
He is the one who owns the land;
Biong, our great grandfather, is the owner of the land
And Arob, our grandfather, is the owner of the land
And Kwol, our father, is the owner of the land.
He is the owner of Ngok
He is the owner of Abyor.
The Arabs were in El Obeid far away in the North.
The Governor challenged Arob

161

'If you are contesting the land with me,
Then bring your son out
And you will have your land.'
He cut the throat of his son
And the land of the Ngok was saved;
Our land was saved
The land of our forefathers was saved.

The singer stages a discussion over Arob Biong sacrificing his son to secure the leadership:

You our elders, I ask you
'Why was the child killed?'
'It was a sacrifice to God.'
'Is the son of a Black Man so cheap
To be killed in sacrifice?
I still ask you,
'Why was the child killed?'
'It was a sacrifice to God.'

These recollections demonstrate that leadership among the Ngok Dinka is the product of a long history of struggle and sacrifice whose legitimacy is deeply rooted in the traditions and experience of the people. External interference is seen as illegitimate and spiritually repugnant. And yet, implicit in the struggle is continuous confrontation with external forces, mostly hostile, but occasionally cooperative. Indigenous leadership has often been reinforced by external involvement and influence. Our father's leadership was therefore part of that legacy, although somewhat exceptional in that it involved a feud within the family. My father thus succeeded to both the Chieftainship of the Government and Divine Authority of the Spears with a great deal of bitterness from many members of his own family. But being a great politician and diplomat, he lost no time in winning over most of his enemies. It was indeed strange in the eyes of many that some of those who had been vehemently opposed to him became among his closest courtiers and companions. Those who had also backed him got their rewards, though of course in subtle ways, except for Achwil Bulabek who clearly became the most favored. All in all, my father was acknowledged as one of the most impartial chiefs the Dinka had ever known. One man praised him in a song of which I remember these lines:

I say, Deng, son of Kwol,
Deng, as encompassing as the Spirit Deng;
Deng does not know his father;
Deng does not know his mother;
Deng the Black-and-White Patterned knows no favor
The Chief cannot be bribed.
Deng, remain in the lead,
Keep the Lead;
Sit at the Head of the Tribe
The soft spot of the tribe is throbbing.

Paul Howell, a legal anthropologist who served as District Commissioner in the area, has written an appraisal of the process that gave Deng Majok the Paramount Chieftaincy against the will of his father, posing the question of whether it was right. Howell was thinking of the strict application of Dinka law, according to which, in his interpretation, the will of the dying Chief should prevail. Although there are, of course, people among the Ngok Dinka who believe that this should have been the case, hardly anyone questions the fact that Deng Majok was a successful Paramount Chief and an exceptionally great leader. Even Howell concedes that he was the most qualified by administrative standards.

As for Father's decision to remain under the administration of the North, instead of reverting to the South, was now complicated by the current crisis of the unresolved status of Abyei between Sudan and South Sudan. The responsibility for that situation also involves our great-grandfather Arob Biong, who pioneered the link with the North back in the 19th century, and our grandfather Kwol Arob,

163

who continued that connection and passed it on to our father. Minyiel Row, a famous Ngok Dinka composer and singer, captured this aspect of Ngok history in these lines:

This feud began with our ancient leaders
When Arob Biong left with Allor Ajing
And traveled all the way to Khartoum
Where they met with the Mahdi
And they prayed facing East-Sabah
Allor asked with his head still down in prayer:
'Arob, son of Biong, have you seen God?'
Arob said—'No, Allor, I have not seen God,
But let us leave matters as they are.'
They were told: 'When you return home
Let the child born to Arob Biong be named Mahdi
And let the child born to Allor Ajing be name Sabah.
You are the people of the Mahdi
Now that you have prayed facing Sabah.'
When they returned, their sons were born
And they received the name Mahdi and Sabah.

Minyiel then presents the decision of Deng Majok to play a bridging role between the North and South:

It was decided that the land be divided
So that each person remains with the son of his father.
But Deng Kwol swore and said,
'I will not abandon the word of my grandfather,
We are the Dinka of Kordofan.'
We lived for ten years,
Then suddenly the Arabs burned Dinka villages
They burned the home of Sabah.
Deng began to quarrel with Babo
But Babo had the Arab Government behind him,
We remained suspiciously together.

164

Thirty years passed,
Then suddenly the Arabs burned Abyei.
They burned the village of Kwol Arob,
The home blessed by the Mahdi.
Those who did not know wondered:
'Why are the Arabs destroying the land of Deng Majok?'

With the deteriorating relations between North and South, reflected in two devastating wars, the Ngok Dinka became the worst hit, turning their area from a bridge of peace and reconciliation, to a point of violent confrontation. Having failed to find justice against repeated aggression, burning of their villages, and capture of their cattle, they prayed for divine intervention. Minyiel Row had these lines of lamentation:

God, it was You who gave the Dinka the cow
And You gave the Arabs their wealth in money;
The Arabs have consumed their wealth
And they have come to capture our cattle
And there is no one to whom we can take our case
So, it is to You God that we must take our case:
Our cattle have been captured
Our children have been abducted
And our villages have been burned down;
We are now clustering under trees like birds.

Interesting enough, the value of kinship ties binding the Arab founding fathers and their Black African mothers, traced back to the slave trade, is invoked as having established a spiritual bind which can inflict a curse upon the violators:

We wonder why the son of our sister captures our cattle.
Yes, the Arab is the son of our sister:
When the Arabs came following the river Nile
They came without their women

It was the daughters of the Dinka who gave them their children.
We wonder why the sons of our sisters capture our herds
Do they not know the curse of wronging a maternal uncle!?
The curse of the maternal uncle is as deadly as the curse of God.
The Arabs captured the Pied Bull of the Spirit Dengdit
They captured the Pied Bull of the Dinka
And they captured the Brown Spotted Bull of the Spirit Garang.
Their case will be seen on the Day of Judgement
These are Sacred Bulls
Their case will be seen on the Day of Judgement.

With the crisis the Ngok Dinka are now in, the wisdom of the decisions made by the ancestors is being questioned and criticized. That is the essence of these lines from Minyiel Row, calling on the Ngok people to:

Rise and suffer the decision of your forefathers
When you were joined with the North
Placing you between North and South
So that you play the role of the sewing machine
That binds pieces together;
So that we unite the Browns and the Blacks
Unite the Africans and the Arabs.
Why are we left swinging like children on trees?
The North pushes us away, saying,
'You, Ngok Dinka are part of the South.'
And the South pushes us back saying,
'You are the Dinka who chose to remain with the Arabs.'
O my Bull, the world has darkened?
We called and called
And no one asked why we were calling;
We cried and cried
And no one asked why we were crying;
We talked and talked
And no one asked what we were saying.

So, we left and went to Babanusa
There, we also called and called
And no one asked what we were calling for.
Anyone who came to visit us in prison
Was treated as though he had visited John Garang.
What we have endured is known only to the Creator.

It is clear that the wisdom of the decision to remain in the North as the best way of safeguarding the interests, not only of the Ngok Dinka, but also that of their kith and kin further South, under the circumstances then prevailing in the area, is not appreciated or even understood. Indeed, if it were understood, I believe the current leaders of the Ngok Dinka would have much to learn from that experience, as their people are now facing similar challenges in the sensitive and volatile border area between the two Sudans.

Seven

The Maternal Link

The Dinka bias in favor of the paternal line implies that a mother's genealogy is generally far less traceable than the father's line. But just as the child is emotionally closer to the mother, though rationally more identified with the father, so is the special bond that ties a person to his maternal kin. Their affection, support, and reinforcement are recognized as unfailing and pivotal in shaping the character and destiny of a person. The Dinka believe that the blessing and curse of the maternal kin are stronger than those of the paternal kin, which signifies the role of the maternal kin.

Most of the story of my maternal line came from my mother's brother, Ngor, and my sister, Ayan. But a number of elders made comments in my conversations with them over the story of my father's life which, though incidental, broaden perspectives on the link with my maternal kin and provides a useful background to the accounts of Ngor and Ayan.

Your mother's father, Mijok Duor, was not from Abyor tribe— said an elder called Monyluak Row.

He was from our tribe, Bongo. Even your grandmother, the mother of your mother, called Ayak Deng Ngor, was a girl of our tribe. Abyor has no claim over any one of them. Our home was Ngol, the land we now dispute with the Arabs. Our section was called Biar, the large section called Biar. Your maternal kin were the central members of Biar section. And Biar is the largest section of the entire Bongo. Should this dispute over land be discussed, you, Mading, will hear the name Biar mentioned in relation to Ngol. Bongo is divided into Biar, Yom, and Adhaar. Those were the three main divisions. Then they sub-divided. Biar produced Awet, and Awet produced Kwac.

Monyluak Row then gave some details about the circumstances under which my maternal relatives migrated to Abyor Chiefdom:

I will now tell you how your maternal kin migrated to Abyor. Your ancestor, Maluk Atokbek was friends with someone. The name of the man who was his friend is what I do not know. I am only a child in relation to that history. They used to go together. And when people would assemble, your ancestor was the expert who mended words. Your maternal kin have always been known for verbal skills and wisdom. For instance, with your grandfather, Mijok Duor, if he were absent from his age-set, Koryom, people would wait for him before talking. If it were a subject which required the gathering of the age-set for consultations, they would say—'We must wait for Mijok before we open the subject for discussion.' When your grandfather begot children, the first set of children came as girls. And Ngor was born last. Ngor is a member of the junior Chuor age-set. And when Chuor used to meet and discuss as an age-set, Ngor used to be waited for if he were away. He is a man who weighed words this way and that way. The whole Abyor would recognize him immediately as Mijok Duor, his father. So, people like our fathers and we ourselves knew Mijok Duor as originally our man, but we would only hear of his words through the relations of Abyor and Bongo, being neighbors that they are. Mijok Duor became a member of Abyor, but his grandfather was a man of the Bongo tribe. So, as I was saying, Mijok's grandfather had a friend with whom they used to be together a great deal. That was Mijok's grandfather Maluk. And whenever Maluk said anything, this friend of his would say—'Maluk is right.' Every day he said—'Maluk is right.' Then it happened that Maluk's brother killed a person. I do not know whether he killed him over girls or killed him in secret or killed him after some conflict on the way; I do not know.

When he killed the man, Maluk's friend was with him. The man disappeared and nobody knew where he was or what had happened. So, they searched and searched and searched for him without success. The relatives of the man could not find out what had happened to their man.

One day, the friend of Maluk left. The cattle had then been released from camp for grazing. But the calves were still tethered to their pegs. People were sitting by the cattle-hearths. The friend of Maluk went and reported to the people of the man who had disappeared. He said— 'Have you found the man who has killed your man?' They said—'We

170

do not know where he is or who has killed him.' Then he said—'Very well. Then you go to that gathering. That was where Maluk and his brothers were.' He said—'Take your spears and take your clubs and run toward that gathering. As you approach them, the person who killed your relative will emerge.'

So, they took their spears and their clubs. Maluk was seated in his assembly. They ran toward them. Others ran behind them shouting— 'O please stop the people from fighting.' Maluk's brother realized that he had been exposed and that he was now known as having killed the man. Their cattle were seized by the relatives of the dead man. So Maluk got up and left the tribe. That was what took him away from Bongo. He called his friend and said—'Friend, I am leaving; you remain in your tribe. Whenever I said anything, you always stood by me and said I was right. Had you been truthful to me this would not have happened this way'.

The spiritual powers of Maluk are then presented in terms of the curse he cast on his tribe as he left, willing that they would be made to scatter for the wrong they had inflicted on him:

That's how he left. Then he uttered a curse and said—'You Biar will disperse and scatter all over the land in the same fashion that I am now leaving.' Biar began to scatter according to the curse of Maluk. He left and was welcomed by Abyor. That was how Biar dispersed according to the word Maluk had said. That is why we say he was our Divine Chief. Some people from the Biar went to Awet, others went to Kwac, and others went to Abyor and others went to Mannyuar and others to Diil. That is how Biar all dispersed. Some are at Adhaar. There is no section of the Ngok in which members of Biar are not found. What destroyed Biar was the curse of your ancestor, Maluk. His clan was our Divine Chiefs. They were the Dhienagou clan. Any illness or disaster that befell the tribe was cured by them. They were our Divine Chiefs. Biar were our Chiefs and the clan Dhienagou were the Chiefs of Biar. Today, nobody has remained who can claim the leadership of Biar other than your maternal relatives. Only they are known as the leaders. Had the descendants of Maluk returned to Bongo and claimed the Chieftainship, people would have stepped aside and said to them—'Yes,

171

this is your position, take it.'

These people of ours, like our people in Patour at Awet, we have never abandoned them. There is a special breed which carries weight, and when they leave, their absence is felt; there is a lightweight breed which even if they leave, people say—'Let them go, we shall find other people.' The people of Maluk, we have never abandoned. The people of your maternal kin are still our people. Even as you are here, you Mading yourself, we consider you the son of our daughter; it is just that man sometimes carries on into other relationships. You travelled first as the son of the girl of Bongo tribe and you will continue to travel in the future into other relationships. For instance, Deng's ancestress was originally a girl from Anyiel and his mother became a girl of Diil, and here he has given birth to you as a son of a girl from Abyor. And you in turn will have children who will be known as children of a girl from another area, as you have now married from America. That is how girls extend relationships.

Pagwot Deng, the Chief of Bongo, also said of my maternal kin: *The section called Biar was theirs. They were in fact the central leaders of Biar. They were the Chiefs of Biar. In those days, there was no Government, but Chieftainship was determined by divine authority. So, they were the divine leaders of Biar.*

*Your maternal kin were the center of the very ancient Bongo—*said Achwil Bulabek, Chief of Abyor.

Maluk Atokbek, son of Dau, was the man who immigrated into our tribe. They then followed in successive generations until your grandfather Duor was born. Duor, the son of Maluk, was then born and Duor begot your grandfather, Mijok. They were the center of Bongo. Then he was followed by the son of his maternal aunt called Tor of the Patuor clan, now also with us in Abyor. People like the lineage of Kaac and people like Monywac of Nyikuac. These people are a continuation of those original people. But they came very early. That is why you hear of the war song of Abyor:

Milk Ayan, the cow from the Nuer;
Milk Ayan, the Cow of Maluk, the Buffalo.

172

The origin of Bongo Section is said to be linked to the Nuer, which is why Maluk's cow is said to be from the Nuer. When Arob was the Chief, he called your grandfather and said—'Mijok, here is my son (Kwol); take good care of him.' Mijok and Kwol were of the same age-set called Koryom. Agoth Akwei later said a word to your grandfather, Mijok. Mijok was so close to Kwol that every single day, Mijok would be with Kwol from the early morning. That is when Agoth said— 'Mijok, son of Duor, you people have overreached for Chieftainship too early in your youth. Chieftainship is a thing for elders.' But Mijok was only performing a duty that had been requested of him by Arob Biong.

According to Matet Ayom, Mijok said:

Your grandfather, the elder called Mijok Duor, was a man of exceeding wisdom and verbal skill. He was a man who spoke extremely well and spoke great words. He was also a great friend of Kwol Arob.

The story of how my father, Deng, married my mother, Achok, is later told by Uncle Ngor and my Sister Ayan with meticulous details, but some of the evidence which I obtained from a number of elders in our conversations about my father also sheds useful light on the situation, at least as viewed from the perspective of my paternal relatives. Matet Ayom relayed:

When your father saw your mother, he went and told his father— 'Father, that small daughter of Mijok Duor, I would like to marry her. Mijok is in any case a great friend of yours.' Kwol said—'My son, Mijok Duor is a great noble man. But the girl is still a child. Why don't you wait for a while?' Your father waited for a little while and then proceeded to release betrothal cattle on his own without informing his father. His father said—'Deng, why have you proceeded to release the betrothal cattle without my knowledge?'

Mijok Duor had reacted rather negatively, saying—'Deng Majok, if yours is a marriage of a son without the involvement of his father, then I shall not accept. Kwol Arob is my age-mate and my associate. If he has not shown interest in the marriage of my daughter to his son and it is only the desire of the son, I cannot accept.' When Kwol heard this, he sent a message to Mijok Duor saying—'Please tell Mijok Duor that he is not a man I can reject. It is just that my respect for him inhibits me.

173

I have already married for Deng Majok with a lot of cows. I am afraid of his getting involved with Mijok's daughter at a time when he does not have the same number of cows at his disposal as he had for his first wives. I fear that Deng may not afford a bride wealth appropriate for the status of Mijok Duor, a great man in whom I find support, for it is with the words of Mijok Duor that I am running this country. So, it is just that I felt embarrassed and fearful, but my son had told me about his marriage plans. I know of the proposed marriage. But it is now for Deng to secure his own wife from his own herds. I will no longer pay the bride wealth.'

Matet Ayom gave as a reason for Kwol Arob's reaction the fact that Deng Majok had already married several wives in close succession: *Kwol had attended the marriage of Deng's fourth wife, Aker Tiel, who had been married in Twichland and had not yet come home when Deng Majok wanted to marry Mijok's daughter. Kwol therefore felt that Deng's marriages were occurring in too close a succession. So, he refused to get involved in his later plans. This attitude offended your father. What provoked your father to become independent in marriage to the point where he never consulted his father any more was the case of your mother. Why his father did not attend the wedding even though he, Deng Majok, had informed him of his plans offended your father very much. The only thing your grandfather, Kwol Arob, did was to apologize to his friend, your mother's father, Mijok Duor, explaining to him—'I cannot attend this other marriage of Deng. I shall not take responsibility for yet another marriage by Deng. This should now be his entire responsibility.'*

Matet Ayom told me what I was later to hear from other sources, that my grandfather's attitude was what made my father start marrying excessively to prove to his father that he was capable of affording his marriages without his father's support. Although this is probably an overstatement, it is possible that it could have been to some degree a contributing factor.

I believe this is what provoked your father to indulge in excessive marriages. He was challenged by his father's attitude. He wanted to prove to his father that he would do it on his own. Then, he overdid it

174

and got married to all those wives. In the past, girls were not married by men independently of the men's fathers. A man had to inform his father of his intentions, and even if the father did not share his son's views on the marriage, he would send his acknowledgement of his son's interest to the relatives of the girl. He would say 'This proposed marriage is the will of my son. I am not a party to his plans, but if he has his own cows to pay the bride wealth, then let him marry the girl. It is not that I am opposed to his marrying into the family of that gentleman of our tribe.'

Deng Majok had younger brothers whose turn to marry was also coming. That was why grandfather objected to Deng getting into another marriage. But he said that if he could find cattle to pay the bride-wealth, then Mijok Duor was not a man whose daughter he could reject. 'It is with the words of Mijok that I am running the tribe.' Then the marriage of Biong Mading, your father's brother, came immediately after that. The cattle he had were not sufficient. He would take some cows and send them to Biong's marriage. And then Arob, his younger brother, made a girl pregnant. So, his own marriage was also added to these other marriages. All four marriages were performed by your father at about the same time. So, the marriage of your mother got completed only much later. But your maternal grandfather was a cool-hearted man. He said—'Tell Deng Majok, if his father says that it will be for his son to perform his marriage with me, then let him not concern himself with paying me the bride-wealth. Let him occupy himself with other urgent matters. I have cattle for my food; I am not in need. I shall also not reject his marriage on account of cattle. Let him perform the marriages of his younger brothers.' That attitude from your grandfather was very pleasing to your father.

According to Achwil Bulabek, Kwol Arob's initial objection was based on the fact that the girl was already engaged to a close relative: *Your mother had been betrothed to a son of your paternal aunt who was therefore your father's cousin, a man called Kweng, the father of the man you heard was recently killed in the fight with the Arabs. Kweng was the son of Achai, the daughter of Arob. The girl, your mother, also rejected Kweng. Deng Majok proceeded and released his cattle for the*

175

marriage. Then your maternal grandfather took out the bull, Mading, after which you were named and slaughtered it in sacrifice to bless your mother's marriage to Deng. You were then born and named Mading after the sacrificed bull. But you had another clan name. Arob was your clan name. But your maternal grandfather, Mijok, said—'His name is Mading.' So, the name Mading captured you, but your clan name was Arob.

Chol Piok had a different motive for Grandfather Kwol Arob's opposition to my father's proposed marriage to my mother. To him, Kwol saw Deng's increasing marriages as outpacing Deng Makuei whom he saw as the son of the first wife and should therefore have priority over Deng Majok even in marriages:

Why your grandfather Kwol Arob refused at first was the fact that Deng Majok was already marrying more than Deng Makuei. That he did not like. That disturbed him deep inside. He did not want Deng Majok to be an equal of Deng Makuei. You see, that grandfather of yours, if Deng Majok had not stood firm, he would have been left far on the periphery of things.

Uncle Deng Makuei himself gave me an elaborate explanation of the circumstances surrounding Grandfather Kwol Arob's position:

Our father opposed your father's marriage to your mother because he felt that Deng Majok would not pay adequate bride-wealth to Mijok, your mother's father. Mijok was a very dear person to my father, a friend with whom they would share one bed. When (your father's first wife) Nyanboldit was married, I do not recall whether my contribution was twenty or sixteen cows. Then I married Nyannuer. Deng Majok contributed to that. Then I engaged Nyandeng Adija with initial payment of cattle. Then your father turned on Nyanbol Amor. With Nyanbol Amor, some relationship was involved between us and the competitors. Pakany lineage was my father's maternal kindred. Nyanbol Amor had been engaged to Dan Deng Piok. The lineage of Dan Kiir and the lineage of Wun Mou were one. When your father eloped with her, my father said—'You have committed a wrong. The girl is the wife of my maternal aunt's son.' But when my father was prevailed upon to consent on the grounds that things had gone too far,

176

my father released an atonement cow and persuaded the other side to withdraw their claim.

Then we released our cattle into the marriage of Nyanbol Amor. Your father had helped me with five cows in the marriage of Nyandeng Adija. When we contributed for the marriage of Nyanbol Amor, my father said—'Since you are the senior son, you have to contribute more and then claim future help from him.' So, I contributed six cows and a bull. We sent them into the marriage. Father then celebrated that marriage. He was initially opposed to the marriage because of his maternal uncle's son.

As for Kwei, he did not marry her; he only made her pregnant. When he made her pregnant, she was engaged to Deng Monytoc Deng who had paid cattle for her. But then my father said—'Since she has borne a son, she should no longer be allowed to go to someone else. So, you, Deng Majok, release your cows and marry her.' So, Deng married his third wife, Kwei, with his own cattle.

When it came to your mother, my father was opposed because your grandfather Mijok was close to my father and also to me.

Deng Makuei's account alludes to the importance of tobacco to the Dinka as a much sought for commodity and which, as we saw earlier, was one of the elements my father used in showing his generosity and hospitality: *Even after your mother was married, I used to keep tobacco for your grandfather. I would insist that no one should touch it. 'It is for my Uncle,' I would say. He would then have it fetched in the gloomy season of morning rains.* Deng Makuei then emphasized his father's concern that Deng Majok would not be able to afford a decent amount of bride wealth for the daughter of Mijok Duor:

When your father wanted your mother, my father said—'Mijok, Deng is going to create problems between you and me. He and Deng Makuei are now independent, and no one can expect the other to arrange his marriage. I fear that he will not be able to afford a good bride-wealth for your daughter. It is better to let Deng Majok find a wife wherever else he can and you and I remain in the close relationship our families have enjoyed for long. You and I have been very close; your father and my father were also very close; your grandfather Maluk was also very

177

close to my grandfather; and your great-grandfather Dau was also close to my great-grandfather. Let us not allow this proposed marriage to generate conflicts between you and my children.'

That was how my father refused. He was concerned about a close relationship that might be affected by the marriage. Both families had an important role to play in the welfare of the tribe. Your maternal relatives were also people of divine authority. If disease appeared in the tribe, my father would call Mijok to perform curative rituals. And he would offer him a cow for the clan spirit of disease prevention. That was that. I don't even know how much Deng Majok eventually paid for Achok. But our relations had been so close that I used to buy clothes for your mother and her sisters when they were girls. You see, ours was an extremely close friendship.

I once made a public speech to the Ngok Dinka in Abyei on the theme of our role in the South/North borders, upholding and re-inforcing our ancestral heritage of being bridge-builders or the link between the Africans of the South and the Arabs of the North, thereby assuming the important symbol of national unity and stability. It was an attempt to turn the negatives of a disputed area into positives that could give the area a national significance and promise considerable advantages to the people. As I left the meeting, paving my way amidst the security forces and the crowd, Patal Biliw, one of the leading personalities in the tribe, managed to draw my attention and say—*Mading, remember that the words with which you speak so well are not merely those of your father, Deng Majok, or even of your grandfather, Kwol Arob; they are also the words of your maternal grandfather, Mijok Duor and your line of maternal forefathers. Just remember that.* I was very pleased to hear his words, although it was by no means the first time for me to hear that line of argument.

The balance I now feel toward the heritage of my paternal and maternal lines is of course a late realization. But I have no doubt in my mind that in all kinds of subtle ways, the message about the heritage of my maternal ancestry has always been there, discreetly but effectively filtering through the depths of my consciousness. But Uncle Ngor was to give me deeper insights which moved me profoundly.

The rest of this chapter is a translation of a tape-recorded conversation with Uncle Ngor Mijok, my mother's only brother, in the mid 1970s in Khartoum, about the past, present, and future of his lineage and its connection with my paternal line, not only through generations of his ancestors but more specifically through my father's marriage to my mother.

Francis Mading Deng: *Uncle, as I told you last time, I am very much preoccupied with the desire to record the affairs of our people. I do not know whether you have heard of the books I have written on the Dinka. Some are here and others are not. And all of them contain words from the Dinka. It is what is recorded in books to be taught to children that constitutes education. And even when a person proceeds for higher degrees to the point of receiving a doctorate, these are the kinds of works that they consult to acquire their education.*

So, today, I would like to talk to you about a variety of issues starting with the affairs of my maternal relatives, your own family.

Ngor Mijok: *Mading, you have just said what I wanted. I have been dissatisfied with your not having heard about the affairs of our family. There are several people: there is my father who is your grandfather, the man called Mijok, whom you knew. His father was Duor. And there is Maluk, who begot Duor, a man of Bongo section. His father was Dau. What took Maluk away from Bongo is a long story. He was the son of the Chief of Bongo. In the olden days, the land was governed by the power of the Sacred Spears. Such was the case of your paternal great grandfather, Arob Biong.*

Like Arob Biong, Maluk was a single son. What really made him a single son was that his brother had killed a person accidentally. And of course, a Chief must be covered and protected. But one man went around and spread the message among the relatives of the dead man, saying: 'Under that Big Tree of the Chief is the person who killed your brother.' The relatives of the dead man ran to attack the people under the tree in the hope of deterring the killer to identify himself. They were stopped. The son of the Chief, Maluk's brother, then went to his father, Dau, and said—'I must leave the land and go into the wilderness!' Dau said—'Why?!' 'Because I am afraid that our cattle will be seized

179

by the people of the dead man. It was I who killed him.' That was how Maluk's brother left and went away. Then the cattle were seized. Dau said—'So what my son feared has come true!?'

Through his spiritual powers, Dau, the father of Maluk, caused himself to die because of the tragic situation in which he and his family found themselves. Before he died, he said to his son Maluk—'Leave this tribe and go somewhere else. And after you leave, this tribe will be accursed and destroyed. A disease called Akoi (smallpox) will come and destroy this tribe. As for you, nothing will destroy you or your descendants. You will find a good place where you will go.'

Much of the story reflects rituals and symbols that do not have much meaning and should be taken as mythology that should be taken on face value without explanation:

'How do I begin?' he asked his father. 'Take an empty milk-gourd and urinate into it. And milk my Sacred Cow into the gourd to mix with your urine. And hang the gourd from a post. In the evening, after nightfall, take an axe and cut the peg of the Sacred Bull into two. Throw one part away in one direction and the other part in the opposite direction. Then let the hanging gourd with urine and milk drop from its height so that it breaks. After it has fallen and broken, speak out loud to the tribe and say—"People of my grandfather, I am leaving; I will find my place in the wilderness."'

That evening, as darkness fell upon the camp, he did all that. He urinated into a gourd and he milked the Sacred Cow into the gourd and hung the gourd with the urine and the milk. Then he cut the peg of the Sacred Bull into two parts with an axe and threw one part in one direction and another part in another direction. And then he released the gourd and let it fall to the ground. He took with him the Sacred Bull and the Sacred Cow which he had milked into the gourd. Then he left. That was how Maluk Dau left his tribe.

Maluk had heard of the cattle-camp of Biong Allor, your paternal ancestor. It was at the time of your great, great, grandfather, Biong Allor, that my great grandfather, Maluk, came into Abyor section. Biong Allor had also heard of Maluk's father as the Divine Chief of Bongo, a great healer who controlled epidemic diseases. In the middle of the night, Dau went and walked quietly along the fence of Biong's cattle-camp. The Dinka used to fence their camps in much the same way your house is now fenced in. As he walked along the fence, he saw a fire kindled in the cattle-hearth of the Chief. Maluk saw Biong lying next to the fire with a skin over him. Skins were then used as blankets. Maluk got into the fence and approached Biong. He caught Biong's big toe of the right foot and shook it gently. Biong withdrew his legs and said—'Is this a creature wanting my death!?' Maluk said—'No! It is a person!' Biong then removed the skin-blanket over him and said—'Who are you!?' 'I am Maluk, son of Dau!' he said. 'Maluk, son of which Dau!?' Biong asked. 'Maluk, the son of Dau-Dau, the son of Ajing.' Biong said—'You are playing a joke on me!' Maluk said—'I am not. It is truly me, Maluk, son of Dau, Dau, son of Ajing.'

Biong then got up and kindled the fire to increase the flame so that he could see better. He saw him and found him to be the man he said he was. Biong had heard of the destruction that had occurred to the family of Dau, Maluk's father. But he was not expecting Maluk to come to his camp. Abyor and Bongo were warring sections with a great deal of past hostilities between them.

When he recognized him, he made him lie down and covered him with his skin-blanket. And then he got up, went onto a tree and cried out loud to his people: 'O people of my father, O people of Allor!' He was invoking his father, Allor (Adenhjok) Monydhang. People got up in response to his call. Then he said—'I am about to kill myself!' 'Why!?' they all cried back. 'Why, our Chief, would you think of killing yourself?' He said—'Why you always see a stranger and kill him instead of adopting him to reinforce your strength has upset me a great deal.' 'Who do you have in mind!?' they asked. 'There is someone about whom I hear rumors!' he said. 'Tell us and we promise not to hurt him!' they said. 'Do you really promise so that I can show you this one very special person who is now with me!?' They said—'Yes, please show him to us!' He said—'In that case, lift that blanket of mine!'

The blanket was lifted. People said—'This man looks like Maluk, son of Dau!' Maluk said—'Yes, it is me!' The camp boomed with war-songs to welcome Maluk. Biong said—'Now that you have seen him,

181

take a lamb and go outside the camp. Sacrifice the lamb and whirl it over his head and throw away the sacrificed lamb. Then I will come down from the tree.' That was done. And when the people came back into the camp, Biong came down from the tree. Then he said to the people—'Now, leave me alone with Maluk.' People left. He turned to Maluk and said—'Maluk, son of Dau, what has brought you here!?' Maluk said—'My grandfather's tribe is destroyed.' 'What has destroyed it!?' Biong asked. He said—'My brother had killed a man and our cattle were seized. And when my father died, he cursed the tribe to be destroyed by disease.' 'So, what do you now say!?' Biong asked. 'I came looking for you as the Chief. As our tribe is destroyed, I wanted to join another Chief.' Biong said—'So, it is me you wanted!?' 'Yes!' said Maluk. 'Are you alone!?' 'I have a bull and a cow with me,' replied Maluk. 'They are somewhere there on an ant-hill.' Biong again called his people and said—'The Bull of Maluk Dau is there with a cow in the forest—fetch them.'

Maluk said to them—'Do not look for them. Just walk toward that area. If you see a bull and he does not bellow, then he is not my bull. But should he bellow then that is my bull, and I will not go with you. I will stand here at the gate of the fence.' The bull bellowed. The people went and found the bull with the cow. They were brought back and were about to be taken inside the fence of the cattle-camp. But Maluk refused and said—'Let them be tethered outside the camp.'

Chief Biong said—'Why?' Maluk said—'I will tell you my word tomorrow.' So, the bull and the cow were tethered outside the camp. Maluk slept outside the camp with them. Biong Allor too slept outside with them.

In the morning, Biong Allor said—'I am taking you into the center of the camp.' Maluk said—'I am not going into the center.' Biong said— 'Why?' Maluk repeated—'I am not going to the center.'

Biong said—'Do you still have any lingering doubts about me?' Maluk said—'I do not have any doubts about you, but I am not going to the center.' Then Biong said—'What would you want me to do for you?' He said—'Think of anything.' Biong said—'I will give you a girl for your wife!' He said—'No! That will not do!' Biong said—'Well, I will give you a herd of pure breeds of cattle!' Maluk said—'No, that will not do.' Then Biong said—'In that case, tell me what you really want.' Maluk said—'And if I tell you what I really want, will you grant it to me!?' Biong said—'Yes, I will!' Maluk said—'Where the cattle go to graze when they are released from the camp is what I ask of you.' Biong said—'What is in that?' Maluk answered—'There is something in it.' 'What is in it?' he asked again. 'There is something in it,' Maluk answered again. 'What is it!?' Biong emphatically asked again. 'When the cattle return to the camp after grazing,' said Maluk—'if there is a cow straying into the camp whose owner is unknown, that will be my cow. Any animal that will stray into the herd or break into the fence at night, whether during peace time or in times of war or any other destruction, will be mine—let any such animal be brought to me.' 'Is that what you have chosen?' asked Biong.

'Yes! that is all I want,' said Maluk. 'I shall remain at the periphery. And if any disease should come into your camp, it will hit me first before it reaches you. And from now on, I can say that the epidemic disease called Akoi will no longer hit your cattle-camp. Your camp will flourish. Your section, Abyor, will multiply and flourish to the point where it will become the biggest section in this tribe as long as I am here.'

Biong Allor then called the whole of Abyor and said—'Here is the issue!' They said—'There is nothing much in this request; it is a modest request.' So, he was granted his request. Then Maluk said: 'Provide a bull for sacrifice; I will bless you.' A bull was provided and sacrificed. The bull was sacrificed at the gate of the fence which then became known as the gate of Maluk Dau. People then herded. Cattle would be released for grazing, and when they came back to the camp, any straying cow without an owner would be brought to him. A slave who came wandering into the camp without a master would be given to him. And if a disease came into the camp, Maluk would be the first to detect it and heal it. That is how things went for Maluk Dau.

The most important thing about this account is that Maluk entered the tribe with the background of leadership and from the start was connected to the leadership of his host tribe. That initial relationship became the foundation of close ties that would be sustained for generations. The story of the family is then told through successive generations of Maluk's descendants through the upheavals of the nineteenth century.

Maluk begot children. He bore his son Duor. He was an only son. Maluk suddenly stopped having children. Duor had only one sister called Achwei. Then came the destruction of the land. When the destruction of the land came, Duor was married. He married Nyanger Weldhow, from whom descended the people who are waiting for us outside. Nyanger begot Mijok. When destruction came, Mijok was still an infant child. The destruction of the land broke Duor and Nyanger apart. Duor went into his own wilderness while Nyanger went into a separate wilderness.

Nyanger was with Duor's sister, Achwei. They hid together. And they slept. Nyanger slept with her infant baby called Mijok and her sister-in-law slept next to them. While they were sleeping, the horses of the Arab slavers came. The Arab picked Nyanger, the one with the baby, and took her away. When he placed her on the back of the saddle on his horse, her sister-in-law woke up, raised her hands and appealed to the slaver: 'Please wait for me.' The Arab stopped and looked back to the girl and said—'Did you see me!?' 'Yes, I did,' she said. 'Do you not see her breasts full of milk!? The heat of the sun will burst her breasts. And the baby you are leaving behind will afflict you with a curse. Please release the mother and take me instead. If you want me to be your wife, I will be your wife. If you want to sell me to someone else, so will it be.' 'Is that what you say?' remarked the Arab. 'Yes, that is what I say. I have given you my word of honor.' The Arab dismounted from his horse. He tied the hands of Achwei, and said—'Is that all!?' Achwei said— 'Yes, that is all.'

Achwei then turned to her sister-in-law and said—'Nyanger, let me tell you my word. My father, as you know, is Maluk, son of Dau. This disaster has hit our tribe before. You will be united with my brother, Duor. Tell him that his sister has been taken away by the Arabs. Mijok has been left with his mother. And if I am truly the daughter of Maluk and my father is truly a leader of spiritual powers, and if I have a share of those powers as a child begotten by him, then I say that this destruction will end with me; you will never see the horses of the Arab slavers anymore.'

She went on to say—'Take care of Mijok. May God let him grow up to become a man. And when he has grown up, tell him that he once had an aunt called Achwei. That she was taken away by the destruction of the land and that she went away in order to redeem him. Tell him that I would like to be remembered through children. Let them beget children on my behalf to continue my name. If that is done, the family will flourish with children to continue the lineage and they will no longer witness the destruction we have seen.'

Duor is of course my great grandfather and the baby Mijok is my grandfather, Mother's father. What follows is therefore recent history. *As soon as Nyanger and Achwei separated, Nyanger met her husband, Duor. She said—'My dear husband, Duor, Achwei has been taken away. She gave herself up to redeem me and the baby.' Duor said—'If I run after her, will I not catch up with her!?' 'No, you cannot find her,' said Nyanger. 'Besides, I cannot let you go. The horses that took her are horses that cannot be reached. They were going to take both of us, and it was only when Achwei surrendered herself to them and begged them to save us that they left us.' Nyanger went with her husband. Mijok grew up to become an adult and became well known as Mijok Duor, the son of Duor. He was told the story of Achwei and how she had surrendered herself into slavery to save Nyanger and her baby son, Mijok. The world was destroyed again. Mijok then said to his brothers: 'Here is the world destroyed again. If we die, so be it; but if we live, let us remember Achwei who was among the first to be taken away by the earlier destruction. Let us find a way of remembering her.' In the fight with the Arabs, our people captured an Arab boy and a girl. Mijok said—'These children will be a compensation for the enslavement of Achwei. The boy will be called Ater (The Feud), because he represents a settlement for the feud of enslavement by the Arabs. He will beget children to honor the name of Achwei. And as for the girl, she will be considered the daughter of Achwei. She will be married and Ater will use the cattle of her marriage to acquire a wife who will beget more children to the name of Achwei.' Ater became known as Ater Wun-Mijok—Ater, son of Mijok's father—that is, son of Duor. He grew up and begot the children whose descendants you hear of referred to as the family of Ater. When he was captured, he was still a small child. The world continued. Peace was restored. The children of Achwei, begotten by Ater, included five sons and one girl. And none of them died. They have multiplied and have had many descendants. One is now in Halfa. Others include the young men who are sitting outside. So, you Mading, you have heard the story of Maluk. His grandson Mijok then grew up and begot children. His first born from our mother was Nyanaguek.*

Francis M. Deng: *What about from his other wife who was in fact his first wife?*

Ngor Mijok: *That wife was Nyandeng, the mother of Koc; her first child was Awut. That was why Mijok was called Wun-Awut. Then he had a second daughter whom he called Nyanaguek. So, he had three daughters, Awut and two Nyanagueks, one from Nyandeng, Koc's mother, and the other from our mother.*

Awut was the first to be married. And the two Nyanagueks were contested by men. Koc's sister, Nyanaguek, was eventually given to one of the contesters. Our sister, Nyanaguek, was contested by Bol Malek and another man from Bongo section by the name of Arob Kwol Ditjok. She was eventually given to Arob Kwol. But she rejected him and wanted Bol Malek. Bol eloped with her. My father insisted that she not be given to Bol. 'I will not give my daughter to a man who is imposing his will on me,' he said. So, she was taken and given to Arob Kwol Ditjok. But then, it turned out that she was pregnant with the child of Bol Malek. She gave birth to her daughter, Ajang. My father, Mijok, took Nyanaguek back to raise the baby in our family. When Ajang was old enough to be weaned, her mother was again forced to go back to her husband, Arob Kwol, the man she did not want to marry. She became pregnant from him. While she was pregnant, she again escaped and came back home. At home, she poisoned herself by drinking the milk of the sacred cow of our clan spirit called Akudum. Women were not supposed to drink from the milk of sacred cows. And

186

if they did, they were supposed to contaminate themselves to death.
Her idea in drinking the milk was to kill herself. After she drank the
milk, she spoke to our father and told him what she had done. 'Have
you truly drunk from the milk of the sacred cow?' Father asked. She
said 'Yes, I have.' He said Then, I have repudiated you with all my
heart. You are no longer a daughter to me.'
Nyanaguek fell ill and died. She was killed by the milk of the sacred
cow. In your family, for instance, the milk of the cows dedicated to
the spirit, Deng-dit, cannot be drunk by a woman. When the other
Nyanaguek, our half-sister, heard of the death of her half-sister, she
came running. She was married to a man here in Abyor. He had paid
fifty cows for her. But he was lame and Nyanaguek did not want him.
She opposed the marriage. All the same, my father insisted on giving her
to him. She eventually succumbed and went to his home. She became
pregnant by him. But when she heard of what our sister had done, she
too came and drank the milk of the sacred cow to kill herself. After
having drunk the milk, she said to our father—'Father, I am going
to follow my sister!' 'Why?' asked Father. She said—'Because I am
still opposed to this marriage.' 'So, what do you want to do?' asked my
father. 'I want to follow my sister and I have already drunk the milk of
the sacred cow of Akudum,' she said. She died shortly afterwards.

Needless to say, suicide by drinking the milk of sacred cows is part of
a metaphysical belief system that is not subject to scientific authen-
tication. Traditionally, the Dinka would not question or doubt its
authenticity.

So, you see, Mading, when both girls died, father collected the cattle
and repaid their husbands. He called each one of them and said—'Are
these not all your cattle?' Each one said—'Yes!' 'All I now want from
you are the three customary cows of rwok (compensation for having
made a girl a married woman).' He was then given back the cows of
rwok. When all was over, our two sisters dead and our wealth of cattle
depleted, my father made a ritual invocation and spoke, symbolically
addressing cattle: 'Cattle, I have abandoned you. If I should someday
come across a strong man among my descendants, one who is inclined to
seek cattle-wealth, I will tell him to seek you, cattle, on his own. As for

187

me, I have given up all ambitions for cattle-wealth.'
Atiu, our other sister, the mother of Maper, was then given to Dau
Athian virtually for nothing. He paid only a few cows. Then our half-
sister, Nyanyaath, was given to a man called Kon Kur Ayuel, also for
virtually nothing. Father then saw us, the sons he had begotten. The
house of our mother, Ayak, had me. And the house of Ajing's mother
had Ajing, who was my age. Koc, the senior son from his first wife, had
become something of an imbecile. He was only good at farming but
was hopeless with words and was hardly worthy of the leadership of the
family, despite his position as the eldest.

Achok was the one their father decided would be the girl whose marriage would bring cattle to the family. And in fact, her engagement
brought in many cows and many more were expected to come with
payment of the whole bride wealth.

My sister, Achok, your mother, was beginning to emerge as a young girl.
Father then said—'Achok will be married to bring some cattle with
which I will raise these small children of mine. Since I had disclaimed
ambition for cattle in front of God, I will now have to slaughter an
animal in sacrifice to God to repudiate what I had said.' He took out a
large bull and prayed over it and then sacrificed it to God. He sacrificed
it to remove the curse he had cast on himself of no longer wanting
cattle. Mading, it was then that a man called Kweng came and said—
'I want the daughter of Mijok Duor.' Kweng spoke to his mother, Achai,
from your clan Pajok. His mother came to see the girl. She saw Achok
and approved.

When the people came back to negotiate the marriage, Father said—
'Achok is the daughter with whom I intend to raise my children. If a
man wants to marry her, he must make a betrothal payment of twenty
cows. As she has not yet reached puberty, this payment will only be for
engagement. When she reaches puberty, so that the man is more assured
of her becoming his wife, I will then say my word.' The people went and
returned with twenty cows and two excellent bulls: a huge tawny bull
and a dark bull with a white stripe across the shoulders (Mabil). They
were brought. I was now old enough to be aware. The bull, Mabil, was
given to my mother. It was handed over to my cousin, Kat, the son of

Nyanawel, the brother of Monyjur, who was taking care of our cattle.
Mabil was the color-pattern allotted to me in the family distribution of
colors. But as I was still a child, Kat used him as his song-bull. Achok
was still small; she was still a child. Father talked to the members of his
clan and said—'My kinsmen, here are the cattle. Divide them among
yourselves. The single cow that will remain, I will use to help provide
my children with milk.' So, the cattle were distributed to the clan that
very year, while Achok was still a child.
Deng Majok saw Achok at a dance and desired to marry her although
many betrothal wealth had already been paid by the family of Kueng.
That began the contest for Achok that would escalate into a conflict
between Deng and his father, Chief Kwol.
The following year, as the rains began to fall, Achok went to a dance.
Deng Majok and Deng Makuei were at the dance. Deng Majok talked
to Deng Makuei and said—'Deng, I have never seen that girl before.'
Deng Makuei said—'I know her; she is the daughter of Mijok Duor.'
Deng Majok said—'Let us catch up with her.' They did.

Approaching girls, especially after a dance, was a typical way of ini-
tiating courtship conversation. The conversation begins with self-in-
troductions, names, clan and section of the tribe from which one
hails. This is in part to avoid the risk of breaking exogamous rules
prohibiting marriage between blood relatives and these cover any
traceable blood ties, especially through the paternal line. On the maternal side, after five generations, a ritual of severance of ties can be
performed to make an exception.

Deng Majok then spoke to Achok and said—'Are you the daughter
of Mijok Duor?' Achok said—'Yes!' Deng said—'And who is your
mother?' Achok said—'My mother is Ayak.' 'From which section of
the tribe?' Deng Majok asked. 'She is from the Bongo section,' said
Achok—'the daughter of Deng Ngor.'
Deng Majok went and told his father—'I want to marry the daughter
of Mijok Duor.' Chief Kwol said—'She is already engaged to Kweng,
the son of Achai.' Deng said—'No, I will not accept that.' Kwol said—
'Deng, you will not marry from the family of Mijok Duor. You will
bring conflict into my relationship with Mijok. This chieftainship of

*mine is protected by the family of Maluk. Abyor has become as large
as it is because of the family of Maluk. You will not marry Mijok's
daughter. You will only drag our relationship into problems. If you were
not already married, I would have encouraged you to take your wealth
to marry the daughter of Mijok as your first wife. But you have already
married several wives. Your wealth has been exhausted. You will not
give Mijok enough from the cows with which you are now sustaining
your family. And as you know, Mijok has lost his senior daughters.
It is from the marriage of this girl that he hopes to acquire some wealth
to maintain his children.' Deng said to his father—'I will not accept
your word.' Kwol then said—'In that case, consider me out of this
matter.' They discussed the matter a great deal but could not agree. Kwol
remained opposed while Deng persisted.*

*Deng went to Kweng and said—'Leave the girl and take back your
cows.' Kweng said—'How can I take back my cows from a girl I have
married?' Deng said—'Take them back!' Kweng said—'I will not, son
of my maternal Uncle; I will not.' Then Deng said—'In that case, I am
afraid we may have to kill one another.' Kweng said—'That would be
better than having to withdraw my cattle from a girl I want to marry.'
'Then you had better bear that in mind!' said Deng Majok.*

Here again, the story takes an aggressive turn that is hard to believe
and is probably an exaggerated dramatization that is intended to emphasize the gravity of the conflict.

*Later, at a public dance, he just attacked Kweng and started to dart
him with spears. He darted and darted him with spears, barely missing
him, until the man ran and jumped into a river. Deng went after
him. Even after Kweng had jumped into the river, Deng continued to
spear him in the river. It was then that a man called Biong Ngar-Chol
stepped in to defend Kweng. Deng and Biong began to throw spears
at one another until they were eventually restrained and separated.
People said—'Deng, why did you try to kill the son of your maternal
aunt?' He said—'If anyone wants this conflict to end, then let him take
Kweng's cattle from the marriage.'*

*Achai, the mother of Kweng, Deng's paternal aunt, then approached
her nephew and said—'Deng, this is a child whom I raised and*

weaned among you, his cousins, the sons of Kwol. His father died and left him with me. And this is not a girl that you yourself had courted before my son saw her. She is still a small girl. I want to marry her to Kweng because I want someone who will raise the name of my son. If you are determined to have her as your wife, even if you should succeed in doing so, I will not part with her; you will have her together with me; you will have us both. But I will go all the way to secure her for my son. Even if you should compete by paying a hundred cows, I will fight for her.'

Deng said to her—'Aunt, even if your eyes should shed tears that have never been seen before, she will never be your son's wife.' Achai said— 'In that case, I shall move to the home of Mijok Duor. Her feet and mine will move together.' And indeed, Achai moved to our home. My father decided to stop his daughter from attending dances. The whole situation was baffling. People did not know what should be done. Kweng himself no longer went to the cattle-camp. And he could no longer attend the dances.

At this point, members of Kwol's age-sets, Koryom then interceded to mediate in favor of Deng. Membership in an age-set creates a relationship akin to comrades in arms as fellow warrior. It is a relationship that in fact forbids marrying each other's daughters since members consider themselves as relatives.

The age-set, Koryom, which was the age-set of both your grandfather, Kwol Arob, and my father, came to our home at Nok-Jur. They came on horses. They all gathered there and tethered their horses. Father slaughtered in their honor and after entertaining them he said— 'Gentlemen, my dear age-mates, what brings you? Is anything the matter?' They said—'We have something to tell you.' He said—'Very well. What is it?' They said—'You have lost two of your daughters. This issue of Deng Majok is going to associate your daughter with blood. No one will be able to face the feud of Deng Majok. Please, give up the cattle of Achai. Your daughters are still small. They should not be confronted with this. We say, give the girl to Deng.' Mijok said— 'Gentlemen, is that why you came?' They said—'Yes!' He said—'Is the man for whom you are speaking without a father's voice behind him?'

191

They said—'There is no one to speak for him with the tongue. He himself has spoken with the spear. And he stands alone.' 'But where is the voice of Kwol?' he asked. 'Kwol has excused himself to us,' they said. He said—'Gentlemen, age-mates, I am out of this. Deng is putting Mijok Duor and me in a potential conflict. Should Mijok accept, Deng will not be able to match the intentions of Mijok. So, I better keep out of it.'

Another part of story-telling that might not be easy to understand is that Kwol is reported to have been ambivalent about the proposed marriage, publicly appearing opposed to his son's wanting to marry Mijok's daughter while privately advising him not to give up his pursuit.

Kwol Arob would talk to Deng Majok privately and say—'Go ahead, my son. Take the girl. No one could easily surrender marrying into this kind of breed. Work hard to win her. But let me keep out of it.' A man called Matiok Malek overheard Kwol's conversation with his son, Deng Majok. He came to my father and said—'Mijok, what you are really struggling with is Kwol Arob behind the scene. He has been instructing his son not to give in.' Mijok said—'I know that.' The issue was most bewildering. People could not find a way of resolving it.

My father then summoned his clan, the entire clan, and said to them— 'Sons of Maluk, I have surrendered. And let me tell you what Deng Majok once did to me when he was only a small child. Our age-set, the Koryom, had laid down their spears in the home of his father, Kwol Arob. So many were the spears that they covered the tree on which they rested. Deng Majok came and examined all the spears. When he came to my spear, he placed it on his lap. And when the people were leaving his father's court, his father said to him—"Son, give the spear to your uncle." Deng refused. And when people tried to take it away from him, he threatened to pierce the spear into his stomach. So, I told them to leave the spear with him. That is one thing Deng once did to me. So, if his father has unleashed him against me when I am only beginning to reacquaint myself to cattle, to raise my children, then I ask you: what do you see in this? After all, I have my people and my grandfather had his own fence. What do you say?' They said—'Give in!' He said—'Is

*that what you say?' They said—'Yes!' He said—'Very well! So, it
shall be.'*

The situation again emerges in a rather confusing way. Deng Majok's
behavior and his father's alleged encouragement or permissive response, though motivated by the positive prospect of marriage affini
ty, is perceived as an aggressive imposition that is posing a challenge.
That challenge is paradoxically being met by conceding to Deng Majok's demand in order to advance an unclarified objective for Mijok's
family and clan.

*After the elders of the clan left, Father called the closer members of his
family and said—'I am giving in!' They said—'What have you seen?'
He said—'I have seen something! I have seen the threat of death.' Our
maternal relatives intervened and said—'Mijok, Deng Majok has come
in our way without the name of his father, Kwol Arob. He is not going
to come and untether the cattle of the man we have accepted. There is
no reason to surrender to his will.' Father said to our maternal kin—
'Your daughter is Ayak. That is where you have the right to speak. But
you are not to speak on this matter of my daughter.' Among our paternal
kin, the man called Ater about whom I spoke earlier, said—'Words
cannot be shared to the last word. It is cattle we wanted. But as far as I
am concerned, I Ater, the last word is yours, even if it means no cattle.'
A man called Deng Michar said—'Mijok, when people are born, there
are those who become the source of food and those who are not. Achok
is the ribbon with which we shall tie our bellies for the loss of the two
girls, Nyanagwek and Nyanagwek. She is a compensation from God. If
we let go of these cattle and Deng Majok fails to compensate us for their
loss, what shall we do?' Father said—'There is Achol, Achok's younger
sister. I will give you my word in front of God that she will be your
compensation.' They said—'And why are you imposing on yourself all
this trouble?' He said—'Because I do not want blood to be associated
with the name of my daughter. And I have even smaller children to
protect. As for the mind that went after my spear when he was still a
small child and is now following me openly in the tribe, I ask you to
leave that challenge to me.'
That way, he persuaded our family to give in. After he had persuaded*

193

them, he turned to Achai and said—'Achai, I am going to release your cattle. You have been defeated.' He took the cow Dan-Akol, with widespread horns, which was his personal cow, and gave it to her, saying—'This cow is to appease you because your cows have been milked here. Go and quarrel with the members of your own clan. If you should cry, and thereby threaten a curse, I will find myself forced to resort to what I have as the son of Duor Maluk.'

Mijok was implying that Achai might call on her clan spirits for divine justice which inflict harm of his family and that if she did that, he too would invoke his own clan spirits to retaliate. It would then be a war of spirits in which Mijok is confident in the powers of his clan spirits.

Achai's cattle had multiplied so much within only one year that calves were running and kicking all over the plains. Mading, all those cattle were sent back. And so that was the situation our family found itself in. Achok had been betrothed before puberty. Deng came and contested her. My father gave into his pressures. Achai's cattle were returned. Time passed, and apart from a token payment of several cows, no cattle came from Deng Majok. Achok reached puberty. And yet no cattle came. During the rainy season, my father called the elders of his clan and said—'What you feared has already come true. No cattle have come from Deng. Now, my daughter will resume going to dances. People will point at her and say—"that is the girl whom Deng Majok captured from Kweng. Who can dare approach her!?" If I tell you something, will you agree with me!?' They said—'Go ahead, and tell us.' He said—'I want the girl to be given to Deng Majok.' They said—'Do you really mean that!?' He said—'Yes, I do.' 'Why?' they asked. 'That's the way it is,' he said. 'As it is now, he is going to delay and put me in suspense, knowing that even if he does not move quickly to marry my daughter, no one else will dare propose marriage to her. I have seen death among my daughters. And I have once rejected cattle. I am again going to reject cattle.'

He then approached Deng Majok and said—'I will give you your wife. All I want from you are the cattle of the clan spirits. You have paid eight, actually seven, cows; give me four cow-calves to dedicate to the

194

spirits.' He went and brought a brown cow and a cow-calf of brown and white descent. Then he spoke of the cattle he intended to pay. My father went ahead and gave him the girl. My father then called Dau Maluk and said—'I have given the girl away. Give me the bull, Mading; your bull Mading will no longer be bartered for a cow-calf. Give him to me to be sacrificed for the spirit Agorot (which according to custom, must be done when a girl is betrothed before puberty. Unless done, it is believed that she may not be able to have children.) Dau said—'Uncle, we had set the bull aside to sacrifice for the spirit of our dead father.' Father said—'Your father will not be honored with a bull of Mading color pattern. We will have to find a bull of Maker pattern for your father. Give me Mading with horns yet untampered with; that is what I want. That is the bull we should sacrifice for the spirit, Agorot.' Dau Maluk went and released Mading.

My father called the members of his clan and said—'This Mading which we are taking to be sacrificed (in Deng Majok's home), I would like to say something to you about the occasion. Do you recall Achwei!?' They said—'Yes, we do!' 'And is she not now represented by Ater, who is among us!?' They said—'Yes!' He said—'Well, Ater means feud and it is with perseverance that a feud can be met. The feud of the arm is met with the determination of the arm; but the feud of the word is met with the strength of the word. The feud with which Deng Majok has confronted me must be met with the word of mouth. Let us take this bull, Mading, and pray to God to give us a son. That son will be the one who will meet the challenge of the feud with Deng Majok. You can no longer kill him. He is the husband of Achok. And you cannot subdue him with the word of the tongue.'

'You have overcome the feud of Achwei. I now want you to go after the feud of Deng Majok until you find it. Even if I should die, I want you to be able to say—"This was what Mijok Duor said. Let us go and pray over Mading and pray to God." He left with a number of people. Among them was a man called Chol Minyuon, an elder. And with them was Miyar Kac, an elder. And among them was Deng Michar, an elder. He called a number of elders. And they went. They stood their sacred spears in the ground and prayed. My father said—'God, what

*I have to say is not much. We ask you to give Achok a son whom we
shall name Mading after the bull we are about to sacrifice. That is all
we ask of you.' My father and the elders with him prayed over the bull,
Mading. They prayed and prayed and then sacrificed him. Then they
left. They said—'It is now up to God to decide whether to accept our
prayers or to reject our word.' That was the way it ended. None of our
family could move in a different direction to look for a cow from your
father.*

*When Achok begot you and gave birth to you, your father sent your
stepmothers, Kwei and Nyanbol. He said to them—'Would you go and
see how Achok will deliver.' And after you were born, Kwei confessed
the purpose of their visit and said—'Achok, the reason why we came
was because we wondered whether there was another man whom you
might confess. But since you have delivered smoothly without confessing
another man, we would now want to return quickly to convey that
message.'*

*After you were born, my father convened the elders of his clan and
said—'Chol Minyuon, do you not see anything pleasing to your heart?
You will die. And I will die. And all of us assembled here will die. I
have only one word to tell you. Is there any other name besides that
Mading?' They said—'No, there is only that Mading.' He said—'Then I
am giving you a lamb with which to wash your hearts and pray to God
and say—'God, our hearts are now pleased; we no longer have anything
bad in our hearts, now that we have our Mading. He will one day hear
all these words.'*

*Days passed. You continued here. Then word came that your family
wanted the baby to be brought home to be seen. So Achok took you.
There, you were given a paternal ancestor's name. Achok stayed longer
than was expected. Word came that you had been given another name.
My father said—'Is that truly so!?' They said—'Yes!' So, my father sent
a number of women. They took with them beer and different kinds of
foods. When the women went, they were told of the other name. Kwei
said that the child had been given the name of Arob. It was then said
that Mading had been renamed to be Arob Biong (after Kwol Arob's
father). The women came back and told my father the story. He said to*

196

them—'Are you sure that you heard it quite accurately?' They said—
'Yes, we are sure we did.'

My father took his spears and left very early before dawn. He arrived
before your father was out of his sleeping hut. He sat outside. When
the women got up and saw him, they said—'What is the matter?' He
said—'Nothing! I was just passing by to visit Achok before proceeding
to Abyei.' Deng Majok was then told: 'Awut's father is outside.' He got
out of his hut and went to see him. 'Father, is all well!?' Deng asked.
'Yes, I was just passing by to see Achok and continue on my way. I am
going to Abyei.' Deng said—'Very well.' A bed-seat was then brought out
and he sat.

My father then said—'Would someone call Deng Makuei for me?'
The villages of the two brothers, Deng Majok and Deng Makuei,
were next to one another. Deng Makuei was called. He came and
joined them. Then my father said to them—'Sons of Kwol Arob, this
tongue of mine was once invoked by Monydhang Biong. He said to
me—"Mijok, come and let us consecrate our tongues." We blessed each
other's tongue. Then he said to me—"Should Kwol fail to become the
Chief, you will be the one to inform me in the hereafter." I was the
most senior member of our entire age-set, Koryom; Kwol was a much
younger member of the set. His uncle was concerned that their clan
might rob him of the Chieftainship since he was that young. It was I
who secured the Chieftainship for your father, Kwol. That was why
one man called Agoth Akuei said—"If Mijok Duor has designated
the leader, then let me tell you that the words of the tribe are slipping
away to the young and you may suddenly find the country taken over
by the younger generation to your utter surprise." I responded to him by
saying—"Uncle, I have heard your words." I knew that he was trying to
repress my bias for Kwol. If I have suddenly become an outsider to this
Chieftainship, then let me know at once.'

They said—'What is the matter, Father!?' He said—'That daughter
of mine, Achok, who is in your home, is not here because your father,
Kwol Arob, went and sat down to arrange her marriage to you. Nor
have you paid for her. Our ancestral spirits are still without their share
of cattle from her marriage. All I wanted was to purchase the Head

which robbed me of my spear and later drove away the cattle of my daughter's marriage, with which I was going to maintain my children.' By the Head, Mijok is referring to Deng Majok's character or personality which is being both condemned and praised for the self-assertiveness and determination he reflected in his childhood seizure of Mijok's Spears and unrelenting pursuit of Achok. He is implying that Achok would beget a child with the strong personality of Deng Majok that is paradoxically criticized and admired.

That was the Head I bought and appealed to God. If God has now judged in my favor and has shown me the fruit of his judgment by giving me my Mading, how could you think of naming him Arob Biong!? If you people have the spiritual power to ask for your grandfather, Arob Biong, to be reborn, why don't you pray so that Achok begets Arob Biong for you next time!? As for this Mading of mine, never ever call him by any other name. Right now, I am taking my daughter, Achok, and the baby, Mading, with me.' They said— 'Father of Awut, how could you react so severely!?' 'Say no more,' my father responded. 'Better maintain your silence, I do not want to hear any more!'

Mading, my father was a tough-headed man. He was a man who could be so severe that once a word had come out of his mouth, he would never retract it. He stood up and went to the door of the hut in which Achol was and said—'Achok, come out with the baby, we are going. After all, you came only to show the baby to the family.' People all gathered and pleaded with him: 'Father of Awut, you cannot take the baby this way. At least leave Achok to be brought to you by others.' Then he said—'I will leave her on the condition that she comes this very day and does not spend another night here.' Achok was brought to our home that same day. We spent the night.

The following morning, Deng Majok got onto his horse and went with a number of elders to see my father. They spoke to my father and said— 'Father of Awut, why allow your heart to be angered by such a trifling thing!? Even if the child is called Mading, as you wish, would he not still be Mading, son of Deng!? There is no issue. He will be Mading as you want him to be.' Father said—'Very well my son; that was all

198

I wanted. If you have now come and apologized, the issue has ended there. We will not quarrel anymore.' Deng Majok returned and told his family—'I do not want to hear the child called Arob anymore. He will be Mading.' That was that. I have told you the story of your mother's marriage and of your own birth.

Remarkably, I grew up not knowing that I had another name. It is much later in adolescence I learned about Arob and the circumstances leading to the dominance of Arob as my active. In fact, I initially felt some complex about being the only son with a name that was not a typical clan name. However, when I got to know the background, I began deeply appreciating my name and feeling proud of it.

Later on, my father sent for the elders of his clan and said to them— 'I do not know the day my end will come. I want to leave you my word today. If any one of you should ever think of raising a claim for cattle against Deng Majok on account of Achok, that person would have invited a deadly curse from me, a curse that will destroy that person. Anyone who would raise a case of cattle against Deng Majok, let it be known that he is cursed to destruction. Leave that whole matter as it is; it will remain my own affair.'

Far from completing the payment of the bride wealth, Deng Majok began to generously receive the share of cattle he was owed as a son-in-law of the marriages of the girls in Mijok's family.

When the daughter of my uncle was married, my father sent for Deng Majok and said—'As a son-in-law, you are entitled to share in the bride-wealth.' Deng said—'I will take five cows. I know that I am indebted to you, but I will complete my marriage. My entitlement in this marriage should be five cows.' My father said—'Take four cows and a bull!' Deng said—'I want five cows and a bull.'

Father said—'Very well! So be it.' When the cattle were taken to him, he did not like the bull. He was given the freedom to choose from the other bulls. When the daughter of Ater was married, Deng came and claimed a cow according to the custom of Pal (whereby a man can claim a cow that was once his if it should accrue to a relative). That cow was found to have three cow-calves. Uncle Ater said—'If this was the marriage of Mijok's daughter, I would have objected to the claim of Deng Majok. But since it is my daughter's marriage, we should let Deng take the cows.' Deng took the cows.

Then our sister Achol was married to Akuei. He made an initial payment of thirty cows. Deng came and made his claim for a share. Father said—'Make your choice.' He picked the bull, Mabil. And he picked a tawny cow with widespread horns. And he proceeded to pick more cows. Elders of the clan came to my father and said—'Mijok, you have forbidden us to raise a case against Deng Majok. And here is Deng Majok finishing our cattle. What should we do?' My father said—'May I tell you one more thing?' They said—'Yes, tell us.' He said—'Women compete and defeat one another in cooking. Achok is not a senior wife; she is a junior wife. She may not be able to excel over the senior wives in cooking. If she is defeated, Mading, her son, may lose Deng Majok's respect and be disregarded. But if Deng were to find that Mading's mother is a girl whose family is supportive with cattle-wealth, he will give Mading his personal attention. It is my share which Deng Majok takes from you. As for what is part of your share, I will not allow it to be affected by Deng Majok's share.' He then proceeded to distribute all the cattle of Achol's marriage, leaving only one cow-calf, Dan-beng-low (a color configuration of gray with a white stripe), as the cow consecrated for us, the twins.

Uncle Ngor began to tell the story of my close relationship with my grandfather Mijok, which I of course remembered from early childhood, but the details of which I only learned incrementally as I was growing. I only got to know the full story from Uncle Ngor only later in life.

Then you became ill when you were still an infant. You were beginning to walk. My father was extremely fond of you. He would watch you keenly as you played around. And very often, he would want you to sit on his lap or hold you and bounce you about as he chanted words of praise for you. One night, while you were severely ill, he did something. It was raining very heavily, with frightening thunder and lightning. He decided to take you out in the rain that night. My mother objected, but he insisted. She cried as she tried to restrain him from going outside with you. At one point, he said to her—'Ayak, did I not fetch (marry) you with my sacred cows?' 'Yes,' she said. 'And how could you question my ancestral duty? Open the door and let me go out.'

She opened the door and he went outside with you in his arms. Then he prayed: 'God, why are you thundering this loudly? I sit in your heart to take my child away from me? If you are thundering because you want to take him, then I pray that you take me instead and leave him for me. Take me this very moment as you are angry, raining, and thundering. And if you should decide not to take me, then let me return into the hut and let your water, which has fallen on him, be a blessing so that he can sleep well tonight and wake up tomorrow morning smiling and playing for me to see.' You were crying as he held you and prayed that way. The next morning, you woke up miraculously well. He held you in his hands and seated you in his lap. And he smiled into your face as he saw you so well and smiling.

Then the following night, he woke up my mother and said—'Ayak, are you awake?' My mother said—'Yes!' Then he turned to me and said— 'Son.' I said—'Yes.' He said—'Get up and sit here. Listen to my words very carefully. Did you not witness what happened last night?' I said— 'Yes, I did.' He said—'Well, I surrendered myself to redeem Mading. I will die. And after I am dead, what you hear happening in Abyor about the Chieftainship will come true. Don't you hear that Deng Majok will take over the Chieftainship from his father, Kwol Arob?' I said—'Yes.' He said—'The Head (Deng Majok's personality) that imposed its will on me will probably succeed in taking Chieftainship from his father. And should it happen that way, this Mading of mine will one day force his way and find a position there. When you grow up, never complain to your brother-in-law, Deng Majok, that he has not paid enough for your sister's bride-wealth. Never tell him. It is Mading who should eventually be told. But Deng must not be told.'

My grandfather still felt the need to justify why he favored Deng Majok over his competitor Kueng over the marriage of his daughter Achok. Much of what he said related to the future of leadership in our family and the welfare of his son Ngor.

And you, Ayak, when you used to say that we should give our daughter to Kweng—I am going to die and you too will die, who is Kweng's father to whom we shall leave our children? You and I might have found in Kweng's wealth a great deal for our own consumption, but what about something to be found by our children in the future? We do not know which of us two will die first. But even when we are both gone, Mading will not miss inheriting from the Head of Deng Majok. And he will not miss inheriting from my own Head, I, Mijok Duor. From these two Heads, something will emerge in him. Should he inherit from the Head of his father, Deng Majok, that too will have become mine. And should he inherit from my own Head that too would have become mine. That was all I wanted, my dear wife, Ayak, daughter of Deng Ngor. With my Mading, I have compensated for the loss of cows. This tribe is ours. It is I who controls the disease of cattle. And it is I who controls the disease of man. That is why the tribe has flourished and multiplied this much. And yet, we have not found the central place in this section called Abyor. Chieftainship is inherent in us, and it has continued to be attracted to us. But we have not found the center in this tribe. Now, I have found the center. I wanted to enter the center.

Ngor then addressed the success of Achol's marriage mostly in terms of procreation which the Dinka consider the core objective of marriage. Ideally, this is seen in terms of the continuation of the paternal lineage through sons. But having one son is often justified with reference to the history of the family and the positive role single sons have played in continuing the lineage.

Deng did indeed establish Achok's house with children. The only thing is that they turned out to be girls, except for yourself. But as we reflected, we realized that this was part of our ancestral blood. In the family of Duor, the pattern is generally one single son among daughters. Duor was first. He had one brother, but that brother disappeared into the wilderness. And his sister was the one taken into slavery. When Mijok came, he too turned out to be one son. And when I was born, I also turned out to be one son. When, we discussed this situation, my father said—'Do not be concerned. Blood flows down the line whether through one son or through many sons. It will go on and on. When it comes to Mading, he will not have only one son. But even if Achok stops

*with Mading as her only son, what is wrong with that? Was I not an
only son? And have I not produced several sons from my different wives?
The house of Koc's mother has sons and the house of Ajing's mother has
sons. Only Ngor's mother has a single son because that is where the
blood of Maluk has gone to produce an only son. So, even if Achok
should stop with one son, Mading will have more sons, and one of his
sons will be the one to bear only a single son. That is the way it goes
down the line. So, do not be concerned about Achok. Because of those
girls, Mading's father will give him weight. When they get married, his
father will realize that Mading has the weight of wealth behind him. I
will not be there when this happens, but it will happen. And Deng will
turn his eyes with favor on Mading.'*

Ngor then commented on the developments since the time of those
discussions with Mijok and concluded that his father's wishes and
predictions have been fulfilled. And much of that had to do with his
prayers and expectations for my future.

*All the things my father said, God has made them come true. When
he later got seriously ill and you were an older child, people said to
him—'Mijok, shall we send for Mading to come?' He said—'No!' They
said—'Why?' He said—'No, I do not want him to be involved in this
(his death). I have already given him my blessing. The person I want
to come is Koc.' Koc was fetched. Then he said to him—'I want you to
go to Deng Majok. Tell him that I am dying and that I am leaving
no cattle behind. What I want from him is a cow with a calf to be
sacrificed when I am gone. That is the only cow I am requesting of
you.' People said—'Why is Awut's father inviting death upon himself?'
A man called Deng Monyjur said—'I saw Mijok invoking a lamb
yesterday, speaking in the same vein.' People turned to Koc and said—
'Go your own way. Do not listen to the terrible words of your father.
How could he say such dreadful words of death!?' Koc went and stayed.
Later on, my father had Koc called. He said to him—'Have you
been to see Deng Majok?' Koc said—'Well, Father—' 'Go away,' he
interrupted. Then he called for Kat, the son of Nyanawel. He said to
him—'Please go and explain to my son-in-law, Deng Majok, that
I want him to send me a cow with a bull-calf. And it should be a*

203

lactating cow. Let the cow be brought and tethered here. I will die this very season. When I am dead, I want the cow and the bull-calf to be sacrificed.' He repeated those very words to Kat.

And indeed, he was right; he was dying, and he felt it. The cow was brought and tethered. At first, your father was very reluctant to send the cow because he did not like the way my father was talking about dying. The whole thing did not appear to him understandable. When the winter came, he called me and said—'Go to your maternal relatives and bring a big ram. I am dying and I want to perform a ritual.' He looked to us as though he was well, but he was feeling something deep inside himself. I went to the family of Nyanawel who kept sheep. I came back with a large ram. He saw me with the ram through the door of the cattle-byre in which he was lying down. As soon as he saw me approach, he got up and walked toward me. When we came within talking distance from one another, he said to me—'Chief!' That was how he addressed me: 'Chief!' Then he said—'Twin, Ngor, my Ngor.' I said—'Yes, Father!' He said—'This ram will be slaughtered for the ritual of severance—aher.' I said—'What severance, Father!?' He said— 'I am going to sever myself from you. Even if I find a comfortable home in the ground, this ram, Nyongrial, will be the symbol of my oath. They say that a dead man returns to fetch his most favorite child. That is why I want to sever my ties with you before I die and while you watch.' I said—'But Father, how can you do that? Do people sever themselves while they are alive? Is this not a ritual which is performed after a person is dead?' He said—'Never mind, my son, just fetch a spear!' People tried to stop him, but he insisted. He tethered the ram, Nyongrial, and began to invoke: 'Nyongrial, my father has returned for me, and my mother has returned for me, and my grandfather has returned for me. My time in this world is over. I must go. I am going to kill you and make you feel the pain of the spear as a reminder. If I should miss my son, Ngor, and want to fetch him to join me, you will remind me by saying—"I thought you slaughtered me in order to sever yourself from your son!?' You are the symbol of that severance." Then he slaughtered the ram. He cut the animal into two equal parts. And he said—'Let one half remain in this home and the other half be thrown away or given to a stranger.'

Then I went to the cattle-camp. I spent three days at the camp and word came to me: 'You will not reach your father alive.' I came running and found him trembling. He was no longer able to speak. I cried and cried and said—'Father, are you going to die without saying a word?' Deng Michar caught me and said—'What else do you want your father to say? Has he not already said enough to you? Or is it that you are still too young to appreciate what he has done!?' Your mother heard of our father's death with uncertainty. And thus, Father died and was buried. He had said to me—'Ajang is the daughter of Bol Malek. Should Bol come to seek her, do something that will be heard throughout the land, something that will honor her name. It was because of Bol Malek that I gave up cattle. But should he come, I want you to honor Ajang so that your name be heard loud and clear, that you are Ngor, the son of Mijok.' When Bol Malek came, I made him 'recover' his daughter with thirty cows. Your father took a share of a cow, Per-low, with a cow-calf and another cow, Dan-per, a cow-calf of black and white color pattern. That is the story of your mother's background. And that was how your mother, Achok, came into your family. My father was after something in his own heart. As for what he wanted, he declared to his people before he died—'I have found what I was looking for.' Those are the words of the land. And one says what is true, so that saying it leaves you healthy without even a cold-sore on your mouth. It is what you have seen, and not what you have heard, that you should say. All the things my father had seen, he said to me. Achwei is now in an unknown part of the world, but her name has been maintained so that there is now a family known as the family of Achwei.

As for our affiliation in this section of Abyor, it was Biong Allor who welcomed our ancestor Maluk, son of Dau. Then Arob Biong became a Chief in the presence of our ancestor, Maluk. When you used to say as a child that you were Mading, son of Achok of eight cows, your father did not like hearing that from you. But it was not something you heard from your maternal relatives; it was something you heard in your own family. It was not the kind of thing you could say you were told by your maternal grandfather or maternal uncle.

205

Deng Majok listened very carefully to voices from our side. But until he died, he never heard anything from us to take down to the grave with him. He never heard any complaint about cattle and he never heard any insults from us. When the country was destroyed by the civil war, he once spoke to me and said—'Is there someone who tells you that if you settle near Deng Majok you will not find anything to sustain you? Why do you keep away from me?' I said to him—'I have two wives and there is not a single cow from you in any of their marriages. But my father had said something. I fear that if I were to be close to you, I might break my father's oath even unintentionally. That is why I keep my distance.' He said—'Are you the right person to complain about my not having contributed to the marriages of your wives, or should it be for the families of those girls to state their claims to me?' I said—'What about the complaints they state to me? But, in any case, what do you have to be concerned about when I have managed on my own!? That is why I keep my distance; I do not want to prick you, even by mistake.' So, you Mading, those are the words that remain. I have now passed them on to you.

Francis M. Deng: *Uncle, as I grew up, people watched me, knowing the background of my grandfather's expectations from me. They probably knew that my grandfather had condemned himself to death to redeem me, as God's gift to him. How do you think my father took all that, and how did he respond to it, whether in his treatment of me or in his relations with my mother?*

Ngor Mijok: *Mading, it is only you and I talking here. There is no reason to keep anything behind. Achok has been severely tested by your father, but he never found any ground for disrespect. We never saw any disrespect shown to Achok. But whenever I felt provoked, I would think of my father's words and tell myself—'If my father gave up demanding cattle for his daughters, why should I, a strong young man who has succeeded in establishing himself, behave differently!? Demanding cattle from Deng Majok might negatively affect the future of Mading. It might also hurt the future of his sisters. The future belongs to them. I*

206

have had my share in life with my own sisters.'

But it seems that my maternal relatives, according to Uncle Ngor, expected to receive from me social services and other material benefits than I was able to deliver. In fact, until I heard of their complaints from Uncle Ngor, I was not even aware of their expectations and complaints, which were mostly directed to Uncle Ngor and to a lesser extent to my mother. Both defended me, especially as they feared that grievances felt by maternal relatives might carry a curse, even if not intended. Uncle Ngor's account continued:

Mading, our clan of Maluk hold some grievances toward you. They had thought that you were going to be a person to whom they would have access to resources. They know that your life carries a legacy bestowed upon you by the elder of our clan, my father and your grandfather, Mijok Duor. They complain to me. My response has been: 'You members of our clan, have you heard of anything Mading has done against you to alienate him from you?' They say—'No.' I said to them— 'I do not receive my share from the marriages of Achok's daughters, the sisters of Mading. And I have never asked Mading for favors. Why do you feel left out to complain in those words?' They said—'Ngor, what disturbs us as Mading's maternal uncles is that he seems to care only about his clan, Pajok. These are people who did not contribute to the marriage of his mother Achok. And yet they are the people benefitting from Mading. And he is known as Mading, the son of Achok. It is we who know how Achok came to be his mother.'

I said to them—'Fellow members of our clan, you are fighting yourselves. Your anger against Mading can carry with it the curse of maternal uncles. And you know that the curse of a maternal uncle is deadly. Pajok have their hearts in material things. This is something they have always been known for. This is something we can do nothing about. But you people have a bigger interest in Mading as the son of your sister Achok. If people could call on God to make them talk to their dead elders, we should say to my father—"Mijok Duor, the name Mading which you insisted upon has materialized according to your word." We would call on him to protect Mading. It does not matter who eats from him.'

When you decided to establish a farm in our area, members of our clan gathered and celebrated. They felt your presence. They said—'Now that Mading is going to establish a farm here, maybe he has at long last decided to turn his eyes on us?' Your farm was made. And then the cattle-byre was built. They said to themselves—'Any place where a government leader establishes a presence usually receives education, health and other social services. Perhaps Mading is planning to bring government services into our area?' I said—'We will wait and see.' Members of our clan said—'We will take good care of this farm of Mading, son of Achok.'

Then they turned to your mother and said—'Achok, why is your son making his farm in this area and his clan, even his own brothers, seem opposed to the idea? When we ask them for services near the farm, they say—"You will be provided with services," but nothing happens. We tell them that what we are doing is not our own, but their brother's and therefore theirs, and yet we get no response. Is that not hostility to us rather than to Mading? It is not Mading they do not like; it is us they resent because Mading has come to us.' Achok said to them—'That is a lie, do not listen to such words. Put your hearts fully into the farm.' And indeed, they had put their hearts into your farm. It is only that God took me away when I was the only one mobilizing and coordinating the people to work on the farm.

One thing that pleased us all was that Deng Majok educated you. The elder called Choi Minyuon, our uncle, said in his last days—'O you people, my age-mates have all gone and I am the only one who has remained. I now hear that Deng Majok has taken Mading to school. The cattle which would have been used for marrying Achok will now be used for educating Mading. So, do not complain any more about Achok not having been married with enough cows. When a child goes to school, his maternal relatives are expected to contribute cattle for his education. So, you watch closely to see how Mading's education progresses. If Deng Majok does not take good care of his education, then you have a right to speak. But if he takes care of his education, then you should not complain about Achok not having been married; she will indeed have been married.'

What he said was a word of great wisdom. There was a year that you and Bol were on leave. As you came to go back to school, you sold a number of cows for your school fees and pocket money. I believe each one of you sold about four cows. I spoke to Deng Korow and said— 'What is all this wealth of cattle being spent for?' He said 'Ngon, there is something important in this. And that son of your sister has caught the attention of his father. Deng Majok has begun to focus on him, and he has even said—"That child you see will one day be my Head. Now I realize that what my father was saying has come true. People say my father, Kwol Arob, hated me, but it is a lie. When I was about to give up on Achok, he said to me—'Son do not surrender, even though I will not attend the wedding myself. As long as the girl is the daughter of Mijok Duor, go after that Head.' That Head which my father was talking about is apparent in my son, Mading. He will one day be my Head." So, you see, Deng Majok talks quietly in admiration of your sister's son.' Deng Korow told me that.

So, you, Mading, you are a child of destiny. I pray to God and to my father to keep this destiny. I have people behind me, but all I want is the path my father had set forth for us. I only hope that Mading can share this with me. My father said that he was not after winning men of influence; nor was he after the power of magical charms; nor was he ambitious for any particular leadership position. He said—'What I wanted in my heart, I have told you. If you should have any grievances aching your hearts, tell me about them.'

Two things have disturbed my heart. One has to do with what I hear about your eyes having a disease (glaucoma). The other has to do with the future of the girl you have brought from the unknown lands of America. That is why I pray for God to save you so that your children grow up while you are seeing and watching, so that you see which direction they will go, whether they will cease to be Dinka or not; that is something I pray for. I pray that my father does it that way. If one were to do things to be seen and heard long after they are gone, then I wish my father would look into this and safeguard your life to see the future of your children, so that you know where they are heading for and you tell them the sort of words that you and I are now telling one

*another. It is fitting that you yourself tell them the kind of things you
and I are talking about.*

Francis M. Deng: *Let me tell you, Uncle Ngor, that while most of the
precise words you have been saying were not known to me, the gist of
what you said has always been clear to me. And wherever my children
are raised, they will get that message. And the words that you and I
have been saying will be on record. They will grow up and will find
them. But the world ahead is a world that is going to be mixed. And
wherever a person originates from, he may find himself growing up in
an entirely different environment. What is crucial is for a man to know
himself and his background. However far from his background a man
may be, as long as he knows his origins, his identity, and his people, this
is a world in which people and traveling have become so easy that a
man can no longer argue that he is far from his people.*
*So, if God saves my children, they will find these words written down.
That is why I am very pleased with our conversation. If you had not
come on account of your illness, for which I asked you to come for
treatment, I would have asked you anyway to come so that we would
converse the way we have just done. So, in a way, we have hit two birds
with one stone, as they say.*
*There is something which I believe I hinted to you when I was in
school. And I believe I also hinted it to Achok. But I have not talked
to anybody else about it. I grew up knowing that there was something
positive my father saw in me, something he saw and liked as offering
some advantages to him. But as I grew up, I also felt some misgivings
about Father's attitude. There was nothing very explicit. But subtly
speaking, there was some disparity between what I expected and what
I witnessed. I got to compare myself with the sons of the senior wives,
Bol and Kwol, and expected to be treated in identical ways with them.
The idea of being in a secondary position was never something I liked.
But in the Dinka way of doing things, there is always the seniority
of the mother. There is a difference between a first or second wife and
a fourth or fifth wife. For the same reason, there is always that small
indication of the mother's position in people's attitudes toward the*

210

children. For instance, in the distribution of cattle, seniority always counted. On the whole, I felt equal to my brothers, Bol and Kwol. In fact, I appeared to win some favor on account of my words. But a person favored because of his ability to speak well is not the same as a person loved by his father for the simple fact of father's love.

Father noticed my words very early. Whenever we spoke to him, even if it were something we all agreed upon, because my brothers always wanted me to be the first to speak, Father seemed to believe that the idea had come from me. If it were something he did not like, he would always appear to blame me more for what we said. And if it were something he liked, he also noticed. Whenever we met to speak to him, I would always be chosen the main speaker on our behalf, which made me the ringleader.

One small thing almost angered me when we were small children. I used to take good care of my clothes, while Kwol's clothes were usually worn out very quickly. One time he bought some clothes for Bol and Chan because their garments were worn out. I complained openly in front of others. His immediate response was—'But you still have your clothes in good condition.' I said—'Should I be disadvantaged by taking good care of my clothes!?' He then bought new clothes for me along with the others.

On the whole, Bol and I grew up equal as we progressed in school together. He always distributed things equally to us. Nevertheless, I always felt some small shortcoming in Father's attitude. It was never anything explicit or conspicuous. But when it came to speaking about his children, I always felt that Father spoke about me as a son in whom he had positive expectations. One time he sent me to Twichland to fetch his wife, or reclaim his bride-wealth cattle if the woman would not come. Then he left to go to Arabland. Bol and I, accompanied by our cousin Koc Aguer, the son of our Aunt Awor, decided to go to fetch the cattle if the wife were not returning. We went and brought some of the cattle, having decided to repudiate the marriage since the woman, supported by her brother, would not come. We came and sold some of the cattle and then proceeded back to the school. We were in high school. We went on horses. Father was still in the North. But word had

211

gone ahead to him that the children had broken his marriage and had brought back the cattle from the marriage and sold the best cows. I was the first person he had sent and Bol and Koc had merely decided to join me. So, I felt a personal responsibility for what we had done.

As we rode, word came back to us that our father was very angry with us for having broken his marriage and sold the cattle. I was worrying a great deal about our meeting and how he would react. As I reflected in anticipation, a thought came to my mind: 'What if he is very angry and becomes abusive!? What could he possibly say? Supposing he were to insult me, what could he say by way of insult?' It was then that a thought occurred to me—'What if he denied me as his son!? What if he said that I was not his own birth!?' That small thought began to preoccupy me all the way.

Then we met with our father. I was in the lead. He greeted me very warmly. It was the kind of greeting that did not show that he was in any way angry with us. He decided that we should all stop there to rest. He asked me a lot of questions about the affairs of the family and the tribe. Then he said—'Mading, did you sell the cows?' I said—'Yes, we sold some.' 'How many did you sell?' I told him. He remarked—'All those cows!?' But we were both speaking smilingly and in a very relaxed way; no tension or hostility at all. Then he said—'Will you please give Arob some financial help?' Arob was then serving a prison sentence in Nahud.

Then we proceeded to go to school. At first, I was relieved and happy that what we had feared had not transpired. But after we were back in school, that small thought that had occurred to me—'What if he should deny me!?' began to reoccur. I began to think and think and think: 'Am I my really Father's son?' The problem began to grow and grow until it became a mental aberration. I would go to sleep and it was still in my mind; I would wake up, and it was still in my mind; I would go to the class, and it was still in my mind; I would glare with my eyes while my heart was somewhere else. It became such a problem for me that I almost lost my mind. That was why I came and spoke to you.

Ngor Mijok: *Yes, you almost said that. Kweng, the man who first*

*engaged Achok, if Achok was old enough, he would have completed
his bride-wealth and he would have been given his wife. Had Koryom
age-set of Abyor, the age-set of Kwol Arob and my father, not decided
to intercede in support of Deng Majok, the marriage of Kweng would
have been completed. But as it was, Kweng's cattle were withdrawn
and those disposed of were compensated for before Achok even reached
puberty, you see. We spent a season. Achok then reached puberty. Your
father's marriage came shortly after.*

*When Achok reached puberty, my father slaughtered a cow, a Per-nyang
color, whose meat he said should be dried for Achok. He said—'Since
she will no longer drink the milk of the cows because of her condition,
eating food made out of pure millet without addition will give her
stomach trouble. So, she should have the meat of this cow. I was going
to exchange her for a bull, to be slaughtered for a feasting held in
cultivation. But it should now be slaughtered for my daughter, Achok.'
That Per-Nyang was slaughtered at Nok-Jur. It was cut into strips
and dried. So, is there a woman who can conceive before she reaches
puberty? Or is there a woman who can beget a child for a man she has
not been with?*

*What you might have heard was what your father had said—'Let some
women go to witness Achok's delivery.' His idea was that in the past,
according to Dinka traditions, if a woman had known men before
her marriage, when she came to deliver, if she had been with any
man, a stranger or a relative, she would confess the man she had been
with. Your father's intention was to find out whether Achok would
deliver easily or with difficulty. If she had difficulties, then according to
tradition, she would be suspected of hiding something and would have
to confess before she would deliver safely. When Achok delivered with
surprising ease, Kwei immediately revealed the purpose of their mission.
She said—'Achok, the reason for our coming was to see whether you
might confess something. But since you have delivered so smoothly, we
should now leave and go back to report.'*

*If what you were afraid of was the case, our clan would certainly have
told you. Even I—forget the clan—I would have told you. I would
have told you that why Deng Majok did not pay well for my sister is*

213

because she did not give birth to Deng's son, because Mading is not really his son. I would certainly have told you a long time ago. I, Ngor, would never have hidden that from you. For one thing, I would have concluded that this was probably the reason for some of the things in your father's attitude toward me.

So, Mading, that thing is completely out of the question. Achok begot you when she was still virtually a child. If my father, Mijok Duor, was not a man of his own ideas and determination, no one would have thought that Achok was old enough to be given in marriage. But my father said—'How can my child go to dances and be pointed at: "That is the girl whom Kweng betrothed and was taken away from him by force."' Your heart almost led you astray. The heart of an educated man sometimes strays away with false thoughts. My sister, when Bol Malek begot Ajang, don't you see that Father took her away from the man who married her mother and gave her back to her biological father!? He said—'The child must be returned to her father; and what is more, you should do so through a ceremony which all will hear about.' That we did. And that is one thing I must admit Deng Majok did very well. He said—'Bol, what you did, had I already married Achok by the time you did it, I would have been the one in conflict with you; I would have considered it a personal affront.'

Francis M. Deng: *I should tell you that after all that, I once returned home on leave and decided to have a man-to-man talk with my father. He had come as close as Sennar but had returned without proceeding to Khartoum. And he did not write to me. Even the things he wanted to be done for him, such as guns to be repaired, were brought to my attention by the people he had sent and not with a message from him directly. Then I went home. And shortly after I got home, I requested a meeting with him. I said to him—'Father, as I grew up, I saw small things which have disturbed my heart considerably. But I have not let them come out in the open. We have heard you say quite often how your father had treated you and how you yourself have corrected your father's attitude in your treatment of us, your children.'*

'But when I see the way you treat us, I feel that there is a small but

214

*significant shortcoming which I have not understood. How could
you come as close as Sennar and not send me a letter or even a word
of mouth? Even your things that had to be done in Khartoum were
brought to my attention by your messengers on their own initiative.
I have been wondering what it is that has caused this lack of affection
from you. What have I done to my father? You see, a son does not
feel that his father loves him simply because he has sent him to school
and pays for his education. Nor is love expressed merely by providing
maintenance. There is something which makes a child feel that his
father loves him beyond these material considerations. It is not even a
question of calculation that this son will one day do this or that for me.
It is merely a feeling of love between a child and his father. So, what
have I done to deserve this small but important shortcoming of love I
feel from you? Is there anything you see in me which has disappointed
you and which deserves this attitude from you?'*

*He was in his home court when I asked to see him. And we withdrew
from the crowd and sat some distance away protected by the police
from the encroachment of the people. By God, he spoke very movingly.
He spoke again of his relations with his father and his own relations
with us, his children. Then he went on to say that according to Dinka
practice, a man's view of his child is influenced by his view of the child's
mother. 'I see your mother Achok as the wife who even if I am away,
I trust that I have someone responsible at home. I do not see Achok as
junior to my senior wives. I see Achok as though she were a first wife, as
senior as Nyanboldit.'*

*He proceeded to praise Achok a great deal. 'So, there is nothing I can
hold against you on account of your mother. And as for yourself, it is
you and Bol whom I look to for the future of my family and the tribe.
From the time you were still small, the British administrators and later
the Sudanese officials kept telling me that you would be the children
who would in the end prove to be my strength.'*

*Another issue occurred later. He had allotted us some money from his
salary, Bol and myself. Then Bol left to study abroad. Later on, when
Bol returned on vacation and went home while I was in the University
of Khartoum, Father asked him whether I had sent him the money. Bol*

said that I had sent the money to him. Father then remarked—Then Mading has truly proved himself a man.' On another occasion, as I was at home on vacation, and about to go back to the University, Father called Kwol and asked him—'How much money do you think Mading needs for pocket money?' Kwol came and told me what Father had asked him.

Father later came on a visit to Khartoum. I approached him on these issues with a very angry heart. I told him—'Father, I understand that you said I have proved myself to be an honest man by having sent the money to Bol. Did you believe that I would be dishonest and not forward to Bol what was his due? Did you realize for the first time that I was honest because of having sent the money to Bol?' Another issue arose as I was leaving. 'You called Kwol and asked him how much money I needed to go to school. Does Kwol know where I live to be in a position to tell what I need?' Achwil Bulabek was with him. Father reacted in his usual way. He appeared angry and said—'Achwil, why don't you advise the child!?'

He then went on to recall the way he had raised us, the way his father had ill-treated him, and the comparison between his treatment of us and his father's treatment of him. 'Unlike my father,' he said—'I have never discriminated among you, my sons, even for a single day.' First, he denied that he had talked to Kwol about pocket money for me, but then added—'And even if I had asked Kwol, what is wrong with my asking your brother about your needs!?' He also denied having made the remarks about the money to Bol, but added—'And even if I had said so, should my praising you for having fulfilled your undertaking be a reason for quarreling with me!?'

We argued until Achwil intervened to moderate between us. Then we stopped and I left. For two days, I did not return to see him. Word began to reach me that Father was asking about me. Eventually, he sent someone to me to enquire on why I was keeping away. So, I went back, and we resumed our normal relationship. I then accompanied him to his official meetings and also entertained him for functions in which I introduced him to my university colleagues and other contacts in Khartoum.

216

*As I reflect on my relations with Father, it is true that I did not
see anything bad in his treatment of me, but there was some small
indications that he liked me for my mind and my conduct; he saw
me as a son who would one day be useful to his family and the tribe.
He saw me as a son in whom he had hopes for the future. While I
appreciated all that, I felt there was something missing by way of
spontaneous Father's love. But what Deng Korow said to you about
Father speaking favorably of Meissen is something I only vaguely sensed.
When I was still quite young, and I had just graduated from Khartoum
University, I went home before proceeding to England for further
studies. Father called me aside and told me what was going on in the
tribe about selecting one of the two sons, Monyyak and Kwol, who
were with him at home, to be his deputy. First, he said that Bol and
I had become national figures who had gone beyond the tribe. On the
other two, he said people were beginning to argue in favor of Monyyak
on the ground that he was a son of the first wife. He said he told them
that they were both his sons. He then asked me which of the two sons I
thought would be more suited for the position.*

*He had talked to me years earlier about his intentions to have Kwol
appointed, and he had indeed asked me to write a letter to the Central
Government authorities to put the idea forward. But the issue had
been dropped, and we had not discussed it any more until that occasion
of my departure. Before he talked to me, I had heard much talk,
especially from the women, concerning the rivalry that had already
built up in the family. My answer to him was that I had no preference
to express, because, in a way, I saw merits on both sides. Kwol was a
senior son with experience and had already been designated earlier, but
being from Kwol's section, I might be considered biased in expressing
preference for him. On the other hand, Monyyak had considerable
virtues, quite apart from being the son of the first wife, especially in his
politeness and willingness to listen to advice.*

*I told my father that, since I was the son of a relatively junior wife,
I was probably not objective on the issue but that I agreed with him
that mother's seniority should not be the determining factor. The choice
should be for a person who was seen as possessing the qualities required*

217

for the responsibility. Should that person be Monyyak or Kwol, the criterion should be who would best serve the interests of the tribe. I concluded that I did not have a word to say in preference of any one of the two, but I advised him not to delay the decision and allow the people to drift apart on the issue. I told him that if he delayed the decision too long, people would become so divided that it might prove difficult to maintain the unity and harmony of the family. If he quickly decided on any one of the two, his decision would be the way everyone would follow.

We left it at that. He did not comment on what I said. And of course, he never did anything about it in the end. I recall the comment my mother Achok made one night about the issue. She said—'You people are bothering yourselves for nothing. You will never see Deng Majok place one of his sons as his deputy. That would be an indication of a future successor and a possible end to his own leadership; that he will never do.' And indeed, she proved to be right.

Those were some of the indications about Father's attitude toward me. There were also other things which I heard him say about me. But I always had that lingering feeling that while father saw in me some qualities that he thought might be of some benefit to him, the family, and the tribe in the future, for precisely the same reasons, he was perhaps a little afraid that what had happened between him and his father could happen again. He was afraid that one might aspire to his chieftainship and possibly outwit him the way he had outwitted his father. He once asked me. I had been investigating into the customary law of the Dinka while I was at the University of Khartoum. Then I returned with an Englishman who was my lecturer in the University, together with a senior student, to continue investigation into Dinka law. Father asked me—'Mading, this recording of customary law, is it being conducted throughout the Sudan or is it only in the Ngok area that it is being done?'

Word had been going around: 'Mading is being prepared to be appointed as the man in charge of all the appeals from Dinka courts.' People like Matet Ayom even came and congratulated me for that. Uncle Deng Abot said to me when I went to investigate into Dinka law in his court: 'I saw it in your eyes from the time you were still a baby.' When I saw the rumors so rampant, I told my father—'I will no longer sit in court to listen to cases; there are rumors which I hear going around and which have disturbed my heart; I will only investigate with elders and chiefs at home and avoid sitting in court.' Father heard me and laughed in the manner of a person who knew exactly what I had in mind and liked my reaction.

A small thing happened later on during his terminal illness which saddened me deeply. Father had become quite disenchanted with Bol because of Bol's attitude toward him as a patient. Father would say that his ailment had begun in the area of the liver, but Bol kept asserting that it was in the lungs and not the liver. The problem was that Bol became a doctor to his own father, which in medical practice is not advisable. Besides, Bol has never been inclined toward matters of detail about the way the Dinka do things traditionally. His mind tends to go more into the new scientific ways of the West. And therefore, he was more inclined to look at the records of the doctors than value his father's words, not merely as a fastidious patient, whose views should not be disregarded, but also as someone whose opinions about anything mattered greatly and should be taken seriously. As a result, Father became so dismissive of Bol that when other doctors came to see him, Father avoided Bol, and preferred to communicate with the other doctors directly through me as his interpreter. The good thing is that Bol took all with impressive professional calm as a doctor and did not personalize it to hurt him; if he felt it, he did not show it.

The day he died, we went to see him. It was a few hours before he eventually died. He appeared to be in deep agony, and yet there was a retiring look in his glowing eyes, a sense of surrender and submission to the inevitable that he must have ultimately realized was at hand. He was lying back, gazing at us with his penetrating eyes now deep in the sockets of his otherwise skeleton head. All three of us, Bol, Achier, his clerk, and myself—were standing around his bed. Suddenly, as though to make his very last move in life, Father pulled himself up, wrapped his arms around my neck, and pulled me toward him. Achier immediately intervened and disentangled his arms from around my neck, saying—'The doctor said that you should lie still.' Neither doctor had said anything of the sort, and Achier's instinct was probably to protect Father or me. Father fell back and lay motionless on his back, still eyeing us intensely. I was deeply saddened by that. Perhaps to soothe me, Bol tried to dismiss it as the behavior of a dying man that I should not worry about. I must confess that it was a frightening moment, but that he was pulled away from me was to torment me for years and still does.

Ngor Mijok: *There was something important which he wanted to pass on to you. His mind was thinking about major things and it is most significant that he wanted to pull you toward his heart.*

Francis M. Deng: *What pained me the most was that Achier pulled him away. To this day, I feel great remorse that I did not allow Father to let me hear what was on his mind or in his heart.*

Ngor Mijok: *Despite what Achier did, Deng Majok holds* (Note the present tense in the speech of a dead man) *nothing against you in his heart. The fact that he wanted to place you on his heart means that his heart was pure toward you. You see, Deng Majok knew the full story of your life and what my father had done because of you. But of course, anything is subject to the will of God. Father had said something with Deng Majok which I had not known until Deng Majok himself revealed it to me years later. I had eloped with the daughter of his uncle, Mahdi Arob, after breaking my first engagement. Mahdi's daughter had been engaged to another man. For that reason, I was tried and sentenced to imprisonment. I said to the English District Commissioner: 'You have given me one-year imprisonment after I was flogged with thirty lashes. This man whose court sentenced me is my brother-in-law; he is not my brother. But I would like to have a private talk with him.' Your father turned to the English District Commissioner and said—'The man who begot this young man is dead and before he died, he said something to me about his son. So, let him and me have a private talk. I will implore you to reduce his sentence, but we have a private matter to discuss.'*

When we were alone, he said to me—'Ngor, if you were the son of any other wife of Mijok, Nyandeng or Nyanchuor, I would have allowed you to marry the daughter of Mahdi. But since you are the son of Ayak, I cannot let you have her because your father left me with a big responsibility for you. Your father, Mijok, said to me before he died— "Deng, son of Kwol, if my son, Ngor, does not get established to be known as the son of Mijok, what made me give Achok to you will spoil. I, Mijok Duor, am not a man whose neck should be without beads." Your father said to me that you should marry in the family of Pachwol. Now, you want to choose your own wife and push aside the girl I chose in fulfillment of your father's word. I do not want a person with the vile characteristics of a black ant. I want someone with the discreet behavior of a bed-bug. A bed-bug will appear quiet, hidden, and harmless in the daytime, and yet at night, it will surface in the same bed and bite people. Nobody knows where the bed-bug hides in the daytime. As for the black ant, it goes about recklessly in the daytime in front of its targets and openly attacks to bite. As a result, a great many of the ant population get exterminated. If you want to adopt the behavior of an ant, I will not allow you because your father, Mijok, left me with a responsibility for you. Your father said—"I am not a Mijok whose neck is to be without beads". But the day you accept the word of your father, Mijok Duor, which has now come to you through my mouth, then we will leave this and look for a second wife of your choice.'

That was how I married Akwol, the daughter of Mangok, and later married the daughter of his other Uncle, Allor Kwol. When I engaged the daughter of Allor Kwol, people rose in surprise. 'Why is Ngor involving himself with the daughter of Allor Kwol!?' The sons of Allor Kwol got up and went to complain to him—'All Ngor has given for our sister is only ten cows.' Deng said—'You mean he has actually handed you ten cows which you now possess!?' They said—'Yes!' He said—'But when Allor Kwol married the sister of Mijok Duor, how much did he pay!?' They said—'What compares the affairs of that distant past with the affairs of today!?' He said—'Let me tell you something: I will never support your position with a word—Never! If Ngor was interfering

221

*with an earlier engagement, I would listen to your complaint. But if
he is the first to approach you and has in fact given you ten cows, you
have no cause at all. What I now want from you is to sit and negotiate
the marriage in good faith. If Ngor is hiding any cattle from you, then
you will have the right to point those out and go after them. That is all
I will say.'*

*Biong Mading said—'Our clan, you should do as Deng Majok says.'
Deng then turned to me and said—'A nobleman does not marry
cheaply. Marry this girl properly; she is a noble woman.' And it is true,
if I had not listened to him, I would not have married my second wife,
and I would not have had the home I now have which people can point
to with a sense of pride: 'That is the home of Ngor!' So, that part he
did well.*

*But, Mading, Deng Majok has been undermined and exposed by
divisiveness that occurred among members of your family after the
death of your father. Our tribe is oblivious to this grave situation. Now,
you see a few people clustering in Abyei, searching for something to eat,
and people call them leaders of the Ngok. And all this is happening
because of feuds within your own family. That is why disaster has
befallen the family of Deng Kwol. Some eyes are now turned on
you. I see it quite clearly. I spoke to your mother very discreetly and
said—'Look here Achok, a lion that has roared during the daytime
and revealed its presence in the area alerts people to the danger and a
wise person makes his fence to protect his herd. This evil is finishing the
family of Deng Majok. Be careful.'*

*Yes, Mading, some people are not happy about the position you occupy.
One hears a lot said and some names are always associated with all
that. Even the words I now hear voiced on your stand on public issues,
I see something of the same in it. And it worries me. Of course, I want
to bring it to your attention, but it is not really an issue in which I
want to focus on in our exchange of words as you and I are now doing.
I rely more on the words I say at night when I cannot sleep and pray
alone; or words that I say to others elsewhere in my own way; those are
words that count. I have said to Achok—'Never let your tongue utter
a word of anger or complaint. Why you came and gave birth to your*

*children was a fulfillment of your father's will. It was not a house of
your own choice; it was a home your father had willed for you. And
you gave birth to a child which was not your own planning, but an
unknown gift from God in response to prayers. You never knew Mading
before he became. What our father wanted is what you should pray
to God and our father himself. Ask them—"God, and you Father,
whose spirit has risen above, this is what you wanted in this home. I
came and begot an only son, that one Mading, and in a world under
destruction. Please protect him. That is all I will ask for and look to you
to safeguard his life." My sister Achok, that is all you should do. Never
enquire into anything you hear. And never spend any money to hire a
person with magic to retaliate evil or gain advantage by saying—
"I hate so and so," or "I wish my son would get this or that good thing."
Never do that, until the end of your days. If you do that, you will have
associated evil deeds with the name of Mading. All you need say to men
of virtue is: "Wish my son well in your prayers." And when you give to
people, do so without attaching strings; you will have done the right
thing and God will notice. What some people are doing will turn this
area into an abandoned land.'*

*Truly, Mading, the Ngok are afraid to voice their opinion because of
you. People say—'Mading will hear all this and he will think that it
is the work of subversive elements who are after the leadership of his
family.' But Mading, the behavior of some people in your family since
the death of your father is unbecoming. When they speak, they hit the
right words. No son born by Deng Majok can totally miss on words.
But then emerge what sound like words in the wilderness. The Ngok
are bewildered. They say—'If this was truly the breed of Deng Majok,
would they not go to the source of power and explain what we are
suffering from!?' Instead, they move recklessly, associating themselves
with people whose sole interest is to find something to eat, people whose
ancestors have never been identified with any land as the leaders of
this or that area. Your ancestor Biong Allor had the spirit of God in
his leadership. It was through him that God protected the people of his
tribe. Now, your leadership has gone astray.*

Mading, I want to tell you my word, a word to leave with you even

223

after I join our ancestors. Our kind has always been known for predicting into the future. Our kind can tell what will come in the very distant future. Mading, our kind is rich in heart and mind. In our kind, a person may be poor in material wealth, but the words they say are never cheap in substance. And our type never looks at other people's things; there is no envy in our kind. But our kind excels over all others with the wisdom of their words. Our kind can tell what will lead to disaster in the future, and they can tell what will lead to the good of the land.

I tell the members of our clan: 'Mading is a crop of our breed. He is the crop of our breed because he is Mading Achok. I have not spoken to him since he came back from America. When he was in America in a secure environment, my heart was at peace. I was happy because I knew he was well, and names also benefit from the extension of circles. He was extending our ancestral circle to those distant lands. But now that he is back in the Sudan, at a time when the land is in turmoil, I am worried. What is needed is a crop for the future. And when people speak of a crop, it is not anyone who is valued as a crop; it is the crop of a person of prudent heart and mind who, if he is hidden in safety somewhere, even if the land should be destroyed, it will one day return to peace and order. When it does, that crop will return and will enquire in the air about the whereabouts of his people. He will be told—"So and so is there and so and so is there." He will go after them and collect them to become a group again.'

I was telling Achok—'What worries me is Mading's return amidst a conflict. When he was away, and would come occasionally to visit, people were respected. Authorities would fear that if a disaster should befall the area and he survived, he might do something there in retaliation of what happened to his people. But now that he has come inside, it is as though he has fallen into a trap; he is now in the center of a fishing net.' That is what pains me. Truly, as I sit here now, your presence is heavy on my heart. If it were not for your presence here, I would have gone somewhere else. But I say that I should be near where this issue is discussed so that at least I listen. If it were a destruction that might embrace the whole Sudan, one would have no cause for a personal anxiety. Even if it were a destruction of the whole South, one would have no cause for personal concern. But these are things that happen here in Khartoum.

All I do now is sit and pray to God and gaze on God's face: I say, I will keep my ears open and listen to what is being said. And, of course, it is God that one can now look to and see what he will do to your family. It is the name that will remain which is important. And I look to our father who felt that the continuation of the name was what counted. That I am here being referred to as Ngor, son of Mijok, son of Duor, is a good thing. What disturbs me is the frequency with which the atmosphere shifts in Khartoum. One day happiness prevails and another day, anger prevails: a day of happiness and a day of sadness.

If things were as they were when you were abroad and one were to be heard as having fallen victim of illness, one would accept that as the will of God. But now you are exposed to human dangers that people can do nothing about. And what disturbs me is that your people are placed in a situation where you have to address issues which are not in your hands to resolve. I don't like it. People are behaving in a way which is destroying the tribe and you are not the person in control of the Sudan. And the person called Nimeri is not a man who has permanent friends or people he regards as always good. He is a man who is running the country by the day. If death should come his way, he is willing to face it. But in the meantime, he is working to protect his system. If he hears a person say something that does not appeal to him, he will immediately abandon him. That is what happened to the family of the Mahdi. The way things are being done at home; people are quick to resort to force. But Mading, son of Achok, there is no man who is not a son of man with force.

Your father controlled that tribe through a wide variety of ways. There is no tribe without Deng Majok's cows. Everywhere in Dinkaland, he paid cows. Why he did it that way was not because he was lavish with his wealth; it was security he was after. And indeed, your father managed to take good care of the affairs related to his well-being. And truly that is why he begot you people. When he died, many members of

225

his generation had also died; his death was part of what the Dinka call Aghoc: 'generations passing on.'

So, you see, Mading, man dies and passes on, but he leaves behind a progeny to continue the name. These children whom you have borne may appear as a progeny of a foreign land, but they will carry your name and the legacy of your ancestors. The word of the son of man, the way I am now talking, will be recognized. It will go on and on, never letting the name disappear; and if some good should come out of the earth, people will look around for the available names. The only thing that worries me is that you are now their home and their wilderness; for they have not seen the dignity of your family. They are now like people in the wilderness. And yet, the way your wife behaves toward people shows no gap of appreciation. The way I see her heart, I say that she is superior to all white people. If I were not ill, I would hope to show her your maternal side of the family, and if God were to honor good things that were done in history, it would be appropriate for him to let her witness your background so that she would know that she has married into a breed known for virtue and not for evil.

And it will not be otherwise, Mading, son of my sister Achok; it will be as I now say, however long we may look into the future. You have heard the story of the sister of Mijok Duor. Mijok turned out to be an only child after he lost his sister. Her name has been continued in the family. And then Mijok begot his daughters who were married, and they begot children. That is how you are here. And if what he wanted from your mother's marriage and your own birth is to come true, then he will make your children Dinkas. And even if they should be abroad, they will be Dinkas abroad. It will be said that part of Mijok Duor has spread far into other lands.

But we look to God for all that. There have been times when the world was spoiled. And people dispersed. Man does not wait for disaster to befall him in submission. But even when they disperse, blood does not end; it continues. Our blood is never ended by disaster; all down the line, we have continued. It is natural death that kills our people. All the people I recounted to you, beginning with Dau down to Maluk, son of Dau, the only person who died a violent death was Duor, the son of

Maluk who was killed by a lion. The lion killed him and even ate him at Abyei. And when people cried, a man called Kur-Luak said—'Has the lion eaten Duor Maluk' so that he is now dead!?' They said—'Yes!' He said—'Don't let the people go into the forest after the lion. Let them sing their marshall songs and wait. Tell the man called Ayan Athian (whose son later married Atiu, one of my sisters) to lead the songs. The lion will come out in the open. And when it emerges, let me know; I will have some function to perform.'

When the songs were sung, the lion thundered with roars. People laid down their spears and prayed—'God, are you truly close and listening to our prayers so that you have made the lion cry!?' Then he emerged from the forest with a bundle of grass on his head. They said—'Come, you may kill ten people today, but, in the end, we will kill you and cut your stomach open. But you will not leave after having eaten Duor Maluk. An elder man called Wol Luob said—'What sounds like a lion!?' They said—'It is the lion! He has come!' He said—'Lock me inside the hut; and do not open this hut until he is dead. I do not want to see him alive.' The lion was killed in the open space and his stomach opened.

The affairs of our clan are done with the prudence of the mind and the heart. Our kind does not endear itself to others. Today, the words that I have, if I wanted, I could penetrate Abyei, take it over, and be the one advising and directing the sons of Deng Majok. And I am the one working very hard to keep the people together. And it is your formula which I give to them. I tell them the sort of things you and I have been talking about. But I keep my distance. I have been approached for various positions and I have looked down on them all. I say these positions are not equal to the words I will leave to Mading, the son of my sister. I am a man with a prudent heart and mind, and if I leave my words to my sister's son and they register well to him and he preserves them well to remain, I will have done well. And truly, a man who does not run after another person's food is the one who says a word that will remain. But a person who goes after another person's food says the word of a dish; he only buys food with his words.

I once bought a barrel of beer and said—'Let this be taken to Deng

Abot's house.' He had mats and a large rug spread on the ground for people to sit on. When I came, the place was crowded with people. People all gathered to enjoy the feast. His brother Kwaja then said— 'Gentlemen, enjoy your feast, but remember that this man is here to say something to Deng Abot.' They said—'Is it something that we should not hear!?' And he said—'I think it would be better for us to leave them alone.' They said—'It will be done according to your word.'

When we were alone, I said to him—'Chief Deng, what brought me to your home: you will die and join our fathers who have gone before you. If you listen to my words, you will survive for a longer period of time to perform a task in life before joining them. But if you don't, you will die much sooner. Now, you hear that a chief has been designated. The young generation has now assumed control. The young men of the clan of Malek, people like Monychol are there; Minyiel Ayuak is there; and here you are at your side of Abyei—you will not go. But you have a tradition of leadership. People are now saying: "Deng Majok led the tribe this way; Kwol Arob led the tribe this way; Arob Biong led the tribe this way." And what they are saying does not reflect the affairs of your clan because they do not know.

People are only soliciting food; they are begging the wives of Deng Majok. If you do not go, then you call the son of your brother, seat him in your hut, and talk to him. Tell him the heritage of your family. If you should talk to him with jealousy in your belly, thinking that Deng Majok was, after all, your competitor, the son of your father and not the son of your mother, then whatever goes wrong will be your own doing; and it is you who will be dishonored. But if you do your duty and talk to him, should he deviate from your line and things go wrong, you will at least have your defense in front of God; you will not have discriminated against the children of your father's son. Why I am telling you all this is because I would like you to be around with us in this world and to continue to influence our affairs in a positive way.'

He said to me—'Ngor, son of Mijok, let me tell you the truth. My father, Kwol Arob, did not really love me the way people think. Let me correct the myth of what people say. Before Deng Majok married your sister Achok, I had matured, but had not married the number of

228

wives Deng Majok had already married. Then I went to my father and said—"Father, does Mijok Duor have daughters of marriageable age!?" Father said to me—"Why are you asking?" I said—"I thought that it would be the right family into which to marry!" He said—"Deng, you people have missed the right opportunity for marrying the daughters of Mijok Duor. It would have been fitting for any one of you sons to marry a daughter of Mijok Duor as a first wife and to pay a large bridewealth for her. But that you should come and seek his daughters as junior wives, I will not accept." Then he went ahead and allowed Deng Majok to marry your sister, Achok.

You see, the mind that one wanted from marrying a daughter of Mijok is why Mading, the son of your sister, will be the Head of Deng Majok. And why one wanted that line is precisely what you have now said. No one in our clan or Abyor tribe has thought to tell me what you have told me. But Ngor, I have no role because I am being shunned. It is said that I am still after the chieftainship. Even Kwol (who has succeeded his father as Chief) has become convinced of that.'

I said to Deng Abot—'Talk to him in a way that your dead half-brother will recognize as the voice of his brother and as reflecting his own voice. If you should live, well and good. If you should die, you will have left behind words that will continue.' That was never done. Your uncle heard your brothers talk and decided to remain silent.

So, Mading, those are my words. Take care of your children and they will continue the name. People now say—'What does Mading say about this or that. It is Mading to whom we look for salvation.' Mading, the land is the land of your forefathers. But these children of yours are now in your hands alone. If you are with them to pass your heritage on to them, then they will be Dinkas. That is why I pray to God and to my father that you live to raise them and pass your heritage on to them the way you and I have now talked.

One of my form beliefs in life is that in crises there are opportunities to be identified and utilized. I had Uncle Ngor brought from the village to Khartoum on a health emergency that the leading surgeon in the country, who was a friend, found out to be a collapsed lung. He removed most of the lung and saved the life of Uncle Ngor, whom he described as very strong. Ngor lived into a very old age and died shortly after his sister, whose death he denied, insisting that she had not died but "moved on."

My having taken Uncle Ngor to Khartoum and saving his life, and the fact that his being in Khartoum made it possible to conduct this interview means not only having found and utilized an opportunity in crisis but also having fulfilled an important aspect of my grandfather's aspirations for my life—saving the life of his beloved son. There could have been no greater joy for me than that.

Eight

In the Eyes of a Sister

While Uncle Ngor's account provides some fascinating insights into the tensions and potential or actual conflicts within and between families and clans, my mother herself never conveyed to us—my sisters and myself—a negative sentiment about my father or the circumstances surrounding their marriage. On the contrary, what I remember her saying was unequivocally loving and would tend to indicate the manner in which girls bridge between families and factions through intermarriage. The Dinka put it rather negatively, though only figuratively, by saying that the girl is a "stranger" because she will leave her clan and identify herself with the clan into which she is married. It is probably to counter potential hostilities and conflicts that the Dinka observe elaborate rituals of social avoidance between in-laws, which are associated with "respect," but which also leave the desirable effect of minimizing points of contact and confrontation.

I had a conversation with my mother on some of the issues I discussed with Uncle Ngor. Unfortunately, I did not record our talk. But I do vividly remember the essence of what she said. She certainly emphasized the positives of my identification with my father's line without betraying the point of view of her paternal line. It appeared to me as a case of balancing between loyalties. While Uncle Ngor was cordial in his presentation of relations between the two groups, underlying his perspective was a certain element of deep, though discreet, hostility or adversity, a latent tension that my grandfather had referred to as "feud" which I, the son of their daughter, was to pursue from within the family of their daughter's marriage. It should, however, be stressed that what is meant by avenging a feud is paradoxically positive, for it implies having a son who would grow up in the image of both his paternal and maternal sides and distinguish himself into a leading role in his father's family. This triumph would supposedly promote the standing of his maternal kindred, giving them a constructive victory in the so-called feud.

Considering the vigor with which Uncle Ngor restated his views on the situation, and in light of the close-knit nature of Dinka society, it would be difficult to believe that my father was unaware of my grandfather's expectations from my being and, in particular, that there was an element of adversity to my postulated role. On the other hand, because it was to be pursued through identification with my father, and by inheriting from his "head" to combine with what I would inherit from my grandfather's "head," it combined admiration for my father with objections to certain aspects of his behavior toward my maternal kin. Because of the positive aspect of this ambivalence, Uncle Ngor seemed to believe that the destiny set for me by my grandfather was, in itself, a reason why Father could not be adverse to me—*Deng Majok holds nothing against you in his heart*—said Uncle Ngor—*You see, Deng Majok knew the full story of your life and what my father had done because of you.*

In contrast to Ngor's approach, my mother never saw avenging a "feud" in any fashion as the guiding principle in the upbringing of her children, although she nevertheless injected something of the challenge behind her family's investment in my life. This is presumably why she often cited what my father used to say, that a child loved by God was far better off than a child only loved by his father. The difference between the approaches of Uncle Ngor and my mother was only a matter of emphasis. Whereas Ngor tended to emphasize the angle of adversity, my mother was more conciliatory and bridging.

What is particularly remarkable is that these seemingly divergent approaches were represented by two persons toward whom I felt exceptionally close. My relations with Uncle Ngor were unmatched by any relations between a maternal uncle and his nephew that I have ever come across. I do not have a full brother, so I cannot compare on a concrete basis, but I would say that even a full brother would probably not have been much closer in my sentiments of love and affection than I was to Uncle Ngor. As for my mother, I have always maintained that nothing can match the love of a mother and child and this is from my own experience.

While the words of my sister Ayan reflect much of the spirit with which mother raised us, I find myself poised between Ngor and Ayan's version, as my comments in my conversation with Uncle Ngor indicate. As I have said, Ngor is perhaps somewhat ambivalent about the paternal orientation I grew up with, but Ayan is also exaggeratedly positive in a folk-tale fashion. It is interesting that despite our idealization of our mother, she portrays our father in an even more glorified fashion. On the rare occasions that Father's point of view is well-presented or reasoned while mother's position is presented as lacking in reasoning, appearing almost arbitrary, this is certainly unrecognizable to me because of the intelligence, wisdom and ability with words for which our mother was well known. Nor does Ayan intend to portray our mother otherwise.

In the end, one cannot help concluding that while the Dinka would tend to identify the son more with the father and the daughter more with the mother, there is a deeper level at which the daughter has more empathy with the father and the son with the mother. These sentiments are perhaps constrained on the conscious level by acculturation and social conditioning.

The rest of this chapter is the translation of the tape-recorded conversation with my sister Ayan that took place in the late 1970s. In addition to the matters which I have touched upon in this brief introduction, our conversation also subtly reveals some of the polygamous jealousies, tensions, and conflicts that lie suppressed beneath the otherwise tranquil sea of family unity, harmony, and solidarity.

Some people may find it in bad taste to reveal these internal contradictions, and I have, in fact, omitted some of the details that I considered incongruent to the crux of the book. I have, however, tried to be transparent and credible in telling the whole truth about our family. I do so because I believe that our family has a unique and most remarkable human experience which we ought to share with others. Polygamous jealousies are acknowledged, though undesirable, features of life among the Dinka. Considering the unprecedented size of our family and the numbers of wives and children competing for the love and affection of one man, the problem can be expected to be much more severe in the case of our family. But that was certainly not the case. Our family was and has remained exceptionally close— united and harmonious—despite the numbers. In fact, some members of our family have argued that such large numbers could also be a factor in diffusing the tensions and potential conflicts.

One thing we all agree upon is that our father was a man of extraordinary administrative ability who ran his family with much the same iron hand with which he ran the tribe. He was most intolerant of jealousy and saw to it that he repressed any divisiveness. But jealousies still remained a reality that was aggravated by the societal importance of human relations and the proximity of those relations in the close-knit context of our family. While much of this surfaced more openly after Father's death, it was effectively contained in his lifetime. But an outlet to this repression was found in the constant tendency to interpret misfortune as the work of a jealous and envious co-wife having employed witchcraft to inflict harm on a competing co-wife, her children, or her property—usually cattle.

Everything, including accidents, among the Dinka, has a spiritual cause. And the world of spirits is divided into the virtuous, who do good and punish wrongdoing, and the evil, who afflict the innocent with unwarranted harm. The jealous and envious evildoer is believed to employ the services of "medicine men" or practitioners of witchcraft who in turn use the services of the evil spirits, while the innocent who suffers unwarranted harm may call on God or the virtuous spirits to retaliate with punitive harm on the wrongdoer. Since the supposed wrongdoer is most unlikely to acknowledge wrongdoing, what might seem to the adversary as just punishment may be interpreted as the work of witchcraft. The vicious cycle is thereby continued with mutual incriminations.

While I have omitted some of the details, I have kept allusions to these accusations without siding with either of the competing points of view in order to reveal what I regard as a significant sociological phenomenon of the institution of polygamy. I particularly appeal to my family members, stepmothers, half-brothers, and half-sisters, not to take everything Ayan says literally, but more as a figure of speech, included here not with competitive or comparative intentions, nor in self-promotion, but for reasons of sociological and literary merit and to highlight the operative family value system.

Francis Mading Deng: *Ayan, what I would like to ask you about you have stayed at home and you know the words of our family, both the wider family of our father and our mother's section of that family. I have been somewhat withdrawn from the situation by educational and occupational circumstances. Of course, I know some things about our family, but there are also many things I do not know. I would like to write a book one day, a book about our father and perhaps extending to our grandfather and even myself and the whole of our family. That is why I would like us to converse about the things you know, things relating to our family. Let us start with our maternal relatives and then come to how our mother got married and the life in our father's family. I would like you to tell me everything you know, including the relationship of our mother with our father and other members of the family. Where did your maternal kindred originate from?*

Ayan Deng: *Mading, your words are true. You left home rather early. The background of our birth goes to our maternal grandmother, Ayak, daughter of Deng; Deng, son of Ngor; Ngor, son of Got from the section of Bongo tribe of the Ngok Dinka. There is not a single person in this Ngok tribe who does not know our grandmother, Ayak, daughter of Deng Ngor; not a single person does not know her ancestry. And as for our maternal grandfather, Mijok Duor, he comes from the background about whom Abyor tribe has a classic war song that has remained permanent, the song about 'The (Tawny Cow) Ayan, of Maluk, the Buffalo.' That song is about Maluk, the grandfather of Mijok, our grandfather. What made our father go to marry our mother was the legendary name of Maluk.*
Maluk was a very, very rich man. He was rich with cattle, sheep, and goats. Nothing was equal to his wealth. Maluk begot his son, Duor, and Duor begot Mijok. When Mijok was a small child, he used to sleep in the cattle-byre. Our great-grandfather, Duor, then said—'This child

*of mine is an only son. He cannot sleep alone in the cattle-byre. I shall
sleep with him in the cattle-byre.' He was a huge person. So, he used to
sleep with his son in the cattle-byre. A lion would come and visit, and
come and visit. One day, he came at night. Duor was sleeping. The
cattle-byre was never closed. Duor would place his bed at the door. He
made his bed the barrier with which he blocked the way into the byre
to protect his herd.*

*The herd was so large that it came close to the doorway. One day,
the lion came in the middle of the night. He entered the byre. As our
great-grandfather tried to get up, they got entangled. He struggled
and struggled with the lion in the byre until the lion eventually killed
him. The lion broke his neck. Duor spoke to his small son, Mijok, and
said—'Mijok, I am dead, climb up the central poles of the cattle-byre.'
Mijok was a very small boy. He then went up. The lion remained down
with his father. The sun then rose. But no one came from the byre to
the nearby huts where the women stayed. The woman, the mother of
Mijok, then spoke and said—'Oh, my people, why is the cattle-byre
so silent? Why does no one come from the byre?' That was our great-
grandmother, Nyanger. 'I must go to check.' She went. And when she got
there, she found the lion with the remains of the man in the byre. She
screamed. She believed that both her husband and her son were gone.
She cried out loud. The people then ran swarming to the area. The
lion, which had eaten the father of Mijok, was then killed. That is how
that area became known as the Creek of Mijok's Father— the Creek at
Bogek.*

*Our grandfather then remained a single son. He grew up. He remained
alone in the great wealth of his father. He prospered and prospered
in that great wealth. The cow, Ayan of Maluk (referred to in the war
song), was the only sacred cow whose milk he drank. He would not
drink from the milk of any other cow. He only drank the milk of
Ayan. Up to this day, our maternal relatives consider any cow with the
color of Ayan as sacred. If a cow of Ayan color is acquired, she is never
disposed of. If a person disposes of Ayan, the color of the original cow of
Maluk, it becomes a major curse upon that person.*

Our grandfather then married and his children, including our mother, were born. Our mother, Achok, was one of the youngest of the daughters. There were Atiu and Nyanagwek before her. They then grew up. Achok was then betrothed to a man from Abyor tribe. She was still a small child. She had not yet reached puberty. Achok rejected the man to whom she had been betrothed. She refused him with a great determination. Her father also joined her in rejecting the man. But their entire clan was in favor of the man, saying—'This man has offered too large a bridewealth to be rejected. We cannot leave him.' The man was from the marital family of our father's aunt, Achaidit. Our father then said—'I cannot miss from the daughters of Mijok Duor, the Great Strong man who leads Abyor in both courage and wisdom. I cannot accept not marrying into his family.' Our paternal grandfather, Kwol Arob, then said—'But, my son, I am rather embarrassed that it is the son of my sister who has engaged the girl.' Father insisted—'I will not accept.' Grandfather then said—'If she is already betrothed, what shall we do?' Father said—'I will marry her.' He debated the issue with our grandfather for a long time.

Father's brother, Uncle Biong Mading, then said—'This thing will never be! Deng, son of my mother, if we leave this girl, where shall we find a similar crop to marry in this land of the Ngok? What our father is doing shows disfavor for us, the children of Nyanaghar. This is part of the old story that he did not love you, but Deng Abot. This is why he says that you should not marry this girl. He does not want your name to rise above Deng Abot.' Father then said—'I will never accept that. So, Biong Mading, let us release our own cattle for the marriage.' Father and Biong Mading then went ahead and collected the bridewealth by themselves. But our grandfather, Mijok, rejected the cattle. He said— 'Why should I receive bridewealth from children? I must hear from your father.'

So, they returned and spoke again to their father, Kwol Arob. Kwol then said—'My sons, there was nothing I disliked about marrying into Mijok's family. Mijok Duor is my partner in the leadership of this tribe. If you want to persuade your aunt's son to leave the girl for you, and you want to appease him with cattle, then I have no objection. I will go and speak with the father of the girl.'

237

That is how our grandfather, Kwol Arob, went and talked with Mijok Duor. Mijok Duor then said—'Kwol Arob, I do not want cattle from you. I am not in need of wealth.' Kwol said—'Mijok, why are you bragging like that?' Mijok said—'I mean it; I do not want your cows. I will give you my daughter with only a few cows as a token bridewealth so that you know that it is not the need for wealth that has induced me to give her to you. I am giving her to you because of my son, Ngor. I would like him to have Deng as his brother; Ngor is a single son.' Kwol said—'Is that it?' Mijok answered—'Yes, Ngor is presently without a brother.' Kwol then said—'Very well.'
The cattle for the marriage were then released and sent to Mijok for the marriage of Achok. Mijok Duor in turn gave a reverse payment of so many cows that he confused the people. It did not look like the customary reverse bridewealth. He gave all that wealth to Deng Majok. And whenever a girl was married in the family of Mijok Duor, our grandfather said—'Achok must share in the bride wealth.'

Francis Mading Deng: *Did Achok and Deng Majok not elope?*

Ayan Deng: *Yes. The man who had first betrothed Achok went and brought his age-mates to abduct her. That was the son of Achaidit. He said—'Deng Majok will never take my wife from me.' So, he came with his age-mates and they abducted Achok and carried her to his family home. Mijok Duor's family rose with spears to attack. So, she was promptly returned. Then she was taken by Deng Majok and his brothers. Deng Majok's cattle had already been paid. But that man was still saying that he would never leave the girl for Deng Majok. Biong Mading saw that and said—'If we do not take this girl, our father may again be persuaded to support the son of his sister. We better take her.' Though she was returned and then later on given to her husband in the proper way.*

Francis Mading Deng: *Was she still a small girl then?*

Ayan Deng: *Yes, she was still a small girl. She had now reached puberty, but she had not yet completed the rites of puberty, guup. (When a Dinka girl first reaches puberty and starts menstruating, she spends a whole year during which she is ritually barred from cow's milk. After that, she is ritually purified and acknowledged as a matured girl. This rite is known as guup.) Achok went, but she stayed for a long time without conceiving. She stayed for many years before you were born. Agorot (a spirit which is believed to affect a girl who gets married before puberty and prevents her from giving birth until she is ritually purified with appropriate sacrifice of animals), was preventing her from conceiving.*

She spent at least two years without conceiving. Weldhou, her cousin, then brought a bull to be sacrificed for Agorot. It had then been divined that it was Agorot who had been preventing Achok from conceiving. The bull was Mading. Mading was then slaughtered at our home as a sacrifice for Agorot. As soon as Mading was slaughtered, you were conceived. When you were born, you were then called Mading, but your real name was Arob. That was your clan name. But you became known as Mading.

When you were born, Mijok Duor would not allow even women to sing lullabies to you. He said he was to be the only person to take care of you and to sing lullabies to you. He would sit singing and rattling the lullaby gourd all night until morning. He would say—'Achok, you go to sleep.' And whenever our grandmother Ayak Deng Ngor rose and offered to relieve him, he would say—'This is why I gave my Achok to Deng Majok; it was because of this Mading of mine. So, you Ayak, take your rest and go to sleep. You have nothing to do with this child. He is entirely mine. You will take care of the child Achok will bear after Mading. As for this child, it is I alone who will take care of him.'

And when you were taken to be weaned, it was our grandfather, Mijok Duor, who took you and said—'Ayak will remain at home and I shall take the child to the cattle-camp.' It was he who weaned you. He took you to the cattle-camp and spent the autumn with you in the grass plains of toc (dry season grazing lands) and then spent the winter with you in the woodlands of gok (the rainy season grazing land). He took care of you until you were grown up. Our grandfather died shortly after you were brought back into our family. But your earlier years were spent with our maternal relatives.

When our sister, Awor, was born, our grandfather then spoke to our grandmother, Ayak Deng Ngor, and said—'Ayak, there is your child; take care of her.' He would sometimes take care of Awor himself and even sing lullabies to her and then say—'Now Ayak, relieve me in taking care of Awor. Let us leave Achok alone. Why I gave her to Deng Majok was so that she would beget children for me. I wanted the breed of Kwol Arob.' And Kwol Arob also wanted the breed of Mijok Duor. When you grew up, our father then said that you were to go to school. When Achok saw that, she cried and said—'My only son, Mading, how can he be taken away!? If he should go to school, I will leave this home. I will not remain here. What would I do if he is gone?'

Our father laughed and said—'You talk of Mading being an only child, but is that not all I wanted from Mijok Duor!? I wanted this single Mading. I did not want ten children. I wanted a single child who would resemble Mijok Duor. The way Mading speaks now, if God saves him and our ancestral spirit Ring works well, he will grow up to be a big man and his name will be heard in this Ngok tribe. His name will rise to be known that there is Mading, son of Deng. The fact that he is a single son will escape your own mind, you, Achok, and leave me aside, I, the person who sent him to school. His being a single son is insignificant. Education will one day turn him into three sons for me. And there is yet another thing. Our grandfather once said—"If a woman bears five boys or even three boys, then those children are not our kind. They would not be our children. But if a woman comes and begets a single son to be followed by girls, then the son that woman would have born, even if people wait for a long time, the name of that child will one day be heard." That is the nature of our kind. Our kind does not produce many boys. We beget a single boy. Don't you see that our original ancestor was a single son? And when it came to people like my father, the same situation continued. Every woman who would come and beget two sons, her sons did not grow into the right image. But when a woman bears a single son, that is the woman whose name eventually gets heard. For instance, Awor Mou, from whom we have

240

descended, did not have two sons. She bore Kwol, a single son among daughters. When the other boys were called by her name, people like Koor and Mioriik, they were adopted and given to her because she did not have many children. So, these boys were added to her only son. But Kwol was born a single son. That single Kwol, how many homes belonging to him have fires burning now, you Achok? The fires of that single Kwol, how many of them are now kindled? The fires which Kwol now kindles, my Mading will one day kindle. And if we have combined in Mading the hearts of Mijok Duor and Kwol Arob, even if a long time should pass, his name will be heard. And when he begets his own children, he will not beget a single son. His firstborns will be two boys and even five boys. He will not beget a single son. It is the boys he will beget who will have among them one who will bear a single son. So, you Achok, my wife, if it is the heart I wanted from Mijok Duor that has now come with Mading, then you stop crying over his going to school. Mading will compensate for all that. My Mading will be more important than the ten boys in my family if he goes to school. Do not shed tears for his sake. Do not cry.'

Achok said—'A house in which girls are left and a single son is taken away, what kind of goodness is in such a home?'

But Father said—'Never mind. These girls are also like sons. If nothing touches them, they can stay with you and occupy the place of a son. And Mading will go, but nothing will take him from you. He will return to you.'

Those words of our father we have considered and found to be true. When we thought of Kwol Arob, and saw that he was an only son, and then we see his family and the number of children he has produced, how many are they? If all the descendants of Kwol Arob are gathered, they will be enough to hold a dance by themselves alone. And they are all descendants of that single Kwol. We also discussed the matter with Mother while I was still a little child. I said—'Mother, why do you cry? You hear our father say that Kwol Arob, who was an only son, has produced this large family. Perhaps, even though Mading is your only son, he will grow up to have as large a family in the future as the family of Kwol.'

Mother said—'What nonsense! You are just being foolish. Otherwise,
you too would join me in opposing Mading's going to school.' I said—'As
for me, Ayan, I will not oppose it.'
And Awor said—'Why should we oppose his going to school? Is he going
to die? Will he not come back to us? Let him go to school. Don't you see
other children also going to school!?'
Later, when our father said that he wanted to take us to school also,
that was when Achok then said—'Now that you have taken Mading,
please do not also take the girls away. You will destroy my heart.' Father
said—'I would like to take at least Ayan to school. Even if Awor
remains, I want Ayan to go to school. She will join Mading so that they
can later visit one another and see how they are.' Achok said—'That
is what will never be. If you do it that way, then I shall leave this
house.' My father then said—'Very well, I shall not insist. If you are
so adamant, then I will leave your daughters to stay with you. I have
nothing more to say.'
The way our mother Achok lives in that family, the family of Deng
Majok, was well illustrated by Father at Noong when he said—'My
wives, all of you at Noong, the person to whom I have entrusted you is
Achok Mijok. If anything is too formidable for Achok, then it could be
too formidable even for me, Deng Majok. Achok does not care about
the person who will give her something. Nor does she worry about a
person who will gossip against her. She concerns herself with anyone
she comes across doing the wrong thing. She will immediately intervene
and say—"So and so, you are destroying the family of Deng. Why do
you do this or that!?" If she finds any of my children hungry, Achok
will never keep food from my child of another wife and give it to her
own child. So, you in my village, Noong, I have placed you under the
leadership of Achok. Whatever problem will face you here, Achok will
point it out to me.'
And all that is true. Our mother, for as long as she has lived in that
family, has never filled her stomach with food. And it is not because she
lacks anything. It is because she says—'My children, a woman in such
a large family must never fill her stomach. If she fills her stomach, she
may leave a person hungry near her. And that is not good.' Even her

style of talking with other women at home, she has never talked in a manner of pride about her background or her own status. Never. If she sees a proud person, that is the person she will rebuke and say—'That is not the way to behave. A large family of a Chief like this, you care about the poor and the needy and you help meet their needs. You do not brag that you are of noble status. That is bad.'

When we got married, our father made a remark. He said—'Biong Mading, haven't you seen what I was seeking from Mijok Duor? That is why there is now Mading who has excelled with education. If he continues with his determined heart, Mading will one day keep lighting the fire I have kindled and will make it shine brightly. And the daughters of Achok, don't you see the way they get married with cattle that are staggering in numbers. I do not know about her little girls like Aluong and Nyanluak. But as long as they are girls born by Achok, I am confident that their marriages will also produce cattle. Even if I wait to be old, this will come true.' Our father never suspected that he would die that early. He was only concerned about old age.

When I got married, I spoke to my father and said—'Father, you know that Mading is an only son and you want me to marry an only son, when Achok has no sons; I do not like that. I do not want Loth. His brothers have all died. My mother is without sons and then I go to a home without people, that is not right. Now, as we are here, if there is anything troubling our mother, we can see it. And if there is anything troubling Mading and it is something which can be remedied here at home, we can also do it. A sister usually fetches a brother for her brother. If your sister is married by a man with a heart, you can win and capture that man and turn him into a son of your mother. Loth is now responsible alone for his mother's family. And here is Achok without a son to second Mading. How shall I manage to bring Loth to Achok's side? This cannot be. I cannot go with Loth.'

Then he said—'My daughter, have you never heard what I once told your mother?' I said—'What was it you told my mother?' He said— 'When I was so persistent about marrying your mother, I said to her— "Achok, why I am so determined to marry you, it is not because of the wisdom for which you are personally known; it is the breed of Mijok

243

Duor I want. If Mijok has begotten daughters who are so straight-faced, and able to speak such words of wisdom, then if he were to pass his qualities to a grandson from his daughter, that son could do great things for his father." My daughter, leave the issue of a single son. The issue of a single son is not significant. You may see Loth as a single child in his mother's home. But if anything comes in the middle of the night to attack your mother's son, Mading, and it is said that Mading says— "Let this or that be done," all the husbands of your sisters, even if each one of them had ten brothers to assist him, I am sure Loth would excel among them all. Loth would be the first to visit Mading. He would be where Mading would sleep. And should there be anything threatening Mading with death, if it is Loth, he would die together with Mading. I will not withdraw my word and accept someone else's cattle. There are many men each one of whom comes and says—"I would like to marry Ayan." But I have refused them all. Loth is the only man I have accepted. He will marry you.'

I said—'Well, yours is obviously not love! It is hatred.' He said—'Is it?' And I said—'Yes, it is hatred.' Then he said—'My daughter, it is not hatred. And you Ayan, if a man were to take his heart out to stand apart so that you could examine my heart, I am sure you would find that of all my children in their entirety, deep inside me, I, Deng, when I evaluate them, I consider you to be the top of all my children. And why do I consider you the top? It is because whenever I hear the words you say and I look into them, I find that they are not the words of a girl, but the words of a man. Because of your wisdom, I do not want you to go to a house where you will meet any hardships. I want you to be in a place where the person who takes you will recognize that you are a noble woman and you also recognize that person as a noble man. I want you to live with the weight of dignity. But that you should go to a house where you will be disgraced with indignity, where you will be turned into a lightweight, where your husband will not show me the appropriate respect, and where your mother's son, Mading, whom you call a lone son, will not receive appropriate respect, that I do not want. I want Loth.'

I said—'Very well. There is nothing else I can do. I do not want Loth, but I will not escape. I will stay and wait. If God wills that I go there, then it will be according to your word. But if God does not will that I go, then there will one day appear something you do not like in this marriage and you will abandon the idea.'

He thought about it and called Achok. And said—'Achok, do you not hear what Ayan says?' Achok said—'Chief, how can you say such a terrible word?' He said—'What word?' She said—'How can you ask me about the responsibility for the girls? Is that why you sent Mading to school, so that you would ask me why things happen the way they do? Responsibility for girls is not placed on their mother. It is placed on their brother. If you have found them to be girls without a brother, so that I have become the responsible person to be questioned, then I want you to know that I am not a part of it. I, Achok, I do not want to get involved in that. If you have found them to be without a responsible person, you wait for Mading until he returns. You can then ask him—"Mading, is this man suitable for your sister or not?" If he says—"No," then you will discuss with him. If he says—"Yes," then the matter will have ended there between the two of you. As for me, I shoulder no responsibility for the girls. What brought me into this household, and God came and told me—"Achok, you will have only one son and the rest of your children shall be girls," meant that I would not be involved in discussing those matters.

'I shall only hope in my Mading. If the spirits of the clan of Arob Biong protect him for me, that is what counts to me. As for the daughters, what can a daughter do for a person? Is it a share in the cattle of their marriages that is so significant, or what? But if my Mading survives and gets married, I shall one day live with him and I will take care of his children. Should I be too old, he will keep me near him, and I will live near him if I have become incapable of doing anything myself. But as long as I am still able to do things myself, he will always come to find me, holding his name up high, and I will keep my house to be pointed at: "This is the house of Mading's mother." You can go ahead and marry off your daughters to whomever you want.'

Father then laughed and said to me—'Ayan, the words your mother has said have again confirmed that your mother is a person of great shrewdness. I can never outwit her. She has proved too formidable for me up into her old age. She starts a problem, but when I get close to catching her, she explains it all away and swears on all convincing oaths so that I find myself disarmed. So, you, Achok, yours is a great skill which I do not think I can ever succeed in overcoming. I thought I was going to find you involved in this question of Ayan. But if you are out of it, then you walk your clear path. Nothing bad will touch you, Achok. And as for you, Ayan, I shall appease you; I shall marry a wife to be your helper. That wife will fetch water for you; she will make tea for you; and whatever is lacking for you, she will go and look for it. She will come to me and say—"Deng, this is lacking from Ayan." And I will send it to you. She will be with you until you go to your marital home. The girl this woman will bear one day, if she grows up and gets married, even if I am old, you have the right to claim—"This is the daughter of a wife with whom my father appeased me in the past." You will share in the cattle of her marriage. But I urge you to accept my word. Let Loth be a brother to Mading. I do not want anyone else to marry you.'

He then goes into details about what attracted Deng Majok to Loth. There was a fight between the Arabs and the Dinka in which Loth speared and killed an Arab who had killed a Dinka and severely injured others in battle. He was arrested and sent to prison in the North. After a period of time, he was tried and sentenced to death. Apparently, Chief Deng Majok eventually interceded on his behalf and the sentence was commuted to imprisonment and the prison term was further reduced. Loth served the sentence and was released. Father explained the situation to Ayan.

'And why I favor Loth so much is because of a prison he was in. If he were a weak person, he would have suffered and might even have died. But he lived through that imprisonment with surprising courage. They even fixed the days after which he was to be hanged. And yet his courage remained above it all. I found him before the fixed days ended. He said to me—"Chief, the word of my death is not significant. Do not let my death pain your heart. If I were dying for a personal cause or for the sake of my own family, then I would feel pain. But I am dying

for what I did in defense of our people, the Ngok. I am dying for the redemption of the tribe. If my death redeems my tribe, then nothing can be altogether bad about my death. Do not let your heart fear my death.' 'Then I said to him—"If you have truly disregarded your being hanged with such courage, then you will no longer hang. The Power that will insist on hanging you will hang me instead, and not you." My daughter, why he faced that situation with such a determined heart, spending seven years and waiting to be hanged the eighth year—then I refused to have him hanged and he got instead another seven years, and he completed those additional seven years—why he endured all that with courage, is why I cannot let you go with another man. You must go with him. The heart of Mijok Duor and my own heart, I Deng, and the heart of Adija Ajak, if all three combine, then you will one day produce a child like my Mading. And truly, if God were to listen to prayers, you would have a son for your first born, so that he promotes your name in fulfillment of the words I have said.'

I said—'Father, I have no more to say. The words you have now pronounced are spiritual words which can carry a curse with them. My mother, Achok, does not have many children. She has only us girls. There is our Awor, and myself, and the small girls. There is Mading alone, without brothers. If one of us were to persist in her own opinion, and sever relations with you, even for reasons that are not justified, you will insult our brother. You may say—"What else can one expect from a brother of girls who behave the way his sisters did!? I have nothing to do with you children of Achok." Even if there is no wrongdoing by the children of Achok, knowing you Father, you will insult our brother with reference to what you will call the misconduct of his sisters. That will not be. Our mother has reached old age. She cannot be disgraced by a child she has borne. I will stay. There is nothing I can do. I have surrendered to your wish.' That is how I have remained to this day. Now, as we talk, Achok, in Dinkaland, every penny she has ever received from you, Mading, she has never eaten it with her mouth. She has never swallowed it. The day she receives the money, every Deng Majok's wife who is struggling with a child, she divides the money into their hands. And women say—'Mother of Mading, why do you take so much trouble!?' Even tea, when Achok buys tea, she will make tea and divide it into cups and cups and cups. And when people say—'Mother of Mading, what is the matter? Do you think that an elder person is not entitled to eat?' She would say—'O wives of Deng, what do you think makes a man travel a long way to bring the daughter of a stranger as a wife? It is because of old age and the unknown future. No one knows what old age will do and who may die first, the wife or the husband. If Deng has died and we have remained the mothers of his sons who are now walking in this Ngok country, we cannot eat while the junior wives of Deng Majok remain without food.'

When our cattle go to Nainai where Achok is living, she milks the cows and distributes the milk to all the children of Deng Majok and to the wives of Deng Majok. Even during the daytime, if one comes after the cows have already been milked, she will take the gourd containing the milk for butter and will give it to the person. And when she is told— 'Achok, what about butter, are you not going to make butter from the milk?' She would say—'Is butter greater than Deng Majok? If Deng Majok were to be disgraced in his grave that will immediately bring disgrace upon my son. Although Deng is dead, insults are contagious in families.' Today, we the children begotten by Deng Majok and borne by Achok Mijok, wherever we may travel, there is nothing that can make us stretch our backs to peek into other people's situations out of want or envy. There is nothing that can be more delicious than our father. Nothing can be more delicious than the things our father had done.

When you, Mading, went and married, some people who were negatively disposed said—'Now, Achok has become a person of no value. Now that her son has gone and married a white girl, will he ever return to this land? Will he not remain forever in the country of white people? Even the children he will beget, will they ever know Achok? Will Achok ever see the children of her son? So, you, Achok, you better tie your belt with the daughters. What else can you do?'

Achok said—'People, as we talk, we know that Deng has married from the Nuer; Deng has married from the Rek; and it is the children he begot from those marriages who are walking today in this country. Even if Mading has married there, he married there knowing still that he has a mother here. However far he may travel, he will one day come with that wife of his. However white she may be, she will become darker; the children she will bear will be dark. His wife will remain white, but her children will be dark enough to recognize that I am their grandmother. And if God were to listen to prayers, it would be fitting that this woman whom people have prejudged so much should bear children. Deng Majok will bless her to bear in good health so that she bears children to be seen and recognized as the breed of Deng Majok.'

And all that is true. Our father once said something. He gave examples of marriages and said—'My children, in marriage a man can make his wife change to resemble him.'

Mother later referred to this saying by Father and added—'The God who made Mading go to marry there will help make his wife resemble Mading, the same way those men Deng Majok referred to changed their wives into their image. Mading will change his wife into his image. And even though she may be very far from me and we do not meet, I am sure she will one day resemble me, Achok, however far away she may be. The heart that has maintained me in the family of Kwol Arob, I am sure will pass on to the wife of Mading. She will settle her heart down to the point where she will flourish in this country. People will one day say—"So, the wife Mading went and brought from far away has truly settled and flourished!" So, if our clan spirits know the words of Truth, then we pray that her first children be boys and that she may acquire my heart to be like me in this family. Why Deng Majok said those words about wives resembling their husbands, I hope those words will apply to Mading and that his wife will turn out to resemble him so that it will one day be said that "A long, long time ago, there was a man called Mading, the son of a woman called Achok. When he went to school, he went and learned so much that he went abroad to continue learning. There, he went and married. And the wife he brought from there came and excelled among all the wives of the children of Deng Majok." It is fitting that God makes this come true.'

Then I said—'Achok, have you ever seen her? If you go now, you will see her kneeling and advancing in front of the people on her knees to serve just like a Dinka girl.'

249

Then Aunt Achol Mijok said—'My God, is it true, Mother Ayak, daughter of Deng Ngor!? If she has learned to go on her knees, then she will learn to greet in Dinka, Ci yi bak. And once she knows that, all will be well. The name of Ayak, daughter of Deng Ngor will continue to be heard in this tribe.'

They were sitting, three of them: Achok, Achol, and their brother Ngor. Achol went on to say—'Ngor, son of my mother, God will work. If God has saved Mading to remain alive, and he has now married, then all is well. What used to vex us was when Mading remained unmarried. It was then said—"The only son of Achok, how can he not marry to beget children!?" But now that he has married, nothing is bad. If it is Mading as we know him, he will teach her Dinka to the point where she will know us all, the Family of Ayak Deng Ngor.'

Then I said—'You know, Aunt Achol Mijok, when we went, she asked about the son of Atiu and said—"Mading, how are we related to this man!?" It was then explained to her. Then she went and greeted him. Whenever any person goes, she asks—"Are you from the family of Achok or from the family of Deng Majok?"'

Achok then said—'Does she really refer to me by my name?' I said— 'Yes.' Then she said—'Ngor, son of my mother, just hear that! These are the things that will take me to where Mading is in Arab-land to go and see that wife.' Aluong said—'If you go now Achok, what language will you greet her in!?' She said—'Why! Aluong, of course, I will say Ci yi bak.' Aluong said—'What!? Achok, you mean you would not even attempt the Arabic language?' Achok said—'Why should I greet her in Arabic? I will greet her in Dinka so that she knows that we are the true Monyjang—the central part of the Dinka are properly called Monyjang—the race into which she has married. There are different kinds of Dinka. There are the peripheral Dinka who attach themselves to others and there are the Dinka at the very center.' Ngor said—'When I go, I will tell her—"I am Ngor, the son of Mijok, Mijok, the son of Duor, who begot Achok, Mading's mother. Your husband, Mading, when he was born, it was my father Mijok who used to hold him—that Mading of yours who has now married you."

Then Achok said—'Ngor, is that what you are concerned about!? What really concerns me is that God does not do things perfectly well. If he has made my Mading marry, he should have married while Deng was still alive, so that Deng Majok sees the wife of Mading with his own eyes; so that Deng Majok sees with his own eyes the child Mading will beget, and then die. Anyway, there is nothing I can do. These are things that have occurred with the will of God. But if Deng does truly know the words of Truth where he lies in his grave, then he will bless my grandchildren. This is the Mading whom he used to say would beget the breed of Awor Mou, that the same kind of breed which Awor Mou had born would be begotten by Mading. He said to me that the son of Awor Mou—his father, Kwol—was also an only son, and yet he had kindled all those fires. He told me that all the fires of Awor Mou, which Kwol had kindled, would one day be kindled by my Mading. So, if the tongue of Deng Majok proves correct and Mading kindles all these fires, that is what I pray for at night and during the day. Sometimes, when these thoughts cross my heart, I do not sleep; I remain awake praying all night. These are the words I count in my heart.'

Then I said—'Achok, there is no need to speak such words anymore. It is all God's work. There can be nothing better than the children he has now begotten—that Deng of his and Jok and whoever else he may still beget; no one knows whether it will be a girl or a boy. That is known only to God.'

And truly, that wife of Mading, if it could be said that a person generates resemblance in another person, I would say that Achok has found resemblance in Mading's wife even though she is a foreign girl. That heart of hers, when I watch her behavior and all things connected with her conduct, including the fact that she does not care about food for herself, I see her like our mother Achok. Achok does not think about her own hunger or about her own self. The hunger of night or day, Achok knows neither. She never complains of hunger. And that is the way the wife of Mading is. You find her working so hard that you believe she must have already eaten. But no, she will not have eaten at all.

I asked her one day—'How do you live now?' She said—'What do you mean?' And I said—'Why is it that you do not eat?' She said—'Don't I

251

eat now?' And I said—'You take a small bite at the table and then you get up to do this or that. How can you live that way?' She laughed and said—'Ayan, a person who cooks cannot die of hunger. While I cook, I stir the stew and taste it. And then I may lay my hands on small things here and there and nibble on them. That is enough. I become quite satisfied. I become satisfied with my eyes as I cook. I feel no hunger after that.' Then I said—'I see what you mean. That is the same thing our mother had told us. She had said to us—"My children, when a person cooks, remember that a woman does not prepare a separate dish for herself. When you are married and you have your own home, do not prepare dishes for yourself. Once the woman of the house prepares a separate dish for herself, that house is destroyed. A house in which the woman gives herself a separate dish is a broken home. You should prepare the meal, count all the people in your home, and prepare a dish for every one of them. There will be someone among them who will not finish his dish. What will remain from what you have given should be your dish from which to eat. That is the food from which you will gain weight. But if you prepare a dish for yourself, should need arise one day and you lose your separate dish, you will miss it and your heart will keep wishing you had the dish to which you are accustomed. That way, you get reduced and you become lean from wishful thinking. That is how women become skinny in their homes. It is that they become too used to a food and cannot do without, should need arise. A woman should adapt herself to eating what remains when everyone else in her house has had enough. When a woman does that, then her house will remain a home of dignity and decency. Every year will come and you, the woman, will retain your attractiveness. You will not miss food and become lean. But the woman who worries about what to put in her mouth is not a woman."

I said—'But Achok, this is a difficult training you have given us. How can it be good if people do not eat?'

She said—'Never. You girls remember my words, all of you.'

And sure enough, all of us who were born by Achok, when one is found in her house, we are found to be exceptional. That is why our sister Nyannyop said something when she found me having newly given birth on her return from her home in Twichland. We were in the house of our father's wife, Nyanawai. I came out wearing a shirt. We came out of the hut, three of us, Aluong, myself, and Nyanawai's daughter, Nyapath. We greeted Nyannyop. Then she spoke to me saying—'O really, is it you, Ayan, mixing with these little girls and looking as young as they are?' I said—'What are you talking about, Nyannyop?' She said—'Yes, I mean it. You are the only married girl I have found to have retained her attractiveness in this home of Deng Majok. All the girls of Deng Majok who are married in Ngok, not a single one of them has retained her appearance. They have all changed; they have sunken faces. What is it that preserves your appearance so well every single year? Tell me, sister. Your home must be exceptionally prosperous. Perhaps it excels among the homes of Deng's daughters!'

Nyapath then said—'Yes, Ayan's home is not like the homes of the rest.' Aluong said—'Sister, the home of Ayan is a home of vanity. Her husband is vain and Ayan too is vain. It is not a home in which people worry about what to eat. And people do not worry about spending too much on guests. They slaughter lambs whenever any guest arrives. When Ayan runs out of shoes, they sell a cow. Everything is done. What can vex a person under such circumstances!?'

Nyannyop then said—'Daughter of my father, keep your head firm. I always preach to our father's daughter, Adau, and say—"Adau, being so reduced to skin and bones is shameful. Looking as lean as you do is not good. It gives the impression that one is in need. I, Nyannyop, people see me looking well and believe that there is no hardship of any kind in my house. But a person should not permit hardships to make her lean. What is missing today is missing. Tomorrow, when you find it again, you have it." So you, Ayan, keep your heart firm. You children born by Achok Mijok provide us with a model. You continue in that path of yours Sister.'

That was what Nyannyop said to us. And she continued her praise for Achok's daughters: 'When Your Sister Awor was alive as a wife in the home of Deng Luar, she had held the whole of Mannyuar tribe which had been broken down by bad examples. Our name had been disgraced by those examples. But when she went, Mannyuar became good because

*of her. Had she not died; she would be the person receiving the greatest
amount of praise in the family of Deng Majok—as the best person. So,
do your best. We will then wait and see whether Nyanluak will also
be like you. And Aluong's generation will remain to be tested later on.'
Aluong said—'As for me, my way is clear and it is my own. Whether I
am lean or fat, it is all my own. No one should ask me about that. Why
should people be questioned on their weight?'
We all laughed. What was meant was evaluation of a woman's
heart. For a girl, inheriting the qualities of the mother is by far more
important than inheriting from a man. If a mother has passed on to
her children the qualities of her heart, then the children of that woman
will live united and guided by that single heart of their mother. Yes, we
the children of Achok, we are living by the single heart of our mother.
To this day, I, Ayan, the way I see it, we have a good and proud past to
be satisfied with and to build upon. We are living on that past good.
We have experienced good things that some people may dismiss as
part of a long gone past, but we still derive pride and dignity in all
that. And we do not envy anyone. Even if we see a good thing with
someone else, or see someone showing off a good dress, or hear someone
bragging—'I am a person of dignity,' we look down on all that. I
despise it all. No dignity can surpass what we had when our father was
alive. No nobility can surpass our nobility. Even though time has passed
and taken what we had, we remain a noble people of great dignity.
Even if other people may not recognize it, we have a dignity known
to God. And it is God who did everything that way; no one else did
it. So, we only pray for God to save us into the future, we the children
born into this family. Those are things we pray. What one says in prayer
is—'God, if you have taken our father away as you have done, then
save our brother Mading.'
Some days ago, things were being said here in Khartoum about this and
that. And I said to the people—'Please people, I am a person who easily
gets worried. I feel tempted to get close to the family of my brother.' That
was when you, Mading, had gone to Abyei. I said—'Monytuch, how
can you leave Mading's children alone in the house? How can a woman
sleep with the children alone in the house? If you do not want to sleep*

in the house, then I think I better go to keep her company until Mading returns.' Monytuch said—'When you were in your house in Dinkaland, did you not sleep at home alone with the children whenever your husband was away?' I said—'But would I sleep in a hut alone while there would be people in the village? Girls would join me to keep me company. What sort of a home would people lock a woman up and leave?' He said—'A woman guarded by the police, what harm can come to her?' And I said—'All the same! Those children of Mading, don't consider them merely his sons. They are the brothers our father once spoke about when he said that Mading would bear his own brothers. These are his brothers; do not consider them his children. He is still to beget his own children. But these are his brothers—brothers who will grow and catch up with him. Mading is still young; he is not yet old. Both Deng and Jok, give them three more years and they will catch up with Mading; they will become age-mates and will then walk together like brothers. Then, Mading will beget the boys who will be his sons. But these sons are brothers to Mading.'

Whenever I see them, it is God and my father whom I call upon to save Deng and Jok, to be sons to Achok. Before they were born, Achok used to worry a great deal, but now she sleeps well. She now hears it said—'Jok is very much like Ngor Mijok. And Achok, have you seen Deng? He is exactly Deng Majok.' Achok now prays and says—'God and Deng Majok, please save them. This is what you, Deng Majok, had said to me. Now that they are here, let them sleep well so that they will promote my name and people will say—"Achok has three sons" so that my image is enhanced. Before them, I was vexed by the idea of a single son. Now, it is said that Achok has three boys. My sons have become three.'

Adija now says—'Nyanwut, the sons of Achok, when they come, we shall play with them. Achok now says that she has two sons with Mading and that with her son Mading, her sons have become three. We will join them, you and me and Anger, daughter of Nyanluak, and we shall all play together as the children of Achok.' Truly, Achok is now pleased. She now appears to have people. But previously, she nearly died of worrying about not having children. When she looked at me, she saw

*me without a child. When she looked at Mading, she saw that Mading
had not procreated. That worried her a great deal. It almost killed her.
Awor had already gone into the ground with her children. That baffled
Achok. She thought that her name would never be mentioned through
her grandchildren. But now, Deng Majok has compensated her.*

*It is a compensation Father predicted a long time ago when he said
to our mother—'Although you do not have many children, that single
Mading will bear your children.' Now, he has compensated her; if only
God saves Deng and Jok and saves their mother too. It is the woman
who educates the children. Through that good heart of hers, she will
educate them to the point where these sons of Mading will know the
ways of Biong Allor and Arob Biong. Now, they have already begun
to know their people. Deng's ability with words is clearly our father's
ability. We need not even think of tracing it to anyone else. That is our
father's heredity. As for Jok, the things he does clearly show the behavior
of Ngor Mijok. It is not the behavior of anyone else. God did it that
way to make Mading beget both breeds; he did it that way in order to
give both Mijok Duor and Kwol Arob a chance for each one of them
to reflect his own breed, so that Mading may know why he was born a
single son.*

Those are the words I wanted to say in our conversation.

Francis Mading Deng: *Very well, Ayan. This is what I meant when I
said that there might be words you have heard at home which I might
not have heard. Even the words I caught up with, by repeating them
now you add to my knowledge about our family.*

*I have some more questions to pose to you about all this. Let us go
back a long way. I wonder whether we should not go back to maternal
relatives again. Was Duor, Mijok's father, from Bongo to begin with
before he then moved to Abyor, or was it Maluk who moved from
Bongo to Abyor? Or were they originally both from Abyor?*

Ayan Deng: *Our maternal relatives are called Dhienagou. The
Dhienagou in Abyor and the Dhienagou in Bongo are one. They are
from the same lineage. It is just like us, the family of Biong Allor. Some*

from Dhienagou left and came to Abyor and some remained in Bongo. Those who came to Abyor spread and became a clan by themselves. Our ancestors came and became among the central people of Abyor. What made our grandfather Mijok again go back to Bongo was because of a girl. Their daughter was married in Bongo. Then he went to visit and got married there. That is how they became the Dhienagou of Bongo; he decided to settle there in the camp of Ngor Got. That was our grandfather, Mijok. The sons of Deng Ngor became his brothers. He lived with them until he eventually migrated with them back to Abyor. They came, but the main clan of Deng Ngor remained in Bongo. But the household of the mother of Ayak all came. That is the family to which Chuer Deng belonged. Chuer, the brother of Ayak, you know him. He was the husband of Achol Bar. That is the maternal uncle of Achok, the brother of her mother. Chuer died in his home across the Noong River after people like me, Ayan, were grown up.

Francis Mading Deng: *Did they have any relatives among the Ruweng Dinka?*

Ayan Deng: *Yes. What about their grandmother, the grandmother of Mijok called Nyanger? Nyanger was from Ruweng tribe. She was married in Ruweng. People used to go to cattle-camps in the land of Ruweng. And the girl was very beautiful. Our great-grandfather fell in love with her. He married her and brought her home, just as our father used to go and marry girls outside the tribe. So, the grandmother of Achok with the maternal relatives of our paternal aunt Achol Kwol, the family of Thuc Mior, the wife of our grandfather Kwol Arob, are the girls of the same clan. They are related through their Ruweng connections. That is how our maternal line got related to Ruweng. To this day, Achol refers to Achok as her maternal cousin because of their relationship through Nyanger. That is how they are connected with the Ruweng.*

Francis Mading Deng: *When we were growing up at home, there is what is called the relationship of women and their husband and*

257

children, and what is said is that the husband's relations with the wife are good or bad. How was the relationship between Achok and Deng Majok?

Ayan Deng: *Achok and my father, their relationship, as we stayed in our home there at Noong, we never witnessed a bad thing, even for a single day. Minor quarrels sometimes occurred largely because, if anything small offended Achok, she would rise and go to our father with a hot temper, wanting a quarrel. But our father would say— 'Achok, why I do not want to accept a quarrel with you is because you are not the kind of woman who can be called impetuous. You do things knowing very well why you are doing them.'*

Francis Mading Deng: *What about the large scar I used to see on her back which looked as though it was from a whip? Since our father used to lash his wives with whips, did they perhaps quarrel, and she got whipped?*

Ayan Deng: *No! That scar of hers resulted from a fall when she was still a girl. She fell into a large grinding block made from a palm tree in their home. It was during an evening display by the girls of the village. They were performing a backward high jump dance. Achok came dancing backward in that fashion. Then, suddenly, she fell into the grinding block. That block cut deep into her body separating the skin and flesh into two parts. It was a serious wound that shocked everyone. Butter was melted, boiled and then poured into the wound. It was during the days when doctors did not exist in this area. That scar of hers she did not find in this home; she brought it with her. She got it when she was a girl.*

Francis Mading Deng: *In the past, Achok used to blame me that I did not speak with my father to assert my right over cattle. She would say that our share of cattle was inadequate. As you grew up at home, did you ever hear Achok complain about that matter? And you, yourselves, did you ever feel any dissatisfaction with the way our father distributed*

258

the cattle to the family?

Ayan Deng: *No. when Ayan Kwei was married, our mother
complained and said—'You Deng, why are girls married and I get
no share in the cattle of these marriages, while I see your other wives
receiving their shares? Is it that these women have their sons near
you while I have no son to watch after his rights? Is that why I have
remained without sharing in the marriage of the girls, or what is the
reason?'*
*Father said—'I thought that cattle were all alike, whether they came
from marriage or from some other sources. There is no year which has
ever passed without me allocating cattle to you. But if you consider
sharing in the cattle of the marriages as that important, then let us
leave the matter; I shall allot you a share.' A cow, Ajak, with newly
born cow-calf, Danjak, was brought from the marital family of Ayan.
It was given to us as our share in the marriage of Ayan. And another
cow, Aker, from the marriage of Achai Jur, was also given to us. And
in addition to that, we had cattle which our father used to bring from
other sources. We had a cow, Akol, from an Arab origin. It was such
a wonderful cow that we all cried when a lion killed her. We were still
small girls at the time. Our father then gave us a cow-calf, Danakol.
It had not yet given birth. It was brought from the family of Agorot
Suleiman. Father called Awor and said—'Take this Danakol and
tether her; she is yours. She will one day give birth and be your cow.'
Awor said—'Very well.'*
*But the mother of Agorot Suleiman claimed that she had never
consented to Danakol being given to our father. So, she cast a curse
on the cow-calf. Danakol gave birth to a remarkable calf of the same
pattern and was therefore also called Danakol. She was a cow which
produced so much milk that she used to be milked in an unusually large
gourd. She was never milked in the daylight; she used to be milked at
night (to avoid the envious eyes). That was the mother-cow, Danakol.
Her butter-milk gourd was filled by her alone unshared with any other
cow. Her calf Danakol grew up. She then gave birth for a second time
to yet another Danakol. But the Mother of Agorot went on praying*

259

for her doom. She said—'Danakol, if you have truly prospered in the family of Deng Majok, then you were never my cow. It is fitting that something befalls you.'

When our cattle moved to the toc, Danakol was attacked and killed by a lion when she had newly given birth. We cried over her death very much and refused to eat her meat. When our father was told—'Your daughters have lost their cow and have become so affected that they have been crying and have refused drinking milk,' he sent for us to come home from the cattle-camp. He came and gave us a long-horned cow, Yom, and said—'There is Yom. With her, I am drying your tears over the loss. Take her and add her to your cattle.'

When Achok got ill and our cattle had returned home from the camp, Father said—'Achok, whatever the spirit that has brought this illness on you wants, I will give it. If he wants a cow to be sacrificed, I will find her. If he wants a milch-cow to be yours alone, I will find her.' Achok said—'Whoever said that it is lack of food which is giving me the illness?' He said—'All the same, I shall provide the cow.' When Achok's illness seemed to get worse, Father took her to Abyei, and he slaughtered two bulls in sacrifice to the spirits. He also slaughtered two rams in sacrifice. It was divined that the illness was caused by the Great Spirit called Akudum of Achok's family. Father took out a huge dark brown bull, Mithiang. He called representatives of Dhienagou clan; they came and sacrificed the bull in our family. One of the rams was also killed in sacrifice at night. They were both offered to Akudum. Then he went and got a cow, Gak, and said—'This Gak should not even be milked in a gourd. Let her be milked in a bowl and the fresh milk given to Achok to drink. Gak's milk is not to be mixed with the milk of the rest of the cows.'

The milk of that Gak never entered the butter-milk gourd. Achok used to drink her milk fresh. Gak later caught the disease called manthiei. Achok did not know how to distill alcohol from grain which was said to function as a medicine for that cattle disease. So, she went and asked other people for the malt to make alcohol. It was said that only the alcohol-malt was good for manhiei. She said—'Gak is not going to die for lack of alcohol.' She went ahead and tried to prepare a blend of

260

*alcohol from the malt. But she did not succeed in distilling it. So, she
went ahead and gave the cow a strange blend of the malt mixed with
beer. The cow drank that mixture and immediately recovered. Later,
when the cattle were afflicted with the same disease, manhiei, our
father would say—'Why don't people use the same concoction Achok
used for her cow!? I am not going to be bothered! You make Achok
your veterinary doctor! Those of you who do not want to make the
same kind of mixture Achok made and used to treat her cow—that is
their business.' That Gak later died from another disease. But she had
survived for long until she was used for weaning Adau, the daughter of
Kwoldit. That cow which our father had given to Achok was later the
cow that sustained Adau when she was weaned.*

*As for our general share of cattle in the family, not a single year passed
without Father giving us a cow. Never. But then, whenever an epidemic
cattle disease came, it was always our cow that died first. That puzzled
us very much. And still does. Achok used to say—'My children, I believe
someone has bewitched our cattle. It cannot be otherwise.' We would
say—'O Mother, do not hold such thoughts.' As for our father, Deng,
until he died, we, the children borne by Achok, no one among us can
ever say that our father ever ill-treated us in this or that way. Never.
Even our mother has never, even for a single day, spoken to herself and
complained—'Why did Deng do this to me?!'*

*The only thing she once said was something related to her share of
junior wives. Our father married and allocated junior wives to our
mother. Of course, when a man marries, he knows the woman he
marries, how good or bad she is. Our father married in the manner in
which he married. And he brought the wives home. But these women
would come, escape, and leave. They were women who were being
followed by earlier ties. They were women whom he had taken away
from other men. Achok one day went to him and said—'Never bring
any other woman into this house of mine!' Father said—'What have I
done wrong?' She said—'Why do you marry for your other wives' good
girls who come and settle down, and you keep bringing me useless girls
who never stay?'*

Then he said—'Achok, I do not know what I should have done differently. What is left is perhaps for me to play the role of the legendary man in the folktales who turned himself into an idiot and went to live among the women to observe the girls in order to choose the girl with the best qualities for a wife. That is what I have not done for you. But the girls I married for you were girls I had heard about as daughters of noble men. I went and married each one of them and brought her to you thinking she was a good wife. Then, I later hear about her as a bad girl. And she goes away. She doesn't leave because of anything you have done or because of anything I have done. My wife, can you ever blame me for that? Never mind. Let us leave the past aside. I will seek another wife for you.'

He then married Nyanpiok Jipur. When Nyanpiok was brought, she came and eloped with Mading, the son of Thuc Achol-Aboch. My father then said—'Achok, can you again blame me, now that it is the son of Thuc who has taken away your wife? You cannot blame me anymore.' Then, I persuaded Father to marry Nyanthon. I said—'Marry Nyanthon and bring her. If she should leave, I will never blame you again.' The number of Achok's wives who have left, when we try to count them, they are not less than ten. And none of the other wives has had such a large share of junior wives. And they were all hers, except that they left for their own reasons. If she were someone with something dislikable by her husband, would she have been given so many wives? Our cattle never stopped increasing, even for a single year. He used to give me a separate cow and give our late sister a separate cow. He never gave us all one cow, because I drink only fresh milk and not butter-milk or any milk from a gourd. He would give me my own cow and provide the rest of Achok's family with their own cows. And those cows which he would give us, he would never take again for his marriages or for sale. It is only disease which used to kill our cattle. Diseases which would come and pick our cattle and kill them. This is what made us suspicious. Up to this day, it has not disappeared from inside us.

Francis Mading Deng: *Why was Achok allocated to the house of Nyanbol Amor? Was she not the fourth wife after Kwei? Since she was the fourth after the first three principal wives, why was she not*

262

allocated to the house of Nyanboldit?

Ayan Deng: *What made Achok go to the house of Nyanbol Amor? Aker Tiel was engaged before Achok. She was from Twich. And when Aker was engaged, Nyanboldit and Nyanbol Amor contested her, each one saying that she was to be her wife. Then Father decided that she was to go to the house of Nyanbol Amor. That was what was then accepted. People then waited. Our mother was married after Aker but was brought first into the family. While the marriage was still being arranged, Nyanboldit used to visit the family of Mijok Duor saying—'This girl will be my wife. I shall never leave her.' But when she was eventually brought home, the situation changed. Nyanboldit and Nyanbol Amor were not equal. Nyanbol Amor was very much loved by Deng Majok. Something would be agreed in public, but Nyanbol Amor would later go and change the mind of Deng Majok in private. Achok was first married as the wife of Nyanboldit. But when she was brought home, Father said—'Nyanbol Amor is too exhausted with labouring for guests. No one helps her with the work for guests. And this girl is highly reputed as a hard worker. So, you Nyanboldit, you wait for the girl of Twich. She will be your wife and this girl will go to Nyanbol Amor.' Nyanboldit then said—'If the girl who had been allotted to me has now come and has been given to Nyanbol Amor, then this home will remain with Nyanbol Amor. I must now leave!'*
The matter was highly debated. But Father had decided—'Now that I have said my word on the subject, who will change it?'

Francis Mading Deng: *And was Kwei alone?*

Ayan Deng: *Yes, Kwei was alone. She had been placed apart as head of the third division of the family.*

Francis Mading Deng: *But when Aker Tiel, who was the fourth, was married and said to be given to Nyanbol Amor, did Nyanboldit not object to that?*

Ayan Deng: *She objected, and they debated the matter. But Father said—'I will find you another wife. This woman belongs to Nyanbol Amor.' And so Nyanboldit left her to be the wife of Nyanbol Amor. But later on, Father went and confused it. He said—'Nyanbol Amor is suffering a great deal. It is she who has the main responsibility for guests and other things. And this woman has been praised as a woman who works very hard. So, I want her to relieve Nyanbol Amor. And you Nyanboldit, what I said before has now changed; the girl who is in Twichland will go to you.'*

Nyanboldit then said—'Why do you push me around so much? Did you not say before that the girl in Twichland would be the wife of Nyanbol Amor and Achok would be my wife? I accepted that and became acquainted with Achok, visiting her in their home. Why have you now confused the matter?'

He said—'That is the way I now want it.' Nyanbol Amor would never speak when people gathered. She would remain silent. But later, when she met Deng Majok privately, she would then influence him to alter earlier arrangements. That is how she took over Achok from Nyanboldit. To this day, whenever Achok gets into an argument with her, Nyanboldit still says—'My dear, when Deng Majok took you from me, I knew it was planned so that you would come and help establish Nyanbol Amor. That is why Nyanbol Amor has compounded her strength. If I were to face Nyanbol by herself, she would never counter me with words. But Deng Majok has placed the affairs of Nyanbol Amor's house into your joint hands and made you share in the responsibility of Nyanbol's house.' Achok would say—'Is it your desire to submerge Nyanbol Amor?'

Then Nyanawai was married. And when Nyanawai got married, Nyanboldit said she wanted to take her. But Deng Majok refused and said—'No, No! Achok is lonely. So, I am giving Nyanawai to Achok. She will be her junior wife. You now have Aker and Nyanbol Deng. So, Nyanbol Amor should now have Achok and Nyanawai. They will be with her.' Then Amel was married. And when Amel was brought, she was accommodated in the house of Nyanbol Amor. She was said to be the wife of Achok and Nyanawai. Nyanboldit got extremely provoked.

264

She said—'Tea is now prepared by those two wives. Every good thing that is brought into this family is given to those two women to prepare. And now, they are to be given this new wife! Should I remain without tasting tea or the good things of my husband? My present wives do not know how to prepare the sophisticated foods of the chiefs. And all the women who know how to prepare the good foods of the chiefs have been given to one person. If the family has become the family of Nyanbol Amor alone, then I must now leave.' That is when the women in Nyanbol Amor's house spoke to Deng Majok and said—'Chief, if that is the way it is, then you better give Amel to Nyanboldit. We will leave her and remain by ourselves.'

That is how Amel was taken and given to Nyanboldit. People like Agorot Pabut were then married. Agorot Pabut was to be the wife of Nyanboldit's household. She was from a very wealthy family. Achok's family was near Agorot's family at Yom. Achok came and said—'We want Agorot. She is to be our wife.' They overturned the plan of Deng Majok, and when Agorot was brought, they took her and accommodated her in their household. Father said to Nyanboldit's complaint—'That is the way it is. Did they not give you Amel the last time? Don't people exchange hands? Was Amel your wife and was she not given to you? What more can you say?'

Anyiel was then married and given to Nyanboldit. And then Akwol Biong was married. When Akwol Biong was married, Nyanboldit said she was her wife. But Father said—'No! It will not be that way. I must now give Akwol Biong to this side of the family because their wife has gone with you.'

That is the way he did it. Then he got into his multiple marriages which he just threw into the family indiscriminately. But the wives of the early marriages were distributed in an orderly way. So, that is how they were organized.

Francis Mading Deng: *How do women in our family now view the senior wives, our mothers, in light of their children, ourselves?*

Ayan Deng: *Of the young wives, such as the wives of the household*

265

of Abul's mother Nyanbol Amor, who are now in the family, there is Nyanlou, there is Abiong Piyin, there is Agorot Pabut, and there are people like Anyuat and Nyanlou who are sharing the house with Achok at Nainai. They have become members of one household. Whatever appears in the family of Achok, it is they who work for it. Women like Abiong and others, if it is something that involves the whole of Nyanbol Amor's section of the family, for instance at Abyei, then they will all be sent for. Each one will come and another will come and they will all gather in the house of Nyanawai. There, they will then do whatever they plan to do together. How they are living, Achok and Nyanawai and Nyanbol have become their elders. They are the senior women at the head of that part of the family. Even other younger wives of the boys, such as the wives of Monylam (Ali), they of course show special courtesy to Achok. Whatever Achok says, the women defer to her in respect.

Francis Mading Deng: *What I mean is how the senior women, like our mothers, are regarded in the whole family, especially in view of their order of seniority as less senior to the very first wives. For instance, what does our mother's being number four or number five mean to the rest of the wives?*

Ayan Deng: *Today, as we talk, the position of Achok among people like Nyanboldit and Nyanbol Amor, whatever they would discuss as the most senior wives of the family, they would always include Achok to be their third. If it is something important to be discussed by the most senior wives of the family, not even Nyanboldit could decide or pronounce herself on the matter without calling upon Achok and consulting her first. Nyanboldit may harbor some other sentiments because of rivalry between her and Nyanbol Amor, but the good thing Achok did to her when she took care of Bol comes back to her heart.*

Francis Mading Deng: *And how do the women at home view us, the sons?*

266

Ayan Deng: *What about when you went and found me newly delivered and you left money to be distributed to the women!? Today, what Amel says in praise of you, if praise was to harm a person because of the envy of others, it would have harmed you. Amel says—'I am still holding to this family because of Mading. It is because of Mading that I shall remain here and be buried next to the grave of Deng Majok. If it were not for Mading Deng, I would not be in this family today. I would be buried in my home land of the Rek.' When we distributed the money to the junior wives, each woman would say—'Even if Mading left only five piastres for me, that he thought of us when we had not requested anything from him, that he thought by himself and said— "Let this be given to my father's junior wives," this is so sweet to us that nothing can match it.'*

Today, son of my mother, the words we are saying are words meant to be heard and known by God. As you sit here, it is only our father who has entered the earth that knows what Achok used to say. It is God who is there above watching over us here on the ground who knows why you were born a single son. What he will do, how he will save you, how he will let us survive, how he will maintain the child you beget—those are the issues that concern us. Even the prosperity that people speak of at home is not what concerns us. When two of our cows recently fell dead together the same day, Loth cried in the evening and refused to eat. I said—'Loth, just because of the death of the cows!' He said—'What has killed the cows of Mading in this manner?' I said—'My God! You are ignorant of the truth. Have not the cows our father left us died? And these were later acquired by Mading with the strength of his own arm. They are the result of the pen which our Father had placed in his hand. That is how he got educated. And later, he bought his wealth not for himself but for our father. He bought them to be the cows of Deng Majok and to compensate for the cows that had died so that people can still say that Deng Majok has wealth. If our father saw a big evil coming to destroy the family of Achok and he has redeemed us by giving the cattle away instead, and Mading, the son of my mother, survives with his children, so that all we lose are cattle, even if they were all to die including their young, by God that would not take sleep from my eyes, I, Ayan. What killed the cattle without any known disease, to make them fall in the daytime as they were about to go grazing, falling down at the same time on the edge of the village, what killed them in that fashion, may be averting an evil which our ancestral spirits had detected as a threat that might kill Mading or kill Achok and therefore redeemed them with those cattle. Let them go! I will never miss them. I will never mourn their death. And I am a person who loves cattle more than anyone else. But why I am surrendering these without bitterness is because I have seen something in the matter.'

Then I went in the morning and explained everything to Achok. Achok exclaimed—'O my God, what could have killed such strong cows?' Nyanawai intervened and said—'Achok, have you become a fool!? Don't you know the affairs of this family? If Deng Kwol has said—"Let me divert the eyes of the witch from Achok to the cows," then these cattle have died for a good cause as long as they have redeemed Mading to remain alive. Mading will compensate for them. Even this summer, he could buy the same number of cows as have died. And the dead cows would have taken the evil spirit away.'

Truly, son of my mother, as we talk here today, our father, Deng, until he died, only minor quarrels, which are normal between a husband and a wife, occasionally arose and were discussed and resolved in the spirit of people living together in their family. But we have never heard Achok spending a sleepless night and sitting up, complaining to us—'My children, your father has done this wrong or that wrong.' That, we have never, never heard.

I have reproduced my sister Ayan's account without editorializing, even though her perspective on all of us, our parents, our paternal and maternal families, and the children of our mother, my sisters and myself, is exaggeratedly flattering. This is, however, not entirely unusual, for the Dinka nearly always exalt their families, especially their forebears, with unmitigated exaltation. Ayan's almost folktale manner of speech should therefore be viewed as a rather inflated reflection of the normative practice, though with its own literary attributes, all of which I appreciate with due modesty.

Nine

A Legacy at the Crossroads

Father's death in 1969 left the family and the tribe torn apart by rivalry between his sons and without a consensus on one uniting leader. The assassination of the successor to Chieftainship, the accusation of the rival brother as an accomplice to the crime, his eventual dismissal in the face of family and tribal opposition to him, and indeed the confusion and disintegration which has since afflicted the family and the tribe are in no small measure associated with my father's failure to provide for continuity after his death. The opposition which my father had suppressed and subdued found encouragement in the vacuum. The ancient and ongoing rivalries between the Dhiendior and Pajok lineages surfaced more actively, fueled by the opposition groups, both traditional and modern. Even the educated class got involved in this tradition-bound struggle for power. A legacy of leadership found itself at the crossroads.

Within the family, the burdens of our father's marriages and large family size, which we had long anticipated, began to fall on us. The personal obligation Bol and I owed the family was established by the fact that we were not only among the eldest sons, but also the ones in whom the family had made the biggest educational investment. My sister Nyanluak, whom I interviewed in the late 1970s, was later to say to me:

The affairs of our family have continued to deteriorate. The way they are going today, unless you people struggle hard, and keep your hearts firm, things will not go well. Today, your younger brothers are roaming all over the country; they have not yet settled down to gainful employment. Most of them are still pursuing their education.

You and Bol are here today in the positions you occupy because our father had given your education great priority. Even if the burdens on you should prove formidable, each of you must talk to his heart at night and say—'If I should surrender my responsibility, what will become of our family? It is better that I sacrifice my personal interest for the good

269

of my people.' One will talk to his heart that way and think about the condition of his father's family: why God created them to be as large a family as they are; why God made father's heart go after marrying so many wives and enabled him to beget the number of children whom he has now left behind. Truly, as you see them at home, there is no family where such numbers exist; it is only in the family of Deng Majok that such numbers are found. If God has saved you to this day, then you people must follow the logic of the situation and calm your hearts down. If a child comes to you seeking help, even if what he wants is lacking, one must talk to him with a gentle and tender heart—'My dear brother, it is only that I do not have this thing, for otherwise I would gladly have given it to you.'

Father did indeed place you in a position of great responsibility from the start. He took you to school and continued to give great attention to your education. You went abroad to continue your studies. You returned to his death and took his body back to his home at Abyei, where he left you with the responsibility you now have. Father knew all that, and even now that he is dead, he knows what responsibility he has left behind with you. Even if you should be overburdened, you must not cry in agony; your burden is a noble one, it is not a bad one.

The challenge at the tribal level was articulated to me by Matet Ayom in words which I consider pertinent not only because of what they say, but also because Matet was both a friend and a political foe to our father:

I started praising you very early in your childhood. Although you have not done me any personal favor, I have always praised you as the true image of your father. Why I used to call you Bashoum—'The Fox' is for the same reason you have now filled your position so well. A country survives because of the arm of the Chief. It is in the hands of the Chief that a country survives. And a country survives through the son of the Chief. When our people used to walk on foot, the man who would lead the way at night would be the son of a Chief. Even if he be a small boy, it is he who must take the lead. He leads the way and when people sleep, he sleeps in the center. And the following morning, when people take to the way again, he takes the lead. So, remember this small piece

of advice. There is no one else to whom you can entrust the tribe. Your
father is no longer there at home. It is you, Mading, who now occupies
the place of your father, Deng Majok. If things do not go well, it will be
because of you. So, you better abandon the relaxation you enjoyed when
your father was alive. Today, the responsibility of the tribe has been
bequeathed to you.

Matet then contrasted the way our father managed the affairs of the
tribe to the manner in which his successors were performing:

The strong words you say today only Deng Majok was able to say then.
Tomorrow, when you listen to the speeches (the talks with the Missiriya
in 1977), you will be disappointed by the words of many. If it were
during the time of Deng Majok, he would determine in advance the
people who should speak, the people whose words would reflect the
truth. Now, the country is taken over by children. But there is always
one person who is known as the seat of the country. And that is you.
You are the front line and you are the seat on which the tribe rests. And
you are the carriage into which the people will load their belongings.
And you are the dish in which the food will be served. So, do your best.
Deng Majok is no longer alive. And Deng is not going to return from
death. Each person goes with his own fame and leaves the suffering
behind for the remaining generations to face. Then the successor
develops his own fame again by the way he faces those problems. So, you
will develop your fame as your father developed his.

Today, the people may not know you well, but that is because of your
distance from them. Your manner of speaking is that of your father,
Deng Majok. Your manner of speech by which you handle problems
calmly, listen carefully to the viewpoint of another person, and adjust
your words to accommodate the truth as you see it. In you, we find
something of the qualities of Deng Majok.

Matet drew attention to the legacy of my dual paternal and maternal
ancestry:

You are the product of two persons. The man who begot your mother
was a man of great wisdom. He helped keep this tribe in order with
the power of his great words. And so was your own father. So, both the
bull and the cow who begot you are people of equal stature. If anyone

271

should associate you with your mother, he will not have associated you with a bad side. And if anyone associates you with your father, he will not have associated you with a bad side either. The person who says that you resemble Mijok Duor, your mother's father, and the person who says that you resemble Deng Majok, your own father, none of them has associated you with a bad side. Both were great men who maintained this country with the power of wisdom and the truth. So, we shall now end our words, but I again urge you to think of your people and what you should do for them.

A number of elders also discussed with me the suggestion I had made to the government on the problem of Abyei, that instead of suffering the tensions and conflicts of a disputed territory between the North and the South, the area be given a special status that would ensure for the people control over the management of their local affairs within Kordofan and promote the economic, social, and cultural development of the area as a harmonious point of contact and a model for peace, unity, and national integration.

One of the elders who spoke in support of the plan was Mariew Ajak:

What I, Mariew, will now say to you Mading, you are our educated son. You are now our peg. With your coming here, even though we were vexed in our hearts, our hearts begin to cool down. The day your father Deng died, when you came with Bol, and when he was buried and you said to the people—'You will remain to live in the country,' I called you aside and said—'Come here.' And I said—'Mading, now that you have come, the few people who have survived, it is you who has made them survive. While you are here, whenever a person is arrested, you bring him out. Now that you will leave, our front has broken down. Now that you will leave, will our tribe not spoil? Will the land ever be good again?' What I told you, if it were not that people forget words, you would recall. I said—'One day, you will come to respect this area only as a graveyard and not as a country with people. Our people will be finished. We are too delicately poised on the borders, the borders of the South and the North. This will destroy us. The tribe of your father will turn into a graveyard. I want you to be the chief. You should remain here. They will shy away from you, but they will not fear Monyyak.' But now that they are gone, they are gone. That is the way things go with people struggling for their country. Today, we are very pleased. If we have now met with you, all the bad things have passed.

Mariew then proceeded to tell me of a report he had received from Pagwot Deng, Chief of the Bongo tribe, with whom I had discussed the Abyei situation several months before, together with other elders from Abyei.

Pagwot went and told me one thing. He said—'You, Mariew, you disbelieve everything. Even if a man brings a true word, you disbelieve him. This is what Mading said.' I said—'Have you met?' He said— 'Yes, we have met.' And I said—'What did he say?' He said—'Mading said—"Our young men all swarm in anger without arranging their words well." In my heart, joining the South or the North is not a good choice. Our area has always been a border-home. If we were to follow what I have thought out, I would like us to be on the borders, not to be considered part of the South nor fully part of the North. The Arabs will shy away from us. We shall be the people to put the country in order. The area of Abyei will develop in a way free from jealousies. If it were left to me, I say that our area should remain separate. I want to write that down. But the young men of our area begin to complain that I have sold the country away. So, I have given up the case!'

I said—'Pagwot, what you are now saying to me, if Mading were here, I would have said—"Do not listen to the words of your age-mates. Do not let your mind be confused. Do not abandon your word. Write it down and show it to the leaders of the Sudan. We are the people of the borders. Nothing is bigger. The land extending to the South down to Agarland, down to Kiecland, down to the land of Jurcol, and further down to the Southern end of the country—your grandfather, Arob Biong, was the man who controlled the whole country. In the generation of my father, were not people like my father captured and enslaved to the point where their cheeks were scarred? If his mother had not rescued him from captivity, would we ourselves not be the Arabs of today? It was Arob Biong who brought peace into this land so that anyone who escaped could return to his home and not be forced back into slavery. That was how my father returned and remained in Dinkaland. The land was one." So, as I see it, Mading should not abandon his word. He should remain and not give heed to what other people say and give up. If he should abandon the tribe, it will be spoiled; it will be spoiled by those people. If he should say—"I shall leave the tribe to you to do with it whatever you want," the tribe will spoil.'

Mariew Ajak continued with his response to Pagwot—*'When Deng Makuei was there as chief, it was Deng Majok who was guarding him. And when Deng Majok died, he turned into a newborn baby. So, when my heart was on Mading, I said—"I believe you will be the person who will bring our tribe back to order"—it was the truth my heart hit. I am only sad that I shall not be able to meet him. I would tell him—"Son of my brother, hold to your plan. Do not listen to the words of your age-mates. Do not allow them to confuse your words by saying—'We are going to the South.' Your words are the goodness of the land. The land is full of jealousies. If it is the Arab, he will not permit any goodness for the area. He will say—'These young men who are flocking to the area are going to take the area away.' Now they have selected people like wild fruits." The educated children are now afraid, and they claim it is we who have spoiled the land. That is why there are no educated boys at Abyei. There is not a single man. It is only we, the ignorant, who are left there. It is we who have remained exposed. He now fetches a man as though he were fetching tobacco. Any ailment you may have which may keep you to your house for the day suddenly becomes a white disaster. It is only that Mading is far from us. And you, Pagwot, what did you say?'*
He said—*'I liked what Mading said.'*
I said—'It is a pity he is far. If he were near, I would say—"Hold on to it. Do not listen to the words of the children; they are people spoiling the land. Keep writing it down and say—'We are different; we are the people of the borders. We shall be Southerners here.'" That is how they will treat us well. They will treat us well out of self-interest. The relationship of people who have had a feud is like food which has not yet been tasted. Now, the Arab unites the opportunists. It will take us a long time to repair their damage. The Arabs say—"These are the people who have kept the people with us." Their hands will stretch to hold the

food given them by the Arab.
If one travels and happens to find Mading, he should be told not to
abandon his word. We are separate and we are Southerners in the
North. That is how Arob Biong left us; that is how Kwol left us; and
Deng, too, recently left us there. We are people of the borders. The Nuer
come to our land; the Twic come to our land; the Ruweng come to our
land; the Rek come to our land; the Arabs come to our land. We are
suited to our situation as the people of the borders. If peace were to
cease, our country would be the battlefield because it is the border. So
Mading's word is my word. It is only that he is far away.' So, what we
should now say is that what you are doing is correct. Write it down;
write it down. It is the truth.

I need not stress that these glorifying words reflect echoes of fading voices and are as much a condemnation for failure as they are praise for achievement. For years, I exerted considerable efforts to find a decent solution to the Abyei problem, a solution that would create harmony between the various demands currently being made by the local people, the neighboring Arabs, the authorities of Kordofan, and the people of the South. For a while, it seemed as though our efforts were blessed with success, supported not only by important decision-making circles on the national level, but also by the President of the Republic himself. With financial resources provided by the central government, the United States Agency for International Development, and the technical services of the Harvard Institute for International Development, the foundation was set for a significant contribution to the development of the area in an autonomous framework.

While the Arab tribes and the Province authorities in Kordofan mistrusted these measures as favoring the Dinka against other tribes in the region, the major blow that undermined the efforts from the start was the opposition of the educated class. Some of them were merely radical youth who saw too much moderation and compromise in my approach. Some opponents went as far as arguing that any constructive work that would bring significant benefits to the people might lure them to the North and dampen their desire to join the South. Their logic was that the more the people suffered in the North, the more intensified their resolve to join the South would be. Some of my opponents were indeed close relatives who were critical of the policies our father and grandfather had followed in favor of remaining in the North and were trying to correct what they saw as past mistakes and bending over backward to disassociate themselves from that past. And there were those who stood against my approach simply as a matter of principle because they were pursuing old competitiveness or rivalry within and between the leading families. To these people, any initiative that did not emanate from them or that might have the effect of giving credit to a member of an opposing family or faction was by definition undesirable.

Conclusion

I would like to conclude by recalling the words of Chief Arol Kachu-ol about the importance of marriages across divisions which bring together the identities of father and mother into a unity that bridges the cleavages and removes any preexisting hostilities between the two respective groups:

Is [your wife] not from America? And you have brought her back to your country. If you bear a child together now, in that child will combine the words of her country and the words of your country. It is as though God has given her to Deng, your father. So, the way we see it, God has brought peace and reconciliation into your hearts. None of you is to hate the race of the other. Even if a man was a slave or descended from a slave, and he marries into a family, he becomes a relative; he becomes a member of the family. It is then for him to bear both his own blood and... the blood of his wife's kin.

Tomorrow, the people of that tribe or the people of that race, God will take them and mix them with the people of that race. They too will bear their own races through their children. When that happens, whatever hostility might have been between people should no longer be allowed to continue. Relationship kills those troubles and begins the new way of kinship... Man is one single word with God.

These words reflect the wisdom of a particular culture, but principles with universal validity that are unfortunately not being uniformly observed. As people are increasingly mixing and bridging the racial, cultural and religious divides, the logical development should be the commensurate unification and mutual accommodation of diversities. For the Dinka, a critical factor in this unification is the extension of the especial bond between mother and child to the maternal kin. The love and affection for the mother is extended to her kith and kin.

One of the arguments the Dinka hold against Northern Sudanese is that they are the descendants of their women whom the incoming Arabs took, whether as wives or concubines and therefore should show especial deference to their maternal kith and kin despite racial, cultural, or religious differences.

Chief Arol Kachuol had this to say: *"Even if a man was a slave or descended from a slave, and he marries into a family, he becomes a relative; he becomes a member of the family. Even our brothers, who were taken away as slaves, by now they have probably found their circles and have combined with other peoples to create their own kinships."*

Since the words of the elders reproduced in this volume were recorded in the 1970s and 1980s, a peace agreement concluded in 2005 between the North and the South gave the people of Southern Sudan the right to secede, which it did in 2011. The case of Abyei was negotiated and it was agreed that the Ngok Dinka would determine, by a referendum, whether to remain in the North or join the South. However, the Government of the Sudan blocked the exercise of the referendum and rejected the result of a referendum organized by the people of Abyei in which they overwhelmingly opted for joining South Sudan.

Abyei is now ambiguously identified by the peace agreement as a shared area between Sudan and South Sudan, with its future remaining unresolved. The security of the area is being precariously maintained by the United Nations Interim Security Force for Abyei (UNISFA), whose efforts, while much appreciated by the people, are severely constrained by the uncooperative attitude of the Sudanese Government. It is, in any case, a temporary arrangement. As a result, Abyei remains in an administrative vacuum, without services, infrastructure, or socio-economic development activities. The Ngok Dinka are therefore virtually stateless, abandoned by the Government of the Sudan, which paradoxically still claims sovereignty over the area, and the Government of South Sudan, which is only able to extend token support in solidarity with the people as ethnically, culturally, and politically South Sudanese.

Minyiel Row has these moving words in one of his songs, addressing our brother Kwol, the Paramount Chief, who was assassinated by the Missiriya Arabs in 2013:

Kwol, we are doomed to the void of the middle,
Son of Deng Majok, we are like a bat,
A creature which is not an animal,
But it has the ears of an animal,
It is not a bird,
But it has wings like a bird,
Wings with which it flies at night.
Everything has twisted itself.
All that we have left is the spiritual world;
Each man must turn to the spirits of his forefathers
And to the Creator who created man at the Original Byre of Creation;
God is there watching.

I have reproduced the words of the elders to underscore the crisis the Ngok Dinka are still experiencing and the urgent need for self-scrutiny by their modern leaders. Whatever resolution to the problem there may be, it will have to take the form of a delicate, sensitive and creative weaving of the past, the present and the future. In other words, it will have to be a dynamic but careful synthesis that reflects the human dignity of all those concerned: Dinka and non-Dinka, South Sudanese and Sudanese, all participating in an interactive and interdependent, inclusive context.

If in this process we look back to the heritage of our forefathers for some guidance, which we should, I am sure some of us will be surprised to discover the amount of wisdom with which those "uneducated" men and women managed problems that still face us today, and how the insights and principles they used in tackling those problems remain valid and applicable to our "modern" context. In particular, they will find that peacemaking, bridging between conflicting positions, and pacifying adversaries not by naked force, but by persuasion and the power of the truth in words—in short, reconciliation between peoples and communities—are among the most noble goals and tools of leadership among the Dinka, as they indeed are in the global community of humankind.

In Chapter One to this volume, I outlined some of the paradoxes now confronting the traditional assumptions about wisdom accruing with age, and the new trends in which modern education associated with youth are reversing those assumptions. Whatever the merits of the old order, change is imperative and irreversible. However, change should not, and cannot, be adopted wholesale. Selectivity is a desired objective. Toward that objective, I proposed some broad guiding principles for bridging those paradoxes of change to facilitate an enriching transitional integration of values, institutions, and behavioral patterns.

Three major themes need highlighting in this conclusion. The first is the dualism of paternal and maternal streams that constitute the very being of every person. The second is the widening circles of family bonds emerging from intermarriage across the dividing lines of identity. And the third is the universality of these contextualized, yet integrating, principles.

I hope this volume provides a basis for such integration within the specific context of the Ngok, one which can be a modest but useful model for approaching other contexts. In this connection, I hope that the volume sheds light on the principles of the value-system, the distinctive attributes of Dinka oral history and literary expression, and the importance of the dual contribution of both paternal and maternal lineages in accordance with the old Biblical dictum: *"Honor thy Father and Mother"*—a simple, but morally overriding principle.

Special Thanks

The process of recording the names of the wives of Chief Deng Majok and their children has been challenging, not only because of the numbers involved, but particularly because the family is now dispersed both nationally and internationally–literally around the world. In addition to their homeland in Abyei, members of the family now live in different areas of South Sudan, Sudan, Kenya, Uganda, the United States of America, the United Kingdom, the European Union, Canada, and Australia, to give the most obvious countries of residence. Moreover, according to Dinka custom, death does not end marriage, and childbearing wives of a dead man continue to have children to his name. So, although Deng Majok died in 1969, he left behind many young wives who continued to beget children with relatives, thus, they are socially considered the children of Deng Majok. The difficulty of tracing the names of all his wives and children is quite obvious.

Another challenge of collecting all the names of Deng Majok's wives and their children is including the names of those wives who left, but were never divorced, those who are deceased, and many children who were born or died unbeknownst to the mainstream family. So we believe that the estimated numbers of 200 wives, 500 children, and about 1,000 grandchildren are reasonable, and maybe even an underestimation.

Many individuals contributed to collection of this list. Charles Biongdit, with his son Moyak and nephew David Kuol Mading Deng, began the work on the family tree several years ago. The final list was most recently prepared by a number of senior wives and sons and daughters of Deng Majok and a relative. The wives include Achiethke Deng Nyac, Aluel Abangbang Kon, Ayan Dau, Ayei Ngor, Nyanjoh Bagat Alor, Nyanaguek Deng Mayuai, Ayuen Wiew, Nyangeek Bol, and Nyanthon Ayuel Agoor. Deng Majok's daughters included

Adau Deng, Achai Deng, and niece Abul Biong. The sons include Arob (Bar) Deng, Arob (Awal) Deng, Malual Deng, and Ring Deng. Uncle Bulabek Biong Makuei also contributed.

I owe them all my deep gratitude.

Paternal Line of Francis Mading Deng
Dongbek Akurweng (Achai Noh)
Koc Dongbek
Manangau Koc
Athurkok Manangau
Jok Athurkok
Bulabek Jok
Dongbek Bulabek
(Kuol) Kwoldit Dongbek
Monydhang Kwoldit
Allor Monydhang
Biong Allor
(Arop) Arob Biong
(Kuol) Kwol Arob
Deng Majok Kwol (Father)

Maternal Line of Francis Mading Deng
Pagou Yuom
Acuek Pagou
Mon Acuek (Achook)
Tiir Mon (Moan)
Ajing Tiir (Tier)
Dau Ajing
Maluk Dau
Duor Maluk
Mijok Duor
Achok Mijok (Mother)

Ngok Dinka Chiefdoms

Paramount Chief: Deng Majok Wives' List

Paan Man-Adau

Name	Chiefdom/Clan	Sons and Daughters
Nyanbol Arop Kuot	Diil/Payath	Adau,Chan,Ngor,Bol,Moyak
Aker Tiel Yaac	Twic/Padhieu	Bulabek,Adau,Awor,Ayen
Nyanbol Deng Arop	Achueng/Dhiendiit	Miyar, Nyanaar (Nyangei)
Tiet Aguar Liet	Achueng/Dhiendior	Achai
Amel Yual Makuei	Malual/Pagew	Moyak, Nyanwillei
Thiyang Deng Riek	Bongo/Payai	Bulabek, Achai, Monyadhang
Akuol Manyang Ayei	Adiang/Padhieu	Arop, Achai, Adau
Achol Anei Deng Monyjok	Abiem/Pabiil	Alor
Anyiel Achuoth Nyok	Bongo/Paluk	Akuet, Kuol, Biong, Achuol
Awut Wiir Akueei	Lou/Pabaal	Achai, Arop
Nyantholony Juac Chol	Abior/Pangok	Nyanwiir, Dombek, Abul
Aliema Deng Atem	Ruweng/Payath	Arop
Nyaluak Kiir Ajing	Mannyuar/Payuel	Achai, Monydhang, Adau
Nyarek Lueth Aduol	Ruweng/Dhiendior	Kuol, Adau, Malual
Nyanthon Amour Neic	Diil/Paguiny	Achai, Jok, Awor
Nyantibiu Bar Akonon	Mannyuar/Paguil	Ring
Nyanaguen Deng Mayuai	Anyiel/Pagoor	Kuol, Jok, Adau, Alor, Chan, Achai, Mawien
Nyaluak Leu Diing	Abior/Pathiang	Akuet
Ayuen Wieu Dau	Anyiel/Pakany	Jok, Nyanriak,Bol, Nyadit, Ring, Nyanak
Agak Dau Nhial	Diil/Paleng	Akuol, Awor, Mahadi, Athak
Nyanjoh Chol Monybai	Mareng	Achai, Mawien, Ring
Adut Kiir Manyion	Achueng/Pamiokpieo	Awor,Adau, Ngong, Arop, Alor
Abuk Kiir Ajak	Anyiel/Payath	Awor, Kuol,Ring, Adau, Alor
Nyanuer Kuol Yier	Alei/Pagwer	Awor, Nyanbol, Achuil, Chan
Nyankoor Mayii Wour	Bongo/Pangok	Achai, Awor(Ngong)
Nyankuin Achuil Deng	Mannyuar/Dhiendior	Achai, Lal, Mathok
Achol Buk Michar	Bongo/Palual	Adau, Achai
Achethkeh Deng Neic	Bongo/Patoor	Mawien,Biong, Nyanriak,Nyanbol
Nyakieu Aar Ajuong	Diil	Mawien, Biong
Bothon Manyuol Monytung	Achaak	Nyariak, Alor, Chol, Jok
Anot Wunchueei Malual	Anyiel/Patoub	Abul, Alor, Biong
Nyanajith Meer	Bongo/Pangok	Mawien
Atoc Dau Koun	Manyuar/Dhienagou	Kuol, Adau
Ajok Malek Nyuol	Noon Deng/Payei	Mawien,Achai, Jok
Atong Akot Koor	Awan Chan/Padool	Awor, Mawien,Biong, jok, Lang, Ayen
Nyanjor Makuac Kerrigi	Alei/Payaak	Nyanriak, Arop, Kuol, Achuil, Achai
Akuac Ngor Tolwut	Alei/Dhiendior	Kuol
Atoc Abiem Bagat	Mannyuar/Dhiendior	
Abuk Akuangdiing Mou	Mareng/Pachier	Mangok, Nyanriak
Akuol Kuenj Deng	Bongo/Paleeng	Kuol, Nyanpath, Adau, Nyanak
Nyanbol Kur Ajuong	Anyiel/Pathiang	Adau, Achai, Bul, Kuol, Biong Awor
Atoc Mading Ayii	Mannyuar/Dhiendagou	Bol, Achuil
Angeth Akonon Yor	Mareng/Pachier	Kuol, Awor, Biong, Achol, Alor, Arop, Achai
Achol Deng Malek	Abior/Pajing	Abuk, Nyantafag, Alor
Amor Akoon Wol	Awan Chan/Payei	Biong, Adau,Mijak

Name	Chiefdom/Clan	Sons and Daughters
Ayen Monywuac Nyikuac	Abior/Patoor	
Nyangeek Bol Nyinkuany	Abior/Pajing	Biong, Arop, Ring, Achai, Adau, Kuol, Nyanaar, Jok
Akuol Kat Malual	Alei/Pangal	Biong, Adau
Nyandeng Ayom Kueth	Achueng/Dhiendiit	
Alang Chol Kiir	Alei/Paguiny	
Nyanyuat Anyanwil Chol	Alei/Dhiendior	Adau
Nyandhyat Chol Miyom	Mareng/Pakany	
Achok Kueth Deng	Abior/Pakuenj	
Nyaluak	Nuer	
Athak Ajak Jabir	Alei/Dhiendior	
Awol Chol Majluel	Abior/Paguil	
Chuga Akuei Deng	Achueng/Payath	
Achel Aguer Ghaal	Twic/Payaath	
Kowk Miyan Ngong	Achaak/Dhiendior	
Nyankrou Magun Athony	Dhiil/Panai	
Ayak Chol Dau	Ruweng	
Nyankuc Chol Kuot	Ruweng/Pinykuac	
Nyanajith Chok Bol	Achaak/Dhiendior	
Ajuk Kueth Ayom	Anyiel/Pathiang	
Nyanjor Bongei Awer	Acaak/Dhiendior	
Ajok Kueth Ayom	Anyiel/Pathiang	
Ayak Deng Chol	Bongo/Palou	
Nyanyiok Yol Loum	Rewung/Pinykuac	
Anguet Ayiik Kur	Diil/Piorbekwer	
Achuei Ngor Chol	Anyiel/Pakiir	
Nyanajith Yak Mior	Mareng/Pathiang	
Ayak Miorik	Manyuar/Padoul	

Paan Man-Abul

Name	Chiefdom/Clan	Sons and Daughters
Nyanbol Amuor Miorik	Anyiel/Panguiny	Kuol, Abul, Achai, Monylam, Mijak
Achok Mijok Duor	Abior/Dhienagou	Mading, Awor, Ayen, Nyanluak, Aluong
Nyanawai Monyjok Chol	Bongo/Payai	Nyapath, Miokol, Nyantibiu, Ring
Adit Atak Mou Kuac	Malual/Pagew	Biong, Alor, Awor, Akuet, Kuol
Akuol Biong Achuil	Bongo/Pakiir	Ring, Arop, Bulalbek, Pieng, Mading, Abul
Adau Ayual Arop	Kowk (Panaru)/Pamel	Bol
Agorot Pabut Lok	Bongo/Pangok	Adau, Kuol, Achai
Agorot Thilman Deng	Alei/Panyhiar	Abul, Abek, Chol
Anyuat Nyok Rou	Bongo/Dhiendior	Kuol, Kom, Awor, Adau
Abiong Piyein Lual	Alei/Paguiny	Kuol, Piol
Nyanlou Anyiel Chol	Anyiel/Pabil	Mijok, Achai
Aker Adija Chol	Achueng/Padeik	Arop, Kuol, Abul, Jok
Abul Malek Akot	Manyuar/Dhienaniek	Achai, Awor, Adau, Nyanar, Mawien, Jok
Nyanuak Dau Minyiel	Diil/Panai	Adau
Nyanbol Aguek Ajith	Achueng/Dhiendior	Arop, Achai, Mawien
Nyanchar Miyan	Diil/Panai	
Nyanchar Anyang Alor	Mannyuar/Dhiendior	Achai
Nyanyuat Ayuel Kur	Achueng/Dhiendior	Achai, Mawien, Adau, Kuol, Monydhang
Nyanajak Deng Kiir	Bongo/Dhienleng	
Nyanpiok Jupur Alor	Manyuar/Dhiendior	
Achuei Ayuel Agoor	Achueng/Dhiendior	
Nyanyiik Deng Lueth	Ayuang/Pateng	Awor, Ayuen, Kuol, Arop (Mou)

Abil Ngor Yol	Anyiel/Pakiir	Nyariak, Achai
Nyanguen Paguot Deng	Bongo/Dhiendior	Biong, Alor
Kwaja Lual Mukpieu	Abior/Pajiing	
Anot Monyluak Rou	Bongo/Paweny	Awor, Kuol, Alor, Biong
Agorot Juac Chan	Alei/Payak	Akumtweng, Akuet, Biong, Alor
Ayuen Bol Palek	Mannyuar/Pabukjak	Nyariak, Ayen, Abul
Nyanthon Ayuel Agoor	Achueng/Dhiendior	Mawien, Monydhang, Nyariak, Kuol, Arop, Biong, Adau
Ayak Ajak Joh	Achueng/Pakweyei	Mawien
Nyangalou Boudha Arop	Achueng/Dhiendior	
Nyanjoh Kundit Miyan	Diil/Pakueng	
Nyantholong Biong Aguek	Anyiel/Dhiendior	Biong, Bol, Achuil
Aluel Deng Dhal	Noon Chol	Akuet, Achai, Kuol, Mawien, Arop
Nyanyol Mading Arop	Manyuar/Panyiok	
Abuk Yak		
Abuk Nyok Guopjieng	Abior/Pajiing	
Nyanagon Chol		Miyar
Nyankat Bol Twar	Achueng/Dhiendior	Biong (Yusif), Nyanaar
Abuk Dut Aroul	Ajuong/Pagong	Ring, Arop
Achol Nguel Anyiel	Abiem/Dhiendior	
Alek Mayar Cyer	Adiang/Payaath	
Nyanyol Mading Arop	Mannyuar/Panai	
Ading Akoc Ajith	Anyiel/Payuel	
Abul Nyiok Wol	Abior/Pajing	
Ayak Ajak Joh	Achaak/Dhiendior	Mawien

Paan Man-Arop

Name	Chiefdom/Clan	Sons and Daughters
Kuei Deng Agok	Abior/Pajiing	Arop, Achai, Ayen, Abul (Nyannyiob)
Amou Bol Jang	Manteng/Dhiendeing	Nyanjuur, Biong, Awor, Abul, Ayok, Nyanweili, Mijak
Kuei Deng Kiir	Abior/Pajiing	Kuol, Achai
Achuil Miyan Kogror	Achaak/Dhienaniek	Bulabek
Awor Bilieu Miyan	Alei/Pabac	Kuol, Biong, Bulabek (Monychok)
Alang Nuan Kueny Deng	Mijuan/Penykuac	Achai, Adau, Nyanluak, Ngor, Nyariang, Adhar, Bol
Nyanjoh Bagat Alor	Manyuar/Dhiendior	Arop, Achai, Malual
Agorot Bol Ater	Mareng/Pachier	Awor, Anguei
Akuol Monyluak Deng	Alei/Pabac	Arop, Ajai, Abul, Dut
Awal Deng Ajak	Mannyuar/Pathiang	Awor, Arop, Nyinaar, Ngor, Biong, Mijak
Akuol Akonon Lual	Mareng/Dhiendior	Alor
Aluel Ayuel Gac	Bongo/Palual	Kuol, Adau, Arop
Nyandeng Akonon Ajak	Mannyuar/Pajiing	Kuol, Awor, Achai, Nyariak, Arop
Acheng Dau Kiir	Alei/Paguar	Mading, Awor, Achai
Nyantwic Ngor Kieu	Mareng/Pachier	Nyariak, Achai, Nyanar, Kuol
Nyaror Hoc Ar	Mareng/Pakany	Nyariak, Adau (Nyansuk)
Aluel Bangbang Kon	Adiang/Padhieu	Ajok, Abeik, Bol, Adau, Awor, Arop
Aluel Miyan Ar	Mareng/Pakany	Kuol, Awor (Nyantafag), Achai, Biong, Mou, Nyandeng
Nyanchar Deng Kur	Bongo/Payei	Alor, Nyandeng, Awor, Abul, Biong
Nyanajak Deng Mamuot	Achueng/Dhienagou	Abul, Nyanaar
Nyaluak Kur Malual	Alei/Payak	Achai, Awor, Kuol, Arop
Ayei Ngor Agelueth	Anyiel/Palou	Kuol, Ngor
Athak Kuel Deng	Diil/Pabukjak	Kuol, Biong, Achai
Nyankiir Dhieu Bul	Diil/Pagwer	Biong, Ring, Aguek, Achai, Nyanmou
Agorot Ayuel Gungkuel	Diil/Pagwer	Biong, Akuet, Achai, Nyandeng, Ring, Mawien

Ayen Dau Deng	MijuanPadonythiek	Arop, Awor, Nyanaar, Ngor, Mijak
Athieng Deng Kueny	Abior/Pakueny	
Achok Kueth Madut	Adiang/Pakiir	Manut, Nyanut
Achuil Kur Wundeng	Diil/Pagangwer	Achai
Achel Chol Akonon	Manyuar/Dhiendior	Achai, Nyanbol, Achuil
Ayak Jelli Deng	Achaak	
Nyanchel Maker Keregi	Alei/Payak	Kuol, Nyariak, Nyanar, Ngor, Bol, Arop
Nyannyiot Minyiel Ayuel	Bongo/Pakiir	Adau, Abul, Nyanar, Ngor, Monylam (Mading)
Amou Koc Deng	Mareng/Pachier	Mawien, Biong
Nyankiir Leng Deng	Abior/Dhiendior	Awor (Adhonj), Abul
Awut Deng(Magol) Deng	Ajuong	
Nyanamel Deng Cyer	Adiang/Payath	
Achol Minyiel Ayuel	Ayuang/Pateng	
Athak Luat Miyan	Ruweng/Pakueny	
Nyanguor Monychol	Diil	
Awor Miyan Riak	Bongo/Pabong	
Kom Ajak Athuai	Mannyuar/Pajing	Achai
Anok Mijok Biar	Alei/Pakeywei	
Anger Deng Gout	Twic Kuac/Paandhiedyot	
Nyaluak Chol Kam	Achaak/Dhiendior	Anger, Nyanbol, Mawien
Nyannyok Dawood	Achueng/Pajing	
Jalab Kiir	Amaal/Patweekt	
Nyanaroup Bar Biong	Mareng/Dhiendior	Biong
Thioul Nyok Dawood	Diil/Panai	
Achuetway	Ajuong	
Ayak Lual Atem	Nooncholguot	
Awutchek Deng Deng	Rek	

Sources

Books by Francis Mading Deng

Deng, Francis Mading. *Tradition and Modernization: A Challenge for Law Among the Dinka of the Sudan.* New Haven and London, Yale University Press, 1971

Deng, Francis Mading. *The Dinka of the Sudan.* New York, Holt, Rinehart & Winston, 1972.

Deng, Francis Mading. *Dynamics of Identification: A Basis for National Integration in the Sudan.* Khartoum, Khartoum University Press, 1973.

Deng, Francis Mading. *The Dinka and Their Songs.* Oxford, Clarendon Press, 1973.

Deng, Francis Mading. *Dinka Folktales: African Stories from the Sudan.* New York, Africana Publishing Company, 1974.

Deng, Francis Mading. *Africans of Two Worlds: The Dinka in Afro-Arab Sudan.* New Haven and London, Yale University Press, 1978.

Deng, Francis Mading. *Dinka Cosmology.* London, Ithaca Press, 1980.

Deng, Francis Mading. *The Recollections of Babo Nimr.* London, Ithaca Press, 1982.

Deng, Francis Mading. *The Man Called Deng Majok: A Biography of Power, Polygyny, and Change.* New Haven and London, Yale University Press, 1986.

Deng, Francis Mading. *War of Visions: Conflict of Identities in the Sudan.* Washington DC, The Brookings Institution, 1995.

Deng, Francis Mading. *Frontiers of Unity: An Experiment in Afro-Arab Cooperation.* Abingdon: Routledge, 2014.

Publications by other authors

Africa Watch. *Denying "The Honor of Living": Sudan, A Human Rights Disaster.* NY, Washington, & London, Africa Watch, 2014.

Arop, Madut Arop. *The Ngok Dinka of Abyei, South Sudan, in Historical Perspective.* Tolworth, Grosvenor House Publishing, 2018.

Cole, David C., and Richard Huntington. *Between a Swamp and a Hard Place: Developmental Challenges in Remote Rural Africa*. Cambridge, Harvard Institute for International Development, 1997. Cunnison, Ian. "The Humr and Their Land," *Sudan Notes and Records*, 35/2: 50-68, 1954. Cunnison, Ian. *Baggara Arabs: Power and the Lineage in a Sudanese Nomad Tribe*. Oxford: Clarendon Press, 1966.

Davies, Reginald. *The Camel's Back: Service in the Rural Sudan*. London: John Murray, 1957.

Deng, Lual A. *The Power of Creative Thinking: The Ideas of John Garang*. iUniverse, 2013.

DeWaal, Alex. "Some comments on militias in the contemporary Sudan", in M.W. Daly & Ahmad Alawad Sikainga (eds), *Civil War in the Sudan*. London: British Academic Press,1993.

Henderson, K.D.D. "A note on the migration of the Messiria tribe into south west Kordofan", *Sudan Notes and Records*, 22/1: 49-77, 1939.

Howell, P.P. "Notes on the Ngork Dinka of Western Kordofan", *Sudan Notes and Records*, 32/2: 239-93, 1951.

Johnson, Douglas H. "The Abyei Protocol demystified", *Sudan Tribune*, (11 December), www.sudantribune.com/spip.php?article25125, 2007.

Johnson, Douglas H. "Why Abyei matters: the breaking point of Sudan's comprehensive peace agreement?", *African Affairs*, 107/426: 1-19, 2008.

Johnson, Douglas H. "The road back from Abyei"

Keen, David. *The Benefits of Famine: A Political Economy of Famine and Relief in Southwestern Sudan, 1983-1989*, 2nd ed., Oxford: James Currey,1994.

McDougall and Lasswell. *Law, Science and Policy*, 1964.

Miyen Kuol, Akol. *Sudan: Understanding the Oil-Rich Region of Abyei*, CreateSpace Independent Publishing Platform, 2013.

Malwal, Bona. *Abyei of the Ngok Dinka: Not Yet South Sudan*. Malmesbury: Bourchier, 2017.

Maskalyk, James. *Six Months in Sudan: A Young Doctor in a War-Torn Village*. New York & London: Spiegel & Grau, 2009.

Niamir, Maryam."Report on animal husbandry among the Ngok Dinka of the Sudan", *Integrated Rural Development Project, Abyei, South Kordofan, Sudan*. Harvard Institute for International Development, Rural Studies, 26 March: 17-18, 27-30, 95-100, 1982.

Permanent Court of Arbitration (2009), "Final Award in the Matter of an Arbitration before a Tribunal constituted in accordance with Article 5 of the Arbitration Agreement between the Government of Sudan and the Sudan People's Liberation Movement/Army on delimiting Abyei Area". The Hague: The Peace Palace, July 22.

Donald Petterson, Godfrey Muriuki, Shadrack B.O. Gutto, Kassahun Berhanu, Douglas H. Johnson (2005), "Report of the Abyei Boundaries Commission", 14 July

Robertson, James. *Transition in Africa: From Direct Rule to Independence*. London: C. Hurst, 1974; Khartoum: the Khartoum Bookshop, 1975.

Ryle, John. "The road to Abyei", *Granta* 26: 41-104,1989.

Saeed, Abdelbasit. "The State and Socio Economic Transformation in the Sudan: the Case of Social Conflict in Southwest Kurdufan", PhD dissertation, University of Connecticut, 1982.

Salih, M.A. Mohamed. "Tribal militias, SPLA/SPLM and the Sudanese state: 'New wine in old bottles'", in Abdel Ghaffar M. Ahmed & Gunnar M. Sørbø (eds), *Management of the Crisis in the Sudan*. Bergen: Centre for Development Studies, 1989.

Scott, Timothy. *Crisis in Abyei: Notes from an Observer*. San Francisco: Blurb, 2017.

Tibbs, Michael and Anne. *A Sudan Sunset*, Totton: Hobbs the Printers, 1999.

Willis, C.A. "Notes on the western Kordofan Dinkas", *Sudan Intelligence Report* 178 (May), Appendix C: 16-18, 1909.

CPSIA information can be obtained
at www.ICGtesting.com
Printed in the USA
JSHW051907040621
15573JS00002B/2